The Tyranny
of Heaven

The Tyranny of Heaven

Milton's Rejection of God as King

Michael Bryson

Newark: University of Delaware Press
London: Associated University Presses

©2004 by Rosemont Publishing & Printing Corp.

All rights reserved. Authorization to photocopy items for internal or personal use, or the internal or personal use of specific clients, is granted by the copyright owner, provided that a base fee of $10.00, plus eight cents per page, per copy is paid directly to the Copyright Clearance Center, 222 Rosewood Drive, Danvers, Massachusetts 01923. [0-87413-859-0/04 $10.00 + 8¢ pp, pc.]

Other than as indicated in the foregoing, this book may not be reproduced, in whole or in part, in any form (except as permitted by Sections 107 and 108 of the U.S. Copyright Law, and except for brief quotes appearing in reviews in the public press.)

Associated University Presses
2010 Eastpark Boulevard
Cranbury, NJ 08512

Associated University Presses
Unit 304
The Chandlery
50 Westminster Bridge Road
London SE1 7QY, England

Associated University Presses
P.O. Box 338, Port Credit
Mississauga, Ontario
Canada L5G 4L8

The paper used in this publication meets the requirements of the American National Standard for Permanence of Paper for Printed Library Materials Z39.48–1984.

Library of Congress Cataloging-in-Publication Data

Bryson, Michael, 1964–
  The tyranny of heaven : Milton's rejection of God as king / Michael Bryson.
      p. cm.
  Includes bibliographical references and index.
  ISBN 0-87413-859-0 (alk. paper)
  1. Milton, John, 1608-1674. Paradise lost. 2. God—Kingship—History of doctrines—17th century. 3. Christian poetry, English—History and criticism. 4. Milton, John, 1608-1674—Religion. 5. Theology—History—17th century. 6. God in literature. I. Title.
  PR3562 .B75 2004
  821'.4—dc21
                                                                      2003012093

PRINTED IN THE UNITED STATES OF AMERICA

Contents

Acknowledgments 6

1. Of Miltons and Gods 9

2. "His Tyranny Who Reigns": The Biblical Roots of Divine Kingship and Milton's Rejection of "Heav'n's King" in Prose and Poetry 42

3. "Who durst defy th' Omnipotent to Arms": Satan's Fall from Hero to King 77

4. "That far be from thee": Divine Evil, Justification, and the Evolution of the Son from Warrior-King to Hero 112

5. "Tempt not the Lord thy God": The End of Kingship and the Awareness of Divine Similitude in *Paradise Regained* 148

Notes 171
Works Cited 195
Index 201

Acknowledgments

I WANT TO THANK REGINA SCHWARTZ FOR HER INVALUABLE SUPPORT at all stages of the research and writing process; Michael Lieb for his guidance on Milton's use of scripture; and Christina Traina for her questions about Milton's relations to larger theological traditions. I also want to thank Peter Herman for his interest in and encouragement of this project, as well as David Loewenstein, Helen Marlborough, Richard Strier, and other members of the Chicago Newberry Library Milton seminar for an intellectual atmosphere that stimulated many of the questions this book asks.

Most importantly, to my wife, Carrie Bourque, and to my family (Robert Bryson, Naomi Vecchiarelli, Heather Bryson, and Lance Wolstrup) and friends (Jennifer Bortman, Donna Kain, Peat Burnett, Kimberly Segall, John Martin, Brian Artese, Charlotte Artese, Chris Hager, Erin Redfern, Anne Sullivan, Bobbie Saltzman, Mary Serochi, and Bill Curtis): for reasons too numerous to recount here, this book would not exist without your love and support. Thank you.

A version of chapter 2 was previously published as "'His Tyranny Who Reigns': The Biblical Roots of Divine Kingship and Milton's Rejection of Heav'n's King" in *Milton Studies* 43, Albert C. Labriola, ed., © 2003 by University of Pittsburgh Press. It is reprinted in expanded and altered form here by permission of the University of Pittsburgh Press. A portion of chapter 4 was previously published as "'That be far from thee': Divine Evil and Milton's Attempt to 'Justify the ways of God to men'" in *Milton Quarterly* 36, no. 2, Roy C. Flannagan, ed., © 2002 by Blackwell Publishers Ltd. It is reprinted in expanded and altered form here by permission of Blackwell Publishers Ltd.

The Tyranny
of Heaven

1
Of Miltons and Gods

> There are some people, however, who . . . assert that God is, in himself, the cause and author of sin. . . . If I should attempt to refute them, it would be like inventing a long argument to prove that God is not the Devil.
> —John Milton, *De Doctrina Christiana*

Imagining God

History is littered with the corpses of gods. As eras and peoples rise and fall, wax and wane, the gods who once roamed secure and unchallenged in their worshippers' heavens and earth fade and die. Some become fossils—objects of excavation, analysis, and study raised from the earth to shed light on lost epochs.

Homeric gods once breathed boisterous life; these deities' passions for sex, war, revenge, love, loyalty, friendship, and power radiate from practically every page of the *Iliad* and the *Odyssey*. But Zeus is dead, a cadaver whose earthly appearances are now limited to literature classes, low-budget Ray Harryhausen films, and high-budget Disney cartoons.

Likewise the Annunaki—the collective gods of such Mesopotamian epics as *Atrahasis* and the *Enuma Elish*—were vibrant and lively, animated in their jealousy, often petty in their resentments. Yet where once the victory of Marduk over Tiamat was enthusiastically celebrated in annual rituals designed to renew the cosmos, the Annunaki now are obscure relics lifted gently from the grave of a barely remembered past. Perhaps not surprisingly, there are no modern musicals, whether live or animated, about Marduk.

The God of Hebrew scripture is a member of a rare and wondrous species: vital and living gods who, for better or worse, still inspire awe and devotion in the twenty-first century. Whether he is called Jehovah, Yahweh, the Father, or simply God, the ancient Mesopotamian deity first described in writing by a desert-wandering people 3,000 years ago is unique: unlike his extinct peers who vanished with their eras and their peoples, he continues to live for millions of worshippers whose rites and rituals are as diverse a lot as the lands in which those worshippers dwell. He has appeared through the eons in many guises—creator and destroyer, personal god of Abraham who finds a wife for Abraham's son, divine Warrior of Joshua, and the ethically minded divinity of Amos. Imagining him has been a lifetime's job for countless generations.

As full of life as Yahweh remains in the modern world, however, it is safe to say that it has been a *very* long time since he roamed battlefields, found a wife for the son of a human friend, or directly voiced indignation over the inequitable treatment of the poor. Times change, and our images of our gods change with them.

Imagining God has been one of the central difficulties of Christianity since the Gnostics. When they posited the creator of the physical world as evil, the Gnostics were arguing that this god was, for all intents and purposes, actually the Devil.[1] However, despite the assiduous labors of such Church Fathers as Hyppolytus, Tertullian, and Augustine, "Gnostic" doubts about the Christian God have resolutely refused to be dispelled throughout the ages. The Gnostic image of an evil god has not died, as have the images of Greek and Mesopotamian divinities; as late as the nineteenth century, "Gnostic" images continued to appear. William Blake's demiurgic creations Urizen and Nobodaddy (to name works from just one author) manifest the continuing poetic energy and the historical staying power of the idea of divine evil.

But the Gnostics accused the creator of the physical world not to *defame*, but to *defend*, another image of God. When they argued that the creator is a dark and evil demiurge, the Gnostics were trying to account for the existence of evil in the world while simultaneously placing the *blame* for that evil on something or someone *other* than the supreme divinity. The Gnostic move is familiar enough: credit for all good is given to the supreme God, and blame for all evil is placed on a "devil."

The real question, then, that separates the "Orthodox" from the "Gnostic" is not, "Is God good?" but "How is God to be imagined so that his goodness is made obvious?" For both "Gnostic" and "Orthodox" early Christians, the goodness of the supreme God was simply assumed. What was at issue was not God's goodness, but the way in which that supreme God was to be imagined. The "Orthodox," who clung to the idea that physical creation was good, imagined God as the creator of the physical universe. The "Gnostic," who regarded flesh and the physical creation as evil, imagined God as a being *higher* than the demiurge who created the imperfect earth and the sinful human condition.

Each group imagined the other's God as evil; each group believed the other's God to be, in actuality, a Devil. But each group also imagined its own God in terms it perceived as good. In essence, each group invented its own arguments to prove that "God" is not the Devil.

John Milton was not a Gnostic. For him, certainly, physical creation was not evil. But like the Gnostics, Milton rejected as evil the god imagined by his contemporaries. The expression of this rejection, his epic poem *Paradise Lost*, has, almost from the day of its publication, troubled many Christian readers who, to their dismay (and often outrage) see in his Father a character who is as far from the "good" god they believe in as Satan himself. Certainly, Milton's Father has historically challenged and puzzled readers—both devout and otherwise—for long enough that to insist on the unproblematic "goodness" of this character is an act that often accentuates difficulties in the attempt to deny them. But if Milton did create an "evil" Father, to what end did he do so?

I believe that Milton creates in *Paradise Lost* a separate god—the moral equivalent of the Gnostics' creator god—in order to reject, not physical creation, but the one institution that Milton spent the latter portion of his life fighting: monarchy. Kings and kingship; a "heathenish government" given to the people of God as a punishment and, according to Milton, absolutely forbidden to Christians by Christ himself, the institution of monarchy came to be for Milton what the physical was to the Gnostics—a result of evil and the invention of the Devil. To imagine God as a king was, for Milton, to imagine God as if he *were* the Devil.

Paradise Lost and *Paradise Regained* are John Milton's desperate attempt to prove that God is not the Devil. Job-like in their accusations, Milton's greater and lesser epics are an indictment and rejection of a God imagined in terms of military and monarchical power. For Milton, God is not the Devil, but in being conceived in terms of human kingship and the all-too-human desires for power and glory, God has been scandalously and blasphemously imagined in such a way as to be nearly indistinguishable from the Devil. Milton pounds this point home by making the Father in *Paradise Lost* his sublime artistic rendering of the execrable tendency to conceive of God in Satanic terms. The Father is not Milton's illustration of how God *is*, but Milton's scathing critique of how, all too often, God is *imagined*. Similarly, Milton's "long argument to prove that God is not the Devil" does not address what God is, but how God is imagined. Milton writes to re-imagine God.

In like manner, I am writing to re-imagine Milton, to reconcile the Milton I have come to know with the Milton I have long struggled against. The Milton of easy answers, rigid orthodoxy, and pat moral positions is one I have encountered frequently over the years, but only between the covers of scholarly tomes. I cannot find this Milton—a literary prophet unambiguously on the side of the angels—merely by searching through the texts he has left behind. I cannot find the political thinker who favors in heaven the kingship he rejected on earth.[2] The Milton I *can* find never wore the garment of his religious faith easily. The author of Sonnet 7, a young man who imagines God as a "great task-master," is not recognizable to me as a *comfortable* Christian who *loves* his God.[3] Milton's "great task-master" is not a figure of unconditional love, but is, rather, a maker of demands, a setter of standards, a white-gloved inspector looking for dust in the corners of his creatures' souls. Such a God must be dealt with, accounted for, and struggled with, but he is not a figure who inspires love, loyalty, or even admiration. A God imagined as a "task-master" is to be *feared*, and not merely in the mildly apologetic sense of *respected*. In this case, fear of God is terror, and God is a figure of dread.[4]

A God who is a "great task-master" is not the God revered by my Christian acquaintances. Their God is rather closer to the Jesus(es) of popular imagination—the baby of the manger, the preacher of love and tolerance, the challenger of the judgmental who declares that only those without sin may cast the first stones—than it is to the God figure of Milton's greater and lesser epics. The Father in *Par-

adise Lost and *Paradise Regained* is the caster of stones, a construction of God closer to the deity of my own youth, the God of Hebrew scripture who reserves vengeance to himself.[5] While Yahweh is many things, he is not *primarily* a God of love (1 John 4:16 notwithstanding). Milton's poetic God—imagined variously as the "great taskmaster" of Sonnet 7 and the Father of *Paradise Lost* and *Paradise Regained*—is closer to this conception of Yahweh than to the abovementioned images of Jesus.

The fundamental difference between the God-figures of Milton's texts and the God(s) envisioned by many modern (Christian) readers of Milton's texts is wide enough to have caused long-standing interpretive conflicts, disputes based, in part, on an unhelpful conflation of theology and religion. A theological approach to Milton does not necessitate a *religious* or *faith-based* approach to Milton. Determination to prove Milton's orthodoxy or the goodness of his poetic God can be a blinding light that renders those who stare into it unable or unwilling to see the text that is right in front of them. It is this determination that is diligently and responsibly overcome in a Bible-as-literature classroom, so that instructors and students from diverse religious and cultural backgrounds can approach the text on common ground. Failure—or refusal—to take the same approach in a course on seventeenth-century English literature leaves students for whom the theological assumptions of Christianity are alien in the position of unwelcome guests at an exclusive gathering. Learning about the theological background of Milton's poetry is a far cry from having to uncritically accept the assumptions of that background; it is also a far cry from having to believe that Milton himself always uncritically accepted those assumptions.[6]

What William Empson once termed the "neo-Christian" position reads the "God" of *Paradise Lost* as if he were the Absolute of Hellenistic philosophy burdened with the dialogue necessitated by the epic form. This reading enables a critic committed to the goodness of the Father in *Paradise Lost* to ignore the darker implications of belief in a *personal* deity who is imagined in terms of omniscience and omnipotence.

The problems with *personal* deity are manifold. When the absolute, originating principle of the universe is conceived in anthropomorphic terms, it is also often conceived in *exclusive* terms. "No man cometh unto the Father, but by me" (John 14:6). "Thou shalt have no other gods before me" (Exod. 20:3). Historically, *exclusive* terms have also often been *national* terms.[7] Exclusive personal deity denies the validity not only of other exclusive personal deities, but also the validity of deity conceived in terms of an impersonal Absolute. The God of Israel is not merely One (Deut. 6:4): he becomes, by the time of Hilkiah and the "discovery" of the Book of the Law (c. 620 B.C.E.), the *only* One. Exclusive Yahwism makes a claim far different from the Yahwism of the Judges period.

Though Regina Schwartz quite correctly points out that there is "strictly speaking, no such thing as monotheism"[8] in the Hebrew Bible, the exclusivist claims of the minority Yahwist faction among Israelite priests (embodied most famously by Hilkiah, the seventh century B.C.E. high priest who "discovered" the Book of the Law—the basis of our Book of Deuteronomy—during the reign of king Josiah) are thoroughly integrated into the assumptions of Christianity. This can be illustrated by a brief comparison. At Exod. 20:3 Yahweh claims the right to exclusive devotion from the people of Israel: "Thou shalt have no other gods before me." This commandment is not intended as a claim that no other gods exist; in fact, it is because the existence of other gods is taken for granted that Yahweh makes such a claim. This tacit acknowledgment of the existence of other gods is a reflection of *henotheism,* not *monotheism.*

Where monotheism makes the claim that only one God truly exists, henotheism acknowledges the existence of other gods while claiming a special status for one god or a special relationship between one god and one people. In the Hebrew scriptures this is the dominant mode of thought even during the Judges period; in prebattle negotiations with the king of the Ammonites, Jepthah asks the king, "Wilt thou not possess that which Chemosh thy god giveth thee to possess?" (Judg. 11:24). No indication is given that Chemosh is considered somehow "false" or nonexistent; rather, the impression given is one of a system in which different pieces of land are controlled by different gods. This fits rather neatly with Schwartz's description of the Hebrew deity: "the deity will bequeath the land as a gift to the people if they are faithful to him, and he will revoke it if they are not."[9]

The idea of local divinities—however exclusive to local peoples those divinities may be—is entirely different from the exclusive conception of divinity inherent in Rev. 21:6. The deity who claims that he is "Alpha and Omega" is making a universal rather than a local claim. Yahweh's claim of being the "true" God (belonging covenantally to Israel) among many "false" Gods (being alien or inferior in power) is entirely different from a claim of being the only God. This claim is a critical step. The movement from henotheism to monotheism involves a corresponding movement—away from a position that merely expresses a preference for one's own way of life, and toward a position that posits one's own way of life as *the* way of life. To move from "Thou shalt have no other gods before me" (Exod. 20:3) to "I am Alpha and Omega, the beginning and the end" (Rev. 21:6) encapsulates a dramatic shift in worldviews from one in which difference—while not necessarily celebrated—is recognized, to one in which difference is a standing outside of totality. To stand apart from the Yahweh of Exodus is to be no part of the emerging people of Israel. To stand apart from the Alpha and Omega is to be no part of existence itself.

The exclusive claims of the Father in *Paradise Lost* are not the exclusive claims of an impersonal Absolute, an Aristotelian Unmoved Mover. They are the claims of exclusive personal deity, the claims of post-Hilkiah Yahweh, the claims of Jesus at John 14:6. The Father in *Paradise Lost* speaks; this simple fact places the Father firmly within the tradition of personal deity. In some traditions God may be that upon which nothing can be predicated, an unrepresentable transcendent absolute, but the Father in *Paradise Lost* is none of these things. He is a poetic and personal character. Furthermore, a careful analysis of the dialogue between the Father and the Son in Book 3 makes evident that the Yahweh presented in Genesis and Exodus is a powerful influence on the figure Milton presents. Especially in the Biblical writings covering the periods of the patriarchs, the Exodus, and the conquest of Canaan, Yahweh is not presented in terms of exclusive or absolute *goodness*; rather, Yahweh is presented in terms of *holiness*—an entirely different conception. Holiness—that combination of the awesome, fearful, overwhelming and terrifying that Rudolf Otto refers to as *Das Heilige*—is that which inspires fear and trembling in the beholder; it is that which can only be approached by the consecrated, in the Holy of Holies, on the Day of Atonement. *Das Heilige* can be seen, in its full sacrality and terror, by no mere human being, and such holiness is claimed by, and for, the Father in *Paradise Lost*. Just as with Yahweh, the Father is presented not as *good*, but as *holy*.[10] The Yahwistic background of Milton's poetic character makes the argument for (or assertion of) the absolute goodness of that character untenable.

The idea that God is entirely *good* is not one that can be distilled—without remarkable alchemical skills—from the Hebrew Bible. The Christian insistence on the goodness of divinity is more Platonic than scriptural. In the *Republic*, Socrates maintains that the only portrayals of the gods that should be permitted are those that are unambiguously positive. The gods must be portrayed as good because, as Socrates insists to Adeimantus, they *are* good. However, in his insistence on the unqualified goodness of the deities to be worshipped in his ideal society, Socrates is less concerned with the reality of divinity than with the image of divinity. Socrates argues that the gods *are* good, but this seems an afterthought; more important than how the gods *are* is how the gods are *imagined*, specifically, how human beings in his ideal society imagine the gods.

Milton is also concerned with how human beings imagine divinity. Just as Socrates and Adeimantus deal with poetic portrayals—hence, *images*—of divinity, so also is Milton dealing with a poetic portrayal—an *image*—of the Christian God. Milton shares the Platonic/Socratic concern with images of the divine, but he does not share the perspective that only unambiguously positive images must be presented. In *Areopagitica*, Milton clearly insists on the value of considering good and evil together in order to enable a "fit" reader to know good by knowing evil. It is, of course, as Milton argues in *Areopagitica*, only "in the field of this World" (*CPW* 1:514)[11] that such an epistemology is necessary, and the objection is all too easily made that the "fallen" nature of this world renders such a mode of knowledge "fallen" in itself. This objection, however, is quite beside the point. In a context that takes seriously the idea of a Fall, it is not possible (without resort to appeals to direct divine inspiration) to form an image of God that is not itself somehow fallen, and if knowledge in a fallen world is a combination of good and evil, then images of God, and poetry about God—two primary ways of "knowing" divinity—are *themselves* combinations of good and evil.

It simply will not do to argue that Milton highlights good and evil by giving the reader a God who is totally good and a Satan who is totally evil. This argument is not convincing for several reasons. First, the idea of a good God and an evil Satan is a commonplace.

For a poem in search of a "fit audience . . . though few" (*Paradise Lost* 7.31), such a neat distinction does not serve in any way to sort the fit from the unfit, or the few from the many among Milton's audience. Second, in the context of a "fallen" world, a "fallen" human poet could not present an all-good God even if that were his intention. Giving God human characteristics forcibly drags God into the realm of the imperfect, the fallen. Third, the Biblical background of the anthropopathetic and anthropomorphic Yahweh—a figure referred to frequently in the Hebrew Scriptures as the ultimate source of both good and evil—looms over Milton's poetic God-image like the shadow cast over a foothill by a mountain. Careful reading reveals that Milton *uses* this background in several key scenes involving the Father, thus rendering that character an *a priori* combination of good and evil. Fourth, Satan—though he is among the most compellingly drawn characters in all of world literature—is ultimately a marginal figure; it is the Father who is the central figure in Milton's attempt to "justify the ways of God to men." Therefore, it is the Father in whom the unavoidable combination of good and evil "in this world" is to be found in Milton's poetic work.

Neither will resorting to claims of divine inspiration for the poet and poetry of *Paradise Lost* help the cause of those who wish to cling tenaciously to the idea that Milton's image of God is unambiguously good. Though it draws on scripture, *Paradise Lost* is not scripture; its calls to the muse and its pretensions to supernatural aid in the telling of its story are firmly embedded features of a quite unscriptural and unchristian epic tradition (the Italian poets of the sixteenth century notwithstanding). Modern readers (many of whom are not, have never been, and will never be Christian) can no more be expected to believe that *Paradise Lost* is divinely inspired than they can be expected to believe that the *Odyssey* or the *Aeneid* are so inspired. To read such works as if they were divinely inspired is a choice more appropriate to the realm of faith than to that of academic inquiry. The constructions of the Father and of Zeus are thoroughly human in origin, and thoroughly embedded in this world's economy and epistemology of good and evil.

In attempting to "justify the ways of God to men," Milton chooses to present a God who is personal and exclusive. What Milton presents, however, is not God, but an *image* of God, a poetic character drawn from the human imagination—an instrument that is limited and thus inherently unable to create a personal deity in any but its own limited terms.

An anthropopathetic and anthropomorphic image of God is not ultimately what Milton is trying to "justify." Rather, the poetry and prose together indicate that what Milton is attempting in his epic is something far more radical than a defense of a traditional personal deity. In *Paradise Lost* and *Paradise Regained,* Milton is writing an *Eikonoklastes* designed to break not the king's image, but the King's image. In "justifying the ways of God to men," Milton labors to break the very image of God he presents in the form of the Father, while simultaneously laying the groundwork for a new image, conceived in terms of the Son.

Imagining Milton

Milton has long been a hotly contested figure, and so, very probably, he will always remain. I am not alone in objecting to what Stephen Dobranski and John Rumrich refer to as the "present critical settlement"[12] in Milton studies. However, the current "critical orthodoxy"[13] surrounding the figure Rumrich has referred to as "the invented Milton"[14] will not be refashioned in new and interesting ways without a lengthy and determined struggle, a conflict in which at least as much light is shed upon the combatants as upon the ostensible subject of the dispute. For example, a common criticism of William Empson has long been that he wore his atheism on his sleeve, and that as a result he found it impossible to imagine a Milton who did not feel about God as he did. There is considerable justice in such a criticism; however, this kind of critique is a double-edged razor, cutting Empson's detractors quickly and neatly in return. The neo-Christian critics of the twentieth century, who regard Milton as "a champion of Christian essentials,"[15] appear to be just as unable to imagine a Milton who does not reflect their own religious views as was Empson. John Diekhoff, for example, tells us that "Satan was a very bad angel, and Milton knew it,"[16] and "Milton presents his narrative and his ethic in conventional Christian terms."[17] William Riggs argues that "Milton labors to express God's will, not his own"[18] in *Paradise Lost,* as if Milton's epic were an ornate evangelical tract. William B. Hunter's decade-long crusade to take *De Doctrina Chris-*

tiana out of the Milton canon appears to be motivated by a powerful desire to reconcile Milton with "the great traditions of Christianity, being no longer associated with a merely eccentric fringe."[19] Recognizing that the religious investments of *Paradise Lost*'s critics color and even determine their analyses, Empson contended that the "opinions of attackers and defenders of the poem have evidently corresponded to their various theologies or world-views."[20] In short, the Milton you see seems to depend a great deal on the critic you read, and critical opinion—from the beginning—has been (and continues to be) sharply divided.

So prominent an early reader as John Dryden found *Paradise Lost* unorthodox. In "Dedication of the Aeneis" (1697), Dryden suspects that Satan is the hero of the poem, and considers the treatment of Satan to be a major flaw; Milton's epic would have had a greater claim to stand as an equal to the *Iliad* and the *Aeneid* "if the Devil had not been his hero, instead of Adam."[21] The reclamation of Milton for the "orthodox" cause, however, begins soon after Dryden. Joseph Addison, in a series of essays (running in the *Spectator* from 5 January to 3 May 1712 [No. 267–No. 369]) opines that it is "the Messiah who is the Hero, both in the Principle Action, and in the chief Episodes" of *Paradise Lost*, and maintains that the poem is suitably orthodox.[22] Addison directly contradicts "Mr. Dryden's Reflection, that the Devil was in reality Milton's hero."[23] To Satan, such sentiments are given as suit "a created Being of the most exalted and most depraved Nature."[24]

Samuel Johnson seems particularly impressed by the piety of the poem: "In Milton, every line breathes sanctity of thought and purity of manners" and even when the forces of Hell are presented, "they are compelled to acknowledge their subjection to God in such a manner as excites reverence and confirms piety."[25] Johnson's critical take on the "orthodoxy" of Milton's great poem continues to carry the day through most of the eighteenth century. Bishop Thomas Newton, for example, declares in 1749 that *Paradise Lost* is entirely orthodox:

> [I]n Paradise Lost we shall find nothing . . . that is not perfectly agreeable to Scripture. The learned Dr. Trap, who was as likely to cry out upon heresy as any man, asserts that the poem is orthodox in every part of it; or otherwise he would not have been at the pains of translating it [into Latin verse].[26]

It is not until Blake, with his famous so-called "misreading" of Milton in *The Marriage of Heaven and Hell*, that the early questions of Dryden begin to resurface. Blake's famous (or infamous) take on Milton ("The reason Milton wrote in fetters when he wrote of Angels & God, and at liberty when of Devils & Hell, is because he was a true poet and of the Devils party without knowing it") is followed by Shelley's almost equally famous assertion (in his preface to *Prometheus Unbound*) that Satan is the "Hero of *Paradise Lost*."[27]

The "Romantic" readings of Blake and Shelley gain tremendous currency from the 1825 publication of *De Doctrina Christiana*, a Latin manuscript identified as a theological work by the poet John Milton.[28] Milton is immediately branded as an Arian heretic (one who denies the equality and co-eternity of the Son with the Father). By mid-century, these labels are firmly affixed. Henry John Todd, in a book-length introduction to his two-volume 1852 edition of Milton's poetry, writes of the treatise:

> Such are the parts of this treatise of divinity; wherein are some positions, which he who wrote *Paradise Lost* could not have been expected to advance. For in these he is to his former orthodoxy often opposed; and in these he appears no longer in the questionable shape which bishop Newton has described, but evidently attached to the Arian scheme.[29]

Even Milton's late-nineteenth-century biographer, David Masson, concludes that both *De Doctrina Christiana* and *Paradise Lost* are Arian: "[Milton] goes on to propound . . . views about the nature of Christ which are expressly and emphatically those of high Arianism."[30] Masson further opines, in his 1882 introduction to *Paradise Lost*, that "Satan . . . as all critics have perceived, and in a wider sense than most of them have perceived, is the real hero of the poem."[31] By the end of the nineteenth century, Milton's heresy and heterodoxy are taken for granted. Blake's reading of Milton as being somehow of the Devil's party—which is in some sense also Dryden's reading of Milton—is dominant.

In Denis Saurat's 1925 publication, *Milton, Man and Thinker*, the "orthodox" Milton has almost completely disappeared. Saurat is quite unapologetic about reading Milton as at least emotionally of the Devil's party, seemingly anticipating Christopher Hill, who, fifty-one years later, would write "Milton was not of the Devil's party without knowing it: part of him knew."[32] Saurat claims that there is "no lack of sympathy on intellectual subjects between Satan and Milton."[33] He further contends that "Satan is not only a part of Milton's character, he is also a part of Milton's mind."[34] Sauraut's unabashedly Blakean reading of Milton's epic—married to his suggestions that Milton was influenced by sources as diverse as Robert Fludd and the mystical *Zohar*—took Milton so far afield from the tame, orthodox figure of eighteenth-century criticism that a reaction was almost inevitable.

The reaction came in the form of a dramatic resuscitation of Milton for the cause of Nicene Creed "orthodoxy," a resuscitation undertaken in earnest by C. S. Lewis in his 1942 publication, *A Preface to Paradise Lost*. In this work, as Christopher Hill puts it, Milton "is represented as a traditional authoritarian who can be used to rebuke the sinful modern world."[35] Lewis conflates Milton, Augustine, and the entire Christian church in his analysis of *Paradise Lost*: "Milton's version of the Fall story is substantially that of St. Augustine, which is that of the Church as a whole."[36] Lewis's argument, dedicated as it is to assimilating Milton's epic to an orthodoxy comprised of equal parts Augustinianism and Anglicanism, is made with the express intent of, as he puts it, "prevent[ing] the reader from ever raising certain questions."[37] Thus is the goal of nearly all orthodoxies summed up.

Two notable responses to this construction of an "orthodox" Milton come from A. J. A. Waldock's *Paradise Lost and its Critics*, and William Empson's *Milton's God*. Waldock's thesis is that Milton's poem reveals strong undercurrents that are in opposition to his stated intention to "justify the ways of God to men." He argues that the troubles with the Father in *Paradise Lost* begin with the expansion and poetic magnification of the story of the Fall in Genesis. "The story is a bad one for God,"[38] writes Waldock, who maintains that Milton wrote his way headlong into "the problems those first three chapters of Genesis held"[39] without realizing "that every rift would become a gulf."[40]

By far the most infamous of critics in neo-Christian critical circles, however, is William Empson. The prototype of the somehow "anti-Milton" critic, Empson questions the justice of the Christian God in his analysis of Milton's poetic God.[41] God is on trial in *Paradise Lost*, and according to Empson, he didn't get a favorable verdict.[42] Empson raises the issue—which recently has been raised again by the similar experiences of John Rumrich[43]—of the reaction to Milton's God of non-Christian, non-Western readers: of his experiences in Japan and China, Empson says "I gathered that those of my students who became interested in *Paradise Lost*, though too polite to express their opinion to me quite directly, thought 'well, if they worshipped such a monstrously wicked God as all that, no wonder that they themselves are so monstrously wicked as we have traditionally found them.'"[44] Empson insists that "most Christians are so imprisoned by their own propaganda that they can scarcely imagine this reaction; though a missionary would have to agree that to worship a wicked God is morally bad for a man, so that he ought to be free to question whether his God is wicked."[45]

The response by neo-Christian critics against Empson's work was perhaps as predictable as it was swift. In characterizing the reaction against Empson, David Norbrook makes a telling comment: "much later criticism—including Fowler's annotations to *Paradise Lost*—has amounted to a defence not so much of Milton but of God."[46] Just as it is not entirely clear in Norbrook's footnote, so also is it not always entirely clear in the "later criticism" whether the "God" referred to is the character Milton creates, or one of the various constructions of a (loosely) Judeo-Christian divinity. Still perhaps the most influential example of such "later criticism" and "defence" is the work of Stanley Fish. A severely orthodox Milton re-emerges in the pages of Fish's *Surprised by Sin*. Though Fish claims to be attempting to heal the rift between the "pro-Satan" and "anti-Satan" strands of *Paradise Lost* criticism, he frequently reveals his loyalties to the latter camp, creating what appears to be a combination of C. S. Lewis and cognitive psychology. Rumrich refers to *Surprised by Sin* as "a methodologically radical update to Lewis's reading of *Paradise Lost* as a literary monument to mainstream Christianity."[47] One example of the difficulties of Fish's argument lies in its apparent pretensions to omniscience. The argument asserts, as an objective fact, a definition of the experience of reading, an experience Fish claims is universal. Far beyond the claims he makes elsewhere about the *mechanics* of reading, Fish's claims to know what a reader's *experience* of a text must be (an experience that is both subjective and not strictly measurable) enter the realm of the fantastic. Fish's declaration that readers who disagree with him (such as Waldock) "falsify [their] experience of the poem"⁴⁸ is an edict more befitting a god than a mere human being. How, exactly, any critic is privy to the precise nature of other readers' experiences of any text without an "Eternal eye, whose sight discerns / Abstrusest thoughts" (*Paradise Lost* 5.711–12) is a question for which I have no satisfactory answer.

Perhaps even more than Fish, Dennis Danielson is a clear example of the assumptions of neo-Christian Milton criticism. The title of his book, *Milton's Good God,* contains his thesis. The first line of the book ("Does Milton worship, and present, a good God?")⁴⁹ is unmistakable in its conclusions. The question suggests that the character Milton creates is to be taken as if it were interchangeable with the God Milton may or may not have worshipped. This is, in a nutshell, the central problem with the neo-Christian tradition of twentieth-century Milton criticism. Milton *studies* have often threatened to turn into Milton *ministries*; as the distinction between a poetic character and the reader's (or critic's) idea of the divine is erased, the difference between literary study and religious devotion becomes disconcertingly hard to detect.

In order to keep that difference clear and unmistakable, I suggest that when reading *Paradise Lost,* three grounding principles should be kept in mind:

1) The audience sought by Paradise Lost *is a "fit audience . . . though few."*

This poem is not explicitly created simply to reinforce the preconceived notions of an English-speaking, "Christian" majority. In seeking a "fit" minority, Milton positions *Paradise Lost* as a challenge to uncritically accepted orthodoxies—whether political or theological. Sharon Achinstein goes so far as to argue that "Milton did not merely search for an audience, he defined one. . . . Milton also advocated a concept of readers who could foment their own spiritual improvement."⁵⁰ In *Paradise Lost,* Milton is defining his "fit" audience as an audience capable of seeing through the traditional images of kingship with which he imbued the Father in his great epic. "Spiritual improvement" for such an audience comes from the realization that God is not to be imagined as an external king, but to be internalized as the truly "kingly" "inner man" of *Paradise Regained* (2.477). Critical positions regarding *Paradise Lost* that rely on orthodox notions (i.e., the Augustinian reading of C. S. Lewis, or the pro-heavenly-kingship argument of Stevie Davies—both of which would hardly be challenging to the views of mainstream theo-political thought in 1660s and 1670s England) are disinclined to explain why only an especially discerning and especially small audience is the overtly invoked target of Milton's great epic.

2) Milton's "God" is not God.

Milton's poetic character is not an absolute representation of God. Neither is it to be taken as simply identifiable with the God in which Milton believed. *Pace* Dennis Danielson, it is unlikely that the man who labored so hard to destroy the *Eikon Basilike* would set up a poetic *Eikon Theios* as if it were an absolute representation of the real thing. Such an attempt on Milton's part would have amounted to idolatry at worst, and Sisyphean futility at best.

3) The Father of Paradise Lost *is off-putting to many readers because he is supposed to be off-putting.*

Since Alexander Pope's 1737 contention that Milton's "God the Father turns a School-divine"[51] in *Paradise Lost*, both *Paradise Lost* and the Father have been disturbing to many readers, even if they did not quite know why. The nervousness about Milton's portrait of God is palpable in the defense of Milton offered by his mid-eighteenth-century editor, Thomas Newton, who, while insisting on the orthodoxy of *Paradise Lost*, is reduced to arguing that though Milton "was indeed a dissenter from the Church of England . . . and in the latter part of his life was not a professed member of any particular sect of Christians . . . nor used any religious rite in his family . . . it is certain [that he] was to the last an enthusiast rather than an infidel."[52]

It is a long and strenuous path from Newton's hesitant "defense" of Milton to the neo-Christian tradition of the twentieth century—a school embracing both Lewis' confident assimilation of Milton to "the Church as a whole" and Stanley Fish's contention that *Paradise Lost* is "Milton's programme [*sic*] of reader harassment."[53] Fish's description of *Paradise Lost* as a poem designed to scold unwary Christian readers who allow themselves to be tempted by the grand rhetoric of Satan into momentarily pushing aside "the imperative of Christian watchfulness"[54] constructs a Milton whose contemporary audience is neither "fit" nor "few." The mental image of teeming masses of late seventeenth-century Christians readjusting their "fallen" perspectives line-by-candlelit-line as a result of the famous regicide's extended game of poetic "gotcha" would be marvelous and witty were it not for the fact that the paradigm from which it springs leaves no room for opposition that is not somehow inherently either "anti-Milton" or "fallen." Much as the classic psychoanalytic conundrum of "denial" (to deny that one is in denial is the primary symptom of denial), to argue against Fish's cleverly autocratic scheme has been interpreted for too long as somehow to demonstrate both the validity of the scheme *and* one's own "fallen" status.[55]

The time has come to say "enough."

As the long-waged battles in Milton studies demonstrate, Milton's poetic creation and presentation of God is troubling to readers—not because they are inadequately equipped to respond to spiritual concepts, but because they are *well-equipped* to so respond. Milton's portrayal of God disturbs because it brings to light all of the normally hidden ugliness of a monarchical concept of God, giving that concept a voice, a personality, and a volatility that raises disturbing questions about the justice of that God. *Paradise Lost* forces its readers to stare directly into the face of a God conceived in terms of military might and kingly power, presenting a God who is obsessed with his own power and glory, manipulative, defensive, alternately rhetorically incoherent and evasive, and an arranger of political dialogues designed to mold angelic opinion; in short, Milton constructs a God who is nearly indistinguishable from Satan.

In *Paradise Lost* Satan aspires to that very monarchical and military model of divinity. He is both a ruler and a leader of troops. Satan himself says, on rising from the burning floor of Hell in Book 1: "To reign is worth ambition though in Hell / Better to reign in Hell than serve in Heav'n" (1.262–63). The narrator describes Satan as a warrior and battle-chief, "who that day / Prodigious power had shown, and met in Arms / No equal" (6.246–48). Satan's lieutenants refer to him as "leader": "Leader, the terms we sent were terms of weight, / Of hard contents, and full of force urg'd home" (6.621–22). The objection that Satan is perverting monarchy and perverting military leadership and service assumes that monarchy and militarism have a "pure" unperverted form in the image of the Father of *Paradise Lost*. However, in the case of the Father, what Satan "perverts" is already a perversion. Neither a military God nor a monarchical God has any place in the scheme of internal rule put forth by the Son in *Paradise Regained*, or in the "paradise within thee, happier far" spoken of by Michael at the end of *Paradise Lost* (12.587).

Here I should state explicitly that I am comparing, and will be comparing, the Son of *Paradise Lost* and the Son of *Paradise Regained*, not only to each other, but to the Father of both *Paradise Lost* and *Paradise Regained*. I am treating these works as part of a narrative and mythological whole, with the latter serving as a continuation and further development of the former's story. The Son's success in *Paradise Regained* is the moment to which the end of *Paradise Lost* looks forward. In comparing especially the Son of *Paradise Regained* to the Father of *Paradise Lost*, I could be accused of a category error—comparing apples and oranges. The Son is a Man, and the Father is, not only *a* god, but *the* God—or at least so it appears. But, as I must repeat (and will repeat as often as is necessary to get the point across), the Son and the Father are *poetic characters, works of fiction, constructions of a writer's imagination*. The writer, Milton, is not using these characters and constructions, Hamlet-like, to "hold, as 'twere, the mirror up to nature." The writer is not claiming that these *characters* are meant to express the full reality of what is essentially inexpressible—the nature and condition of the divine itself. What these characters are, I contend, are different *imaginings* of the divine, different masks or representations, fragmentary sketches that can be drawn of a divinity that is both invisible, and—for Milton, and for many others since—all-too-remote and curiously silent. Imagining divinity in the embodied and human terms of the poetic character known as "the Son" in *Paradise Regained* brings the transcendent back into the realm of the immanent, takes divinity from the monarchical throne down into the realm of the "private person," allowing the poet to emphasize the drastic and dramatic difference between the idea of God he wishes to reject, and the likeness in which—at least provisionally—he wishes to re-imagine God.

In pursuit of this aim of re-imagining God, Milton presents the Son, at only twelve years old, as having already felt that his "Spirit aspir'd to victorious deeds" and "heroic acts" to "subdue and quell o'er all the earth / Brute violence and proud Tyrannic pow'r" (*Paradise Regained* 1.215–20). Even this young, however, the Son "held it more humane, more heavenly, / . . . to make persuasion do the work of fear" (1.221, 223). In *Paradise Regained*, the Son, as an *adolescent boy*—though a boy with the experience of ages behind him—moves past the Homeric/heroic mode in which Satan operates throughout *Paradise Lost*, and in which the Son himself begins his career in Book 5 of Milton's great epic. The fact that the Son's rejection of a military and monarchical interpretation of "victorious deeds" and "heroic acts" is both "humane" and "heavenly" is a clue to the consistency of Milton's outlook. He does not disapprove on earth what he approves in heaven; it is both humane *and* heavenly to persuade rather than to force. In reading Milton's works, it is vital to keep the Son's axiom in mind—it is "more humane, more heavenly, / . . . to make persuasion do the work of fear" (1.221, 223). Reading with an eye toward those moments when persuasion is used, and those moments when fear is used, continually raises the question, *who is using which technique and why?* That question, I believe, is crucial to understanding the images of kingship and authority in both *Paradise Lost* and *Paradise Regained.*

As *Paradise Regained* progresses, the Son rejects all forms of earthly kingship. The crucial question is, does he also reject heavenly kingship? If heavenly kingship is conceived in terms of knee-crooking fealty, hierarchical (and military) organization, and all of the public trappings of regal power simply transferred from an earthly to a heavenly setting and scale, then the Son does reject such kingship. The "kingdom" of the Son is not to be defined by having angels organized into an elaborate hierarchy or by having "to him bow / All knees in Heav'n." In a kingdom of the Son, the bowing is no more, because its uniting of all as one individual Soul is an erasure of hierarchical distinction, not an enhancement of such distinctions.

However, the model of heavenly kingship that the Son rejects is the same one that both Satanic and Heavenly forces use to imagine the remote and imperious Father of *Paradise Lost.* Milton is not suggesting, as did his contemporary Gerrard Winstanley, that the God most Christians worshipped was the Devil,[56] but he is suggesting something startlingly similar. When Winstanley suggests that a "traditional Christian . . . worships . . . the devil," he says this in the context of a cutting analysis of how such a Christian worships God. Such a "traditional Christian" worships an anthropomorphic image of God, identifies that image *as* God, and so "worships his own imagination, which is the devil."[57] The anthropopathetic and anthropomorphic terms in which the monarchical, militaristic God of the "traditional Christian" is conceived are those of the human imagination, "which is the devil."[58] The human imagination, in worshipping itself, follows in the footsteps of Satan.

The God most Christians worship, as Milton demonstrates, is not the Devil, but he is worshipped *in the image of the Devil.* This demonstration, and not the "programme" described by Fish, is the harassment of the reader in *Paradise Lost*—a harassment that must be addressed if the reader is to make sense of the harsh portrayal of God in a poem ostensibly written to "justify the ways of God." In essence, *Paradise Lost* and *Paradise Regained* together comprise that "long argument to prove that God is not the Devil" Milton referred to in *De Doctrina Christiana* (*CPW* 6:166).

Milton's project is not in the end a simple theodicy—a simple assertion or demonstration of the *justice* of God. Milton achieves in his work something far more complex than a justification of what seems to be an unjust God; he defends God ultimately by illustrating, not that God has been unfair to man, but that man has been unfair to God, using God as an excuse for his own weakness and servility. In the case of "his English-men" (*Areopagitica, CPW* 2:553), placing God in the straitjacket of such human political ideas as kingship merely served to solidify those ideas, making it nearly impossible for the English people to develop the habits of thought, imagination, and action that could have ensured the long-term survival of the Republic and the success of the Good Old Cause.

Much of the pamphlet literature published during Milton's lifetime testifies to the popular image of God as a king. Richard Hooke's "The Royal Guard, or, The King's Salvation" (1662) speaks of God as a King and the source of human kingship; Joseph Fuce's "A special warrant given forth from the spirit of God" (1663) speaks of God in the same human political terms. Even a demonstrably republican work like Henry Haggar's 1652 pamphlet, "No King but Jesus"—though it attempts to prove that human kingship is an aberration and that kingship is reserved to God—takes as its axiom the political image of God as a divine monarch that by 1660 had rendered the English people only too eager for the restoration of a human monarch. By the time Cromwell was offered a crown in 1657, Milton could not have been blamed had he despaired of the English people's ability *ever* to learn to be worthy of political and theological liberty.

In the service of such liberty, Milton's own works demonstrate the inseparability of his theology and his politics. His commitment to republicanism wavers in *The Ready and Easy Way,* but his suggestions for what seem like a perpetual oligarchy are made in desperation. The Republic was dead. The Good Old Cause had failed (or had been failed by those who claimed to work in its service). Milton is both practical enough in his ends and provisional enough in his means to have sought *any* political remedy that might forestall the return of the Stuart monarchy long enough to revive the now-moribund traditions of freedom that had not had time to take sufficient root in the hearts and minds of the English people. However much Milton's republicanism wavered, Milton's opposition to the return of kingship never wavered. At the same time, Milton's opposition to imagining God as a king did not waver. Ironically, despite the royalist and Abdiel-like attitude that (according to David Norbrook) would declare "invalid" the making of "analogies between heavenly rule and earthly government,"[59] Milton is both making such analogies and insisting that those analogies are, in fact, invalid. Making analogies between heavenly and earthly government is precisely what Milton is doing, at least in part as a critique of precisely what Milton's contemporaries are doing. In being imagined as a king, God, who for Milton "transcends everything, including definition" (*CPW* 6:137), is obscured by the limited, and limiting, metaphors derived from all-too-human political institutions. Milton's opposition to earthly kingship should not be dismissed or set aside in discussions of the question of heavenly kingship. The whole Milton—including the politics; the theology; the insistence on freedom to read, write, and think his own thoughts and those of no other; and the willingness to die rather than be silent—needs to be brought into play in the discussion of Milton's vision of heaven and earth. To assume that there is little—or no—political critique represented in Milton's heaven is effectively to silence a man in death who would not tolerate being silenced in life.

Milton presents his Father as a king, and his Satan as an aspiring king, precisely so he can demonstrate that kingship, *both on earth and in heaven*, is part of the larger problem of how God has been misconceived. In presenting the entire course of universal history as revolving around kingship, both the having and the desiring, Milton makes the case that it is not kings who must be overthrown, but *kingship itself*. In portraying God as a king, Milton graphically illustrates the primary hierarchical metaphor that in his time rendered the English incapable of liberty, or, as Milton so acerbically declared in the face of the Restoration of 1660, "worthie . . . to be for ever slaves"

(*The Ready and Easy Way, CPW* 7:428). It is to once again begin the arduous work of preparing for liberty, and to find those few "fit" for such liberty among a nation of "slaves," that Milton takes up his theodical sword in *Paradise Lost*. Milton seeks to justify the ways of God by smashing a slave's image of God and replacing it with a free man's, and in the process, dethroning a kingly Father whose concern is to "be sure / Of our Omnipotence . . . Arms . . . Deity [and] Empire" (*Paradise Lost* 6.721–24) and replacing this figure with a Son for whom to be truly kingly is to "lay down" rather than "assume" power (*Paradise Regained* 2.482–83).

Milton's "Fit" Audience

A "fit audience . . . though few": this enigmatic group comprises the elect for whom Milton intended the message of *Paradise Lost*. Who might this audience be? What traits might they share? What beliefs—religious, philosophical, and political—might they hold dear? The answers to these questions hold the keys to Milton's greater and lesser epics, *Paradise Lost* and *Paradise Regained*. Though Milton wrote in a Christian context for a Christian audience, he was not seeking an audience whose moral epistemology was one of blind acquiescence to *any* authority, whether political, theological, or poetical. Milton's ideal readers would have, like the Bereans of Acts 17:10–11, "received the word with all readiness of mind, and searched the scriptures daily, whether those things were so." Such independence of mind in matters of spiritual judgment is crucial for Milton: not only is the audience for which Milton sought "freed from the judgments of men . . . in religious matters" (*CPW* 6:537–38), but the ultimate interpretive authority is not human tradition but the spirit of God working in each individual believer. Belief, however, is not for Milton a reason to suspend critical and judicious reasoning. Ideally, the Christian believer, through the aid of the spirit within, should be *more* critical than the non-believer in the weighing of evidence.

If readers who come to the poem as non-believers—unburdened by centuries of Christian exegesis (like those Asian students to whom Empson referred)—can see something disturbing in the character with which Milton presents them, why is it that some professional literary critics often seem to work so hard at *not seeing*? Milton's "fit audience . . . though few" would hardly be one to go out of its way to take problematic material and whitewash it, rushing headlong into the obvious and orthodox, the apologetic and approved. The Milton we know from the divorce tracts and *De Doctrina Christiana* certainly did not rush into the mire of received opinion either. In prompting "the age to quit their clogs" on the issue of divorce, Milton made himself a target of the harshest and most personal kinds of criticism from the publicly orthodox, proving that he preferred the Bereans to the Presbyterians as a model of Christian reasoning.[60]

Milton was not a twentieth-century Christian, nor was he a repository of twentieth-century "liberal" or "humanist" values. We may correctly see in him positions that are, in some sense, progenitive of such liberal humanist values as we take for granted today (freedom of the press, divorce, a republican form of government, etc.), but we cannot read back the concerns of a twenty-first-century "democrat" onto the seventeenth-century poet. Why, then, are the same standards not applied to Milton's "Christianity?"

Milton was not a comfortably mainstream Christian by any century's standards. Remove *Paradise Lost* and all of the associations of that poem, and a John Milton transplanted into a modern Protestant church (especially of the more familiar American evangelical varieties) would likely be considered a troublemaker at best, a dangerous heretic at worst. As Christopher Hill puts it, "If a twentieth-century neo-Christian had met John Milton in the flesh he would not have liked him. The dislike, I suspect, would have been mutual."[61] Milton's positions on the nature of God alone (as outlined in *De Doctrina Christiana*) ally his ideas more closely with such "heresies" as Arianism, subordinationism, mortalism, and materialism than they do with any recognizable definition of "orthodoxy."

Milton's position while finishing *Paradise Lost* was tenuous. He was the grand old man of rebellion, revolution, and regicide. Nearly everything that Milton had believed in, fought for, and (as it turns out) risked his life for had failed. The rebellion against Charles I, instead of leading to a Paradise of God's Chosen Englishmen, had returned to the dust from which it came. The attempt to transform the governing structures of English Christianity had failed, and Bishops once again roamed the Earth like the Nephilim of old. The "good old cause" that Milton, and many others, had believed to be the will of God had crumbled into disaster, failure, and ignominy. The long-ago-blinded Milton could "see" only darkness, desolation, and doom for his once-beloved England. Everyone and everything important had failed. The Republic had failed. The Parliament had failed. The Protectorate had failed. Finally, Milton himself had failed. The only critical question left was whether the revolutionaries had failed to correctly perceive and align themselves with the will of God, or whether the ultimate and most degrading failure was God's own. Wars in heaven, carefully orchestrated by poets, may have satisfyingly neat outcomes, but wars between "good" and "evil" in the world of real kings, real guns, and real death all too often turn out differently than planned. Sometimes, Goliath wins.

In the post-Restoration world in which Milton finishes his great epic, the "fit audience" is an audience that rejects, however privately and quietly, the institutions of the New World Order ushered in by Charles II, but this definition does not go nearly far enough. It is both too limited in historical scope for a poet who wished immortality through his verse, and too narrow in its ambitions for a prophet whose struggle with his "great task-Master" God had been documented as early as his seventh sonnet (written somewhere near his twenty-third year).

The questions ignored by a strictly religious (and strictly neo-Christian) reading of Milton are as numerous as they are obvious—and troubling. Why does John Milton, who in *Tenure of Kings and Magistrates* defends before all of Europe the right of subjects to depose—and execute—a king (thus defending the beheading of Charles I of England) portray God as a military king in *Paradise Lost*? Why does the man who declares in *Eikonoklastes* that monarchy was founded, not by God, but by Nimrod, "the first that hunted after faction," portray God as a monarch? The most common answers have suggested that Milton approved of heavenly Kingship, but disapproved of earthly kingship. The integrity of this reading, however, rests entirely upon the following assumption: that for Milton, God as the divine King sets the standard which fallible human kings (even the best of them—like Josiah, the great reforming king of Judah) fail to meet. The flaw in this traditional answer to the kingship problem lies in its failure to adequately address another question: why, if the heavenly Kingship of the Father is a perfect standard by which all earthly kings are measured (and fail), does Milton *also* create a Son who, in *Paradise Regained*, rejects the very model of rule that the Father embodies in *Paradise Lost*?

David Norbrook rightly contends that "the problem of divine kingship is not quite so simply solved" as it might appear in the accounts of those who wish to forestall comparisons between heavenly and earthly realms in Milton's work. "Milton seems to go out of his way to blur the distinctions" between heavenly and earthly kings, and that blurring stems from Milton's "rejection of a sharp split between theology and politics."[62] Norbrook further argues that Milton used the "imagery of heavenly kingship to pose the question of heavenly justice in the sharpest and most provocative way to a republican reader."[63]

Milton's use of monarchical imagery in heaven does more, however, than merely pose questions of heavenly justice; it serves as a portrait of injustice blown up to monstrous proportions, with the rankest corruption located in the idea of *Divine Kingship* itself. A "fit audience" recognizes the problems inherent in conceiving of God as a heavenly, and military, monarch, *especially* in the immediately post-Restoration context of the re-ascension to "divine kingship" of the Stuart family's scion, Charles II. This kind of god-image, ultimately based on *Yahweh tseva'ohth*—Jehovah of Armies—pictures God as a Bronze-Age warrior with a seventeenth-century veneer, Achilles in a Stuart-era wig. The manifest absurdity of such an image of God is only exceeded by the stunning fact that many Christians in the late seventeenth-century still held on to this notion of a heavenly *dux bellorum*, an Arthurian or (in twentieth-century terms) Pattonesque God whose primary glory seems to be military prowess. The idea of a God who sits on a throne and commands angels like legions of troops—this was the belief of the *many*, not the belief of the *few*. Conversely, if the argument of Milton's radical contemporary Gerrard Winstanley—that the Christian God is wicked and should be abandoned[64]—were to be literally interpreted, this would be an argument of the *few*, but not, for Milton, of the *fit*. Milton's position is closer to Winstanley's than it is to that of the teeming majority of Christians whose image of God Milton did indeed consider wicked. The belief that the image of the Christian God as a monarch is a grievous error (an error partly responsible for the failure of the Commonwealth and the re-imposition of earthly tyranny)—would be, for Milton, the belief of both the fit *and* the few. The audience who understands the wickedness inherent in conceiving of God as a monarch comprises the "fit audience . . . though few" Milton addresses in both *Paradise Lost* and *Paradise Regained*.

The Problem of
Heavenly and Earthly Kingship in Milton

Milton's position on kingship—both on earth and in heaven—is inseparable from his positions on authority in general. His position regarding external authority, *no matter what the source*, is eloquently summed up by the Son in *Paradise Regained*:

> That other o'er the body only reigns,
> And oft by force, which to a generous mind
> So reigning can be no sincere delight.
>
> (2.478–80)

For Milton, external rule is inherently inferior to internal rule, self-government, self-discipline, self-control. External rule is imposed because of universal failure in these areas. External rule on earth is a perversion brought about by the Fall. External rule in heaven is a perversion that will be done away with entirely when the Father relinquishes power to the Son: "All Power / I give thee, reign forever . . . / Then thou thy regal Sceptre shalt lay by, / For regal Sceptre then no more shall need, / God shall be All in All" (*Paradise Lost* 3.317–18, 339–41). It is important to note that Milton deliberately muddies the clear water of 1 Corinthians 15:28 in his verse. 1 Corinthians clearly spells out that the Son shall "himself be subject unto him that put all things under him, that God may be all in all." The biblical verse is not a rejection of monarchy or an erasing of hierarchical distinctions in an ecstatic union of all creation with God. Milton's treatment of this passage is all of those things. The Father gives up all power to the Son, and the Son, anointed as "Universal King," relinquishes the "regal Sceptre," because it will never be needed again. The Son will abolish the image of divinity as kingship, and significantly, there is no mention of a resumption of submission by the Son in relation to the Father. God (no longer conceived of as Father *or* Son) will be simply All in All.

Of course, neither the idea of hierarchical erasure, nor the meaning of the phrase "All in All" is uncontested. David Norbrook, for example, argues that the Son *does* resubmit himself to the Father: "the problem of succession . . . does not arise [in *Paradise Lost*] when the son can 'succeed' the father only to be succeeded by him."[65] In discussing the meaning of "All in All," Albert Labriola writes that "Paul's apocalyptic vision [from which the phrase "All in All" is drawn] describes the society in the heavenly hereafter."[66] Labriola goes on to describe the "apocalyptic dictum that 'God shall be All in All'" as having an element of "threatened or actual military might . . . crucial to the process of forming the final society."[67] Describing a *society* implies union, but not necessarily an erasing of hierarchical distinctions. A "final society" in which "military might" (whether "threatened or actual") is "crucial" is a union achieved at least in part through coercion, or—to adopt a bodily metaphor for society—*dismemberment* of those elements (or body parts) that are deemed superfluous or gangrenous. Even without the elements of "might" and coercion, a society is a union of separate though interdependent entities, and this is not what I believe is implied by the "All in All" of *Paradise Lost*. As I will argue later in more detail, the significance of God being "All in All" is more closely akin to an awareness of divine similitude through which any sense of separation between creator and creation—or between creation and creation—is revealed as a "Satanic" illusion.

In the state of union enhanced by awareness of divine similitude, external rule—along with external hierarchical distinctions of any kind—will be no more. For a man whose spiritual and political ideal was "a Nation of Prophets, of Sages, and of Worthies" (*Areopagitica, CPW* 2:554), such an erasure of external rule in favor of an internal government of wise and free consciences would be as close as could possibly be hoped for to a "repair [of] the ruins of our first parents" (*Of Education, CPW* 2:366–67) and a restored Eden.

In the beginning, of course, external rule was not necessary: as Milton famously states, "No man who knows aught, can be so stupid to deny that all men naturally were borne free" (*CPW* 3:198). In *Tenure of Kings and Magistrates*, his infamous attempt to justify the ways of the regicides to men, Milton outlines a theory of the origin of external rule—the universal *failure* of internal rule. For Milton, secular authority originated in the need of free peoples to band together to protect themselves against possible harm. The next step in Milton's narrative is the electing of individuals who seemed wiser and/or more capable of handling public affairs than did the rest, and these governed wisely for a time—but absolute power corrupted absolutely. It was then that laws were instituted, laws that restrained the kings and magistrates from exercising tyranny over their people. The people retained power as kings and magistrates were chosen to function as the people's deputies, not their commanders. Milton argues that since the power of kings and magistrates is nothing but what is derived from the people, then the people may change kings and/or magistrates whenever they like, even if these officials are not behaving as tyrants.

Unlike the top-down familial metaphor of kingship (the king is to the people as the father is to the family) outlined in a work like Robert Filmer's *Patriarcha*, Milton's conception of kingship—and indeed of all power—is bottom-up. Milton's theory of power, and of all true government, is not only bottom-up, but it is, in a sense, inside-out. Despite the quite obvious contempt Milton has for what he calls "the rabble," as displayed most notably in his almost-despairing *Ready and Easy Way*, it is, in fact, the "private person" on whom Milton wants to rest the prerogatives of political and religious authority. Just as the individual spiritual beliefs (as long as they are recognizably biblical and non-Catholic) of such "private persons" are to be tolerated according to *Of True Religion, Heresy, Toleration, and the Growth of Popery*, so also is the freedom of each and every one of these "private persons" to be the ultimate basis of political power in Milton's thinking.

In a system in which "private persons" are those who hold no official political office yet function as the source and the ultimate repository of true government, such persons can be seen as analogous to "the inner man, the nobler part" of which the Son speaks in *Paradise Regained* (2.477). Despite the fact that public persons such as kings and magistrates wield external rule "[t]hat . . . o'er the body only reigns, / And oft by force" (478–79), such public rule exists only as a temporary arrangement until the ability of each and every "inner man" to govern himself properly is restored through education—whose goal is to "repair the ruins of our first parents" (*CPW* 2:366–67) and transform a nation of subjects into "a Nation of Prophets, of Sages, and of Worthies" (*Areopagitica, CPW* 2:554).

Since external rule is a temporary arrangement, it is permissible for private persons to throw off the chains of tyranny. For Milton, unlike his powerful theological forbears Luther and Calvin, it is not necessary to be in the position of a public person—a magistrate—to act against secular power being used in a tyrannical manner. The rhetoric of not allowing "private persons" to act against such authority is part of the very Presbyterian-based politics that Milton rejects so vehemently in *Tenure of Kings and Magistrates*. The Presbyterian divines that he takes to task in *Tenure* as "ingaging . . . sincere and real men, beyond what it is possible or honest to retreat from" (*CPW* 3:191) are trying to defend the very Protestant politics of magistracy-based rebellion that Milton puts into the mouth of his Satan years later in *Paradise Lost*. In both the "council in hell" scenes of Books 1 and 2, and the "council in heaven" scenes of Book 5, Satan speaks in the language of a magistracy-based theory of rebellion. His compatriots are "Thrones, Powers, and Principalities." Significantly, these titles are those of three—out of nine—choirs of angels; these titles seem to have been chosen by Milton to emphasize the political analogy being made between kingship on earth and in heaven. The objection Satan makes to the raising of the Son is clothed in terms of unjust usurpation of power. God is he who "Sole reigning, enjoys the Tyranny of heaven" (*Paradise Lost* 1.124). Abdiel, on the other hand, rebels against the rebels, not as a magistrate acting within the rights and prerogatives of his "secular" power, but as a "private person," one who makes his stand on the basis of conscience, and a variation of Peter's "We ought to obey God rather than men" (Acts 5:29). For Abdiel, it is "I ought to obey God rather than Satan."

This position stands in stark contrast to the claims of Milton's contemporary, Thomas Hobbes, who advocated "divine right theory," claiming that external rule is a permanent arrangement, and that furthermore, a king cannot in any way offend his subjects but can only offend God.[68] Milton maintains that it is indeed the subjects of a tyrant who are injured by tyranny, and that such subjects have the right to remove the tyrant. Milton goes much further, however, than merely granting the right of the people to remove a tyrant. Though Milton is no democrat—the people themselves do not *exercise* power, but merely confer power upon kings and magistrates of their choosing—nevertheless, for Milton, power flows from the very "private persons" to whom Calvin would deny the right to "undertake anything at all politically."[69] In *Tenure of Kings and Magistrates*, Milton argues that "since the King or Magistrate holds his autoritie of the people . . . then may the people . . . retaine him or depose him, though no Tyrant, meerly by the liberty and right of free born Men" (*CPW* 3:206).

All of this is not to suggest, however, that Milton completely overthrows the pragmatic tradition of Paul and Peter on how Christians should stand in relation to the secular authority. External rule is not *always,* perhaps not even *often* to be rebelled against, even for so famous a Christian rebel as Milton. In his *De Doctrina Christiana,* Milton makes a curious statement on the advisability of tolerating even secular tyranny: "I do not deny that in lawful matters it may be prudent to obey even a tyrant, or at any rate to be a time-server, in the interest of public peace and personal safety" (*CPW* 6:801). Though this follows a brief section on the wrong-headedness of political notions that suggest that ideas of divine right in government must be taken literally, it does not suggest, as Davies would have it, that Milton approves the kingship in heaven that he fought to bring down on earth; what it does indicate is an attitude similar to that of the Son in *Paradise Regained*—internal rule is the only kind that really matters, or is legitimate. It may be *convenient* to *tolerate* tyranny, to comply with necessity for "personal safety" rather than renew the titanic struggle against tyranny, because the ultimate form of government is the internal rule of the individual, not the external rule of kings.

Milton's view of both heavenly and earthly kingship becomes plain in light of this preference for internal individual rule. Milton the political writer places the source of kingship in the people; such a profound and radical position should not be strictly isolated and bracketed off from questions of heavenly kingship. If from the moment that the people no longer want the king, that king ceases to be king and becomes instead merely a tyrant (an argument Milton makes in both *Tenure of Kings and Magistrates* and *A Defence of the People of England*), what might that concept threaten where the heavenly King is concerned? In Milton's view, is God still "King" if the people (or the angels?) stop wanting him, or is he at that point merely a supremely powerful heavenly tyrant? Furthermore, within the Calvinist context of double predestination—in which God ordains the justification of some to be saved, and the reprobation, or damnation, of others to be condemned—what incentive is there for the vast reprobate majority to continue to regard God-as-king as legitimate, since in such a context "He" does not reign in the interests of all the people, but only in the interests of "himself and his faction"?[70]

Such unsettling, even potentially disturbing questions, are precisely what Milton wants his "fit audience" to grapple with. Milton's project *is* a theodicy, but by no means is it a simple and straightforward demonstration of the "justice" of the ways of a military monarch who sits on a heavenly throne. Milton's attempt to "justify the ways of God to men" is not concerned with demonstrating the "justice" of his own poetic creation: rather, Milton uses the Father as a foil, a negative to the positive that Milton envisions in the Son.

The problematic nature of Milton's depiction of heavenly and earthly kingship is emphasized by the arguments put forth to accommodate Milton's representations of earthly and heavenly kings. Stevie Davies argues for a Milton who looses on earth the monarchy he binds in heaven. Her method of proof is to argue, from an analysis of the structures of earthly feudalism, that the structure of Milton's heaven is intended as a kind of Platonic form of kingship, a form that earthly kingships do not ever and cannot ever inhabit adequately. Davies assures us that "we are meant to perceive Milton's attribution of royal symbolism to the deity as morally stainless,"[71] but she makes this statement after an analysis of imagery that she admits is "anathema to Milton" whenever it appears on earth. The question of why Milton would go to such extremes in applying to his poetic God the very imagery that he found so repugnant in non-poetic "real life" is answered by making a distinction between "oriental" and "feudal" monarchies. The implication of the distinction, of course, is that Satan's monarchy, described as it is in terms of "oriental" despotism, is oppressive, while the Father's monarchy, being Western, is acceptable, even laudable. However, Charles I was no less a despot in Milton's eyes by virtue of inhabiting a feudal rather than an oriental tradition of monarchy. Davies' analysis finally leaves open the question of how the Father's "feudal" monarchy can be less oppressive than Satan's "oriental" one.

In taking Empson to task for objecting to "the Lord of Heaven's feudal character,"[72] Davies insists that the "assumption that a feudal monarchy is just as repulsive as an oriental despotism" is wrong, and that feudalism "is not identifiable with a condition of servitude." The feudal sovereign is conceived of as *primus inter pares*, first among equals. Milton's God is therefore (according to Davies) "the great giver of good, endlessly passing out to his vassal angels the sovereignty that primarily belongs to himself."[73] The Father's rhetoric when "begetting" the Son in Book 5 hardly seems the stuff of what Davies refers to as a "self-renouncing monarchy":[74] "to him shall bow

/ All knees in Heav'n, and shall confess him Lord" (*Paradise Lost* 5.607–8). This is precisely the model of government that the Son will later reject in *Paradise Regained.*

Davies then argues that the Son is presented to the heavenly hosts as "*primus inter pares.*"[75] But not all the *pares* seem quick to agree that the Son should be *primus*. The Son is a "first among equals" whom the Father seems to think it necessary to elevate to such a status by threatening any who do not "bow" with being "Cast out from God and blessed vision" (5.613), and with "utter darkness" into a state "without redemption, without end" (5.614–15). There seems rather more emphasis on *primus* than on *pares* in this scenario. The Father's approach to announcing the Son's new status is one practically guaranteed to create dissent where none may have otherwise existed.

Rather than simply condemning Satan for his reaction to this event, trying to understand his reaction can help to make clear just how dramatic the Father's sudden proclamation had been. The poem gives no indication that the angel who would become Satan had been nursing resentments and rebellious thoughts before this incident. It is only *after* the Father's announcement that "All seem'd well pleas'd, all seem'd, but were not all" (5.617). This *seeming* is something new, a reaction to the new dispensation: the novelty of dissimulation is made clear by the following lines, "That day, as other solemn days, they spent / In song and dance about the sacred Hill" (5.618–19). No indication of *seeming* is given in reference to these "other solemn days." We have no reason, then, to assume that the resentments of Satan are anything other than absolutely new. Satan may not have been lying when he insisted that the Father "wrought our fall" (1.642).

Davies admits "the elliptical brevity of God's speech sounds despotic, however sympathetically one attempts to read it."[76] How despotic it must have sounded to angels hearing it for the first time is a point Davies quietly skips over. The speech sounds despotic because it *is* despotic. The rhetoric of absolute privilege in this speech is not the kind of rhetoric anyone would expect from a "first among equals," or from a "self-renouncing monarch," or from a "great giver of good, endlessly passing out to his vassal angels the sovereignty that primarily belongs to himself." It is the rhetoric of a capricious and unquestioned ruler: the rhetoric that begets questions.

In arguing that Milton found a feudal system (one he could not but have abhorred as a model for earthly political relations) to have "an obvious beauty when transferred to the heavenly spheres,"[77] Davies constructs a Milton who is the worst kind of hypocrite. For this Milton, human beings are to be more free—in a postlapsarian world—from what the Son refers to as the kind of government that "o'er the body only reigns, / And oft by force" (*Paradise Regained* 2.478–79) than are angels in a supposedly perfect heaven. From what we know of the Milton who wrote *Tenure of Kings and Magistrates*, *Eikonoklastes*, and the bravely despairing (almost Moloch-like in its disregard for the dangers of self-immolation) *Ready and Easy Way*, such a heaven cannot have been an ideal toward which humanity should aspire, but a metaphor beyond which humanity must grow.

For a "fit audience," the Son offers the best indication of the system that had the most "obvious beauty" for Milton. In *Paradise Regained*, the Son expresses withering contempt for the idea of kingship in no uncertain terms. Rule is to be internal, a self-government in which each individual is guided, not by kings, magistrates, or even gods, but by truth, and by "knowing God aright." The key question is what exactly it means to know God "aright." The clear implication is that most do not so know God, and that the "knowledge" most think they have of God (a God conceived in terms of *external rule*, of kingly and military power) is not enabling them to know God "aright." Thus, government "o'er the body . . . / And oft by force" continues.

This is precisely the kind of government, however, that the Son has come to abolish, establishing in its stead a rule of "the inner man, the nobler part" (*Paradise Regained* 2.477). The Son's system is not feudalism; nor is it a "self-renouncing monarchy" in Davies' sense. What the Son promises is *monarchy-renouncing monarchy*. To be truly kingly finally, for Milton, is to "lay down" a kingdom, an action "Far more magnanimous than to assume" (2.483). To know God "aright" is to know as the Son knows, to know that the rule of heaven is internal, a rule not of the body, but of the "nobler part," a rule where there is no *primus*, only *pares*.

2

"His Tyranny Who Reigns": The Biblical Roots of Divine Kingship and Milton's Rejection of "Heav'n's King" in Prose and Poetry

> Kingdom and magistracy, whether supreme or subordinate, is without difference called "a human ordinance."
> —John Milton, *Tenure of Kings and Magistrates*

Milton and His Critics

Reading Milton's poetry and prose side by side raises profound questions that tend to recur. Why does John Milton, the antimonarchical rebel who in *Tenure of Kings and Magistrates* defends before all of Europe the beheading of Charles I, subsequently choose to portray God as a king in *Paradise Lost*? Why does the man who declares by way of condemnation in *Eikonoklastes* that monarchy was founded by Nimrod, "the first that hunted after Faction" (*CPW* 3:466) seem to confound his own position by later depicting the Father as an unabashed monarch? One prominent answer to questions of this nature has been that Milton (the political thinker) rejects Charles's earthly kingship while Milton (the orthodox Christian) simultaneously accepts—even embraces—God's heavenly kingship.

Tensions between Milton's representations of heavenly and earthly kingship, however, are not so much purged as *highlighted* by the strenuous and often contorted arguments put forth to reconcile Milton's parallel portrayals of Charles I and the heavenly King. One such argument insists that there is no parallel whatsoever, or, at the very least, that those who find such a parallel are not to be taken seriously; Joan Bennett, in *Reviving Liberty*, insists that finding such a parallel is "Romantic."[1] According to Bennett, "Romantic attempts to link his God with Charles I as monarchs and Satan with Cromwell and Milton as revolutionaries are widely considered to have been mistaken,"[2] a statement that seems to imply that the widely held *or* widely rejected nature of an idea somehow constitutes evidence of the truth or falsity of the idea itself.[3]

Robert Fallon, in *Divided Empire*, takes a slightly different approach. He suggests that Milton actually has no problem with kingship in and of itself. What Milton *does* detest, according to Fallon, is the Stuart monarchy. Fallon argues from the fact that Milton had nothing to say about "Philip IV of Spain, Louis XIV of France, John IV of Portugal, Charles X of Sweden, and Frederick III of Denmark,"[4] not to mention other absolute rulers with whose regimes Milton would have had at least a passing familiarity in his role as Latin Secretary. Somewhat surprisingly, given the evidence of Milton's prose writings, Fallon maintains that "Milton did not reject *all* kings but reserved his condemnation for those who used their power tyrannically."[5] In support of his contention, Fallon declares that the evidence of Milton's prose is "questionable"[6] as a basis for evaluating his attitudes toward monarchy.[7] Quoting from *Tenure of Kings and Magistrates*, Fallon suggests that Milton approves of "just" kings; however, when Milton says, "look how great a good and happiness a just King is, so great a mischeife is a Tyrant" (*CPW* 3:212), this is offered in the polemical context of a crisis-ridden nation deposing, and executing, a single unjust king. This passage is not, in and of itself, either an argument for or against *kingship* itself; Milton's consistency is not so easily undermined.[8] By the time Milton pens the above-quoted phrase, he has already outlined a teleology by which he makes clear his opinion that kingship is a regrettable consequence of the Fall. The rare individual may be a "just" king; but kingship itself is a curse.

In support of his suggestion that Milton rejected only such kings as failed to steer clear of despotism, Fallon, like Davies, suggests that the kingship of heaven is a kind of Platonic archetype, a transcendent reality of monarchy (for which Milton secretly pined) of which earthly kingships are pale and presumptuous imitations:

> The Kingdom of Heaven had to be seen as the most splendid imaginable with all the institutions of royal rule carried out to their most dazzling extremes, its subjects more numerous, their praise more exalted, their obedience more unswerving, their knees more willingly bent, and their devotion more profound than any earthly monarch could possibly command. . . . in showing how God rules, [Milton] drew a picture of government truly sublime and warned temporal rulers not to reach for it.[9]

Heaven could not possibly be more oppressive, wearying, and grindingly contemptuous of its vassals than could the Stuart monarchy—except in the formulation that Fallon here suggests is Milton's own.

Despite arguing that "Milton frequently states that he has no quarrel with kings,"[10] in his earlier work, *Milton in Government*, Fallon contends that Milton bases his argument in the 1660 pamphlet *The Ready and Easy Way* on "two principles, the rejection of kingship and the delegation of sovereignty to a permanent senate."[11] The "rejection of kingship" is not merely a rejection of the Stuart monarchy. Milton is not only rejecting a specific king (Charles II), but he is casting a wary eye toward all external government. In Fallon's description, "Governments, [according to Milton] are a legacy of the Fall; and only insofar as a people are able to achieve a state of spiritual virtue can they release themselves from the burden of that legacy."[12] Essentially, the more virtuous are the people, the less need they will have of external government: "In brief, people get the government they deserve; and those who decline from virtue can expect to find themselves living under tyrants."[13] If people "get the government they deserve," I cannot help but wonder whether the angels in *Paradise Lost* may also be getting the government they deserve.

The odd thing about the picture of heaven that Fallon sketches in *Divided Empire*, wedded as it is to a larger claim that Milton opposed only *bad* or *tyrannical* monarchies, is that a heaven in which "all the institutions of royal rule [are] carried out to their most dazzling extremes" is a heaven *worse* than the Stuart monarchy, not better. The fawning and scraping, bowing and continual praise singing of a Heaven imagined as the all-too-human Stuart monarchy writ large is not something "truly sublime," but something oppressive, frightening and deplorable. In *Paradise Lost*, none of the characters who live (or lived) under Heaven's monarchy denies its oppressive nature, and many affirm that description. When Satan characterizes Heaven as a place of cringing and servile adoration, significantly, the unfallen angels *do not disagree*. When Satan accuses Gabriel of having "practis'd distances to cringe" in Heaven, Gabriel responds with a taunt of his own: "who more than thou / Once fawn'd and cring'd and servilely adore'd / Heav'n's awful Monarch?" (*Paradise Lost* 4.945, 958–60). Empson has characterized this taunt as evidence of "a very unattractive Heaven,"[14] one in which wincing, flinching, and genuflecting has become so ingrained in its angelic (and demonic) practitioners that the sycophantic point accusing fingers at the obsequious.

Milton's description in *The Ready and Easy Way* of the fawning and cringing that takes place in the court of a human king is of a piece with the angelic and demonic descriptions of Heaven in *Paradise Lost*: "a king must be ador'd like a Demigod, with a dissolute and haughtie court about him . . . to pageant himself up and down in progress *among the perpetual bowings and cringings of an abject people*" (*CPW* 7:425–26, emphasis added). How Milton could possibly have imagined that by using "the very practices that he deplored in temporal monarchy" he would be able to "create a King of Heaven so glorious and a court so splendid that it put his idolatrous imitators to shame"[15] is a point none of the aforementioned critics adequately addresses.[16] There is something almost Gnostic about such a construction of Milton's purposes, something that goes far beyond Milton's own paradigmatic epistemology of knowing good by knowing evil and that enters the territory of imagining good by exaggerating the known terms of evil. By this logic, God is simply an impossibly powerful Charles I.

Nevertheless, Fallon has identified something important here: Milton's poetic God *is* an impossibly powerful tyrannical figure. However, Milton is not creating such an image of God in order to put "idolatrous imitators to shame," but to express his contempt for idolatry itself. Idolatry is worship of an *image*, the confusion of a *representation* with that which is *represented*, and for Milton, the image of God as a wildly exaggerated temporal monarch would be one neither to be worshipped nor to be admired or revered. I believe that Milton offers the monarchical image as an object of contempt, not an object of reverence.

In support of a monarchical image of God, Bennett argues that "Milton propounded a world view which is the same in its essentials as [the late sixteenth-century Anglican divine] Richard Hooker's."[17] Bennett makes this claim after arguing that Hooker's concept of God was one in which the deity is "an absolute monarch voluntarily accountable to law."[18] Thus, by implication, Milton's concept of God must also be one of an absolute monarch, though one "voluntarily accountable to law." Bennett further argues that it is this voluntary submission to law that makes the difference between a tyrant (which Milton abhors) and a true king (ostensibly Milton's ideal).

Fallon rightly points out, however, that Bennett's argument avoids a central point: the fact that the King of heaven makes the laws to which he "voluntarily" submits himself. Bennett "seems to beg the question of the poem, that is, whether [God's laws and decrees] are just or not. God may certainly be said to keep his word and so may be absolved of arbitrariness; but the same may be said of any tyrant."[19] As so often in the rhetoric of critical attempts to defend divine kingship, here the accusations leveled at a tyrant provide an apt description of the heavenly monarch of *Paradise Lost*. Bennett's ultimate justification of the justice of God's laws and decrees is an assertion that "God" and "just" are synonymous: "God is just, he is God."[20] Such a matter-of-fact equation of "God" and "just" seems to render Milton's attempt to "justify the ways of God to men" redundant at best.

Davies, Fallon, and Bennett describe a Milton for whom monarchy is the ideal form of government—so long as it is restricted to heaven—and for whom a commonwealth or republic is merely the best of which poor fallen humans are capable. Constructed in these terms, Milton's ideas more closely resemble those of Herodotus, Plato, or Aquinas than those of a mid-seventeenth-century defender of regicide and would-be demolisher of Salmasius, the monarchy-defending scholar of Europe. In his *History*, Herodotus narrates the argument of Darius for monarchy as the ideal form of government; the Medo-Persian potentate asks "what government can possibly be better than that of the very best man in the whole state?"[21] Oligarchy and democracy lead inevitably to strife and faction, while Darius insists that monarchs are free to rule with the best interests of their subjects in mind. Plato, in the *Republic*, likewise argues that kingship is the ideal form of rule, calling "the rule of a king the happiest" form of government.[22] Aquinas argues that "the best government is government by one,"[23] and that "a kingdom is the best form of government of the people, so long as it is not corrupt."[24]

Classical and scholastic justifications for monarchy would of course be familiar to an educated reader of Milton's time, and were often woven into contemporary defenses of monarchy,[25] but for the truly "fit" audience Milton sought with *Paradise Lost*, a wide gap would exist between an awareness of Plato's and Aquinas' opinions of kingship and any notion that such opinions constituted absolute truth. Milton's own willingness both to use and contemptuously to discard the authority of the ante-Nicene church fathers in his antiprelatical tracts is an important clue to his view of any and all extra-Biblical "authority."

Milton's sometime distrust of "authority" actually goes further than casting a calculatedly jaundiced eye on classical and non-Biblical writings. For Milton, even the Bible is not to be trusted completely without the guidance of the inner light of each believer's inspiration. In *De Doctrina Christiana*, Milton argues that the text of the Bible as it has been transmitted across the millennia to a seventeenth-century reader is corrupt. Each believer possesses what Milton calls "a double scripture" (*CPW* 6:587), one external—the written text—and the other internal—the Spirit within—and each believer is to give the latter priority over the former. The text of the Greek scriptures, in particular, "has often been liable to corruption" (*CPW* 6:587) and should be submitted to the judgment of the individual believer, guided by the Spirit. Since the written text of the Bible is not to be taken as the final authority, much less would be classical, ante-Nicene, medieval, or contemporary texts. Milton would expect his "fit audience . . . though few" to exercise appropriate judgment.

In his prose, Milton departs from ancient—and not-so ancient—authorities in outlining a teleology by which it becomes clear that monarchy is *inherently* corrupt. For Milton, not only is the superiority of monarchy to other forms of government not self-evident (as it was for the classical and medieval writers), but in fact, monarchy is the result of the degradation and deterioration of mankind set in motion by the Fall. Milton increasingly comes to emphasize, both in his prose and his poetry, that the real perversion is not the existence of kings (good, bad, or ugly) but of *kingship* itself. The fact that Milton has no particular criticism of monarchs from Spain, France, Portugal, Sweden, Denmark, or various and sundry countries outside of England is irrelevant. For Milton, England is the country that really and truly matters in a way that none of these other nations can possibly matter.[26]

Quite simply, for Milton, England is—or has the opportunity to be—the new chosen nation of God, the new Israel. That Milton thought this is by no means a new suggestion. Sharon Achinstein refers to Milton's equation of England and Israel as a commonplace idea of his time and place: "Israel was not just a model for England, as Rome or Greece might be, but England was a recapitulation of Israel."[27] Barbara Lewalski has characterized the often-drawn parallels between England with Israel as "genuine recapitulations" in which God "deals with his new Israel as he did with the old."[28] In *Areopagitica*, Milton makes his notion of England's special status abundantly clear: God reveals truth "first to his English-men" (*CPW* 2:553), and England is "a City of refuge" (*CPW* 2:553), a "mansion house of liberty" (*CPW* 2:554), and "a Nation of Prophets, of Sages, and of Worthies" (*CPW* 2:554). England, for Milton, had been chosen by God as a special possession, a light to the rest of the world. Abject cringing and fawning servility in the face of the challenges of freedom rendered Milton's countrymen incapable of living up to the rigors of such an ideal, and the dying cries of liberty in Milton's *Ready and Easy Way* attest to this miserable failure of God's "English-men." But during the time in which Milton is writing such antimonarchical tracts as *Tenure of Kings and Magistrates*, *Eikonoklastes*, and *A Defence of the People of England*, the failure of England has not yet become evident, and Milton has, as yet, no reason to abandon his optimistic view of the English as the newly chosen people of God.

Milton is neither isolated nor particularly radical in adopting the view that England is the modern version of Israel, a new special possession of God. Millenarianism, a movement that had been gaining strength in England since the fifteenth century, had reached a fevered pitch by the 1640s, and Milton is merely the best-remembered and most eloquent spokesman for a spiritual mood that had swept through the time and place in which he lived. Writing in *Areopagitica* that the nation of England was "chos'n before any other, that out of her as out of *Sion* should be proclam'd and sounded forth the first tidings and trumpet of Reformation" (*CPW* 2:552), Milton identifies England with Israel in a manner similar to contemporaries such as Arise Evans, John Reeve, and Lodowick Muggleton (men to the right and to the left of Milton both politically and theologically).

In Milton's day, such hopes fed into phenomena as various as the Leveler fight against enclosures of land (echoing the Israelite provision of the Jubilee year, in which lands and properties were returned to their original owners),[29] the Fifth Monarchists' belief that a thousand-year earthly reign of Christ was imminent, and the Diggers' claim that the poor should be able to cultivate common land (based, in part, on the Israelite provision of gleaning—picking up grain fallen on the ground in the normal course of the harvest).[30]

Regardless, however, of the extent to which Milton's millenarianism is a shared phenomenon among his contemporaries, by the time Milton likens England to Israel, it seems no longer possible to fathom either how Milton could regard heavenly kingship as "a picture of government truly sublime,"[31] or how Milton could himself go on to pen anything other than a wholesale rejection of kingship.[32] Davies' suggestion—that feudal kingship would have been not only acceptable, but also beautiful, in the eyes of the Milton who writes *Paradise Lost*—cannot be reconciled with a view of England as the new Israel. Fallon's contention—that because Milton did not specifically reject foreign kings, therefore Milton did not reject *kingship*—also cannot stand up to the test administered by Milton's equation of England with Israel. England should not have kings, because Israel was not to have kings.

Kings were given to Israel as a *punishment*, not as a blessing. Furthermore, the fact that the nations surrounding Israel had kings was a sign of their alienation and estrangement from God; the fact that Moab had a king was—or should have been—irrelevant to Israel. God's rejection of kingship in Israel was a rejection of *kingship*. Similarly, Milton's condemnation of kings and kingship in England is tantamount to a censure of kingship everywhere. Like Moab, such European nations as Spain, France, and Portugal are alienated and estranged from God. There would be no point in condemning the sins of nations already rejected by God.

I suggest, by way of contrast to the readings of Davies, Fallon, and Bennett, that the pervasive and historically problematic images of divine kingship in *Paradise Lost* may be reconciled with Milton's increasingly emphatic opposition to the institution of monarchy by viewing kingship itself through a different historical lens—one demonstrably near and dear to Milton himself. The earliest portions of the Hebrew Bible (those portions least "corrupted" in Milton's eyes) reveal that the roots of heavenly kingship are no less "oriental"—and therefore, in the terms of Davies' analysis, no more "despotic"—than are the roots of the Satanic monarchy so vividly realized in *Paradise Lost.*

Milton's relationship to the Biblical text is problematic, given that he claims that the text of the Greek scriptures (or the "New Testament") "has often been liable to corruption" (*CPW* 6:587), but here I think we can rely on the correlation between the narratives of kingship in Milton's writings and in the Hebrew scriptures. In expressing the dynamic relationship between Milton and the Bible, Regina Schwartz argues that: "[Milton] makes distinctions between the authority of an external and internal scripture. Furthermore . . . he takes authority away from the external scripture altogether to confer it on the internal scripture."[33] Schwartz makes this observation in the midst of a complex argument that has Milton using the Bible to authorize his own positions while at the same time using his positions to authorize the Bible. In essence, Milton is involved in a continual exchange of authority with the text he at once rejects and refines. As Schwartz argues, "Because Milton authorizes the Bible, the Bible in turn authorizes Milton."[34]

Early Biblical narratives, in fact, offer Milton ample evidence that conceiving of God in monarchical terms is a human custom, one that originated, not with the people of the "true" God, but with those peoples who worshipped the "false" gods of the nations. Because Milton makes a point of using Biblical precedents (validated by his "internal scripture of the Holy Spirit" [*CPW* 6:587]) to overthrow human "custom" in practically every argument he ever makes, it seems not only possible, but obvious, that he could and would employ the same tactic in the service of a complete poetic rejection of kingship.

The Scriptural Development of God as King

In writing about both heavenly and earthly realms, I believe that Milton's encyclopedic Biblical knowledge leads him ultimately to a position more consistent—and more radical, both theologically and politically—than the partial or tepid condemnations of monarchy commonly ascribed to him by modern interpreters. Milton's passions and positions are never half-hearted; what Milton looses on earth, he looses in heaven. Ultimately, drawing from a rich and complex palette of Biblical history and political radicalism, Milton in *Paradise Lost* paints God as a king, not in order to provide a perfect model of the monarchy he abhors, but instead to subject the human custom of commingling the sacred and the profane—divinity and monarchy—to a devastating critique.

Milton is, of course, at least as aware as any of his Bible-reading contemporaries that kingship began in rebellion. In fact, his proficiency in the original languages of the Bible likely makes him more acutely aware of the original Biblical nature of kingship than his more limited, theologically and politically jingoistic contemporaries. Milton maintains that for the public interpretation of scripture, "[t]he requisites are linguistic ability, knowledge of the original sources, consideration of the overall intent . . . " (*CPW* 6:582); as a result of his own ability, knowledge, and consideration, Milton could have been only too aware that the first appearance of the word *mamlakah* (or "kingdom") in the Hebrew scriptures is not in reference to Yahweh, but to Nimrod, "a mighty hunter before the Lord" (Gen. 10:9), whose "kingdom was Babel . . . " (Gen. 10:10). In *Eikonoklastes*, Milton notes this verse explicitly, calling Nimrod "the first that founded Monarchy" (*CPW* 3:466) and later referring to him as "the first King," while noting that "*the beginning of his Kingdom was Babel*" (*CPW* 3:598). Let us be clear about what Milton does *not* say here; he does not say that Nimrod is the first pale imitator of "a King of Heaven so glorious and a court so splendid that it put his idolatrous imitators to shame."[35] Milton does not say that Nimrod is the first that founded *human* monarchy as an imitation of *divine* monarchy. Milton does not say that Nimrod got out of bed one morning to declare that "to him shall bow / All knees" (*Paradise Lost* 5.607–8) on earth because God had long ago made a similar demand in heaven, and Nimrod thought he might like to get in on a little of that knee-crooking action. Milton does not qualify the simple statement that Nimrod was "the first that founded monarchy" except by preceding it with the phrase, "reputed by ancient Tradition" (*CPW* 3:466); however, in this instance the firm Biblical support for the characterization of Nimrod as a monarch puts Milton's often uneasy relationship to tradition and authority to rest. He does not contest tradition's opinion of Nimrod because it agrees not only with the Bible's opinion, but also with his own opinion, of Nimrod.

Milton's thorough awareness of the Biblical background leads inexorably to a series of realizations: first, that kingship is a foreign ("heathenish") invention that walks hand-in-hand with tyranny;[36] second, that the title *melekh* or "king" is not applied to Yahweh in the Hebrew scriptures until *after* the kingship of Nimrod; third, that the concept of God as a king comes from human customs of kingship; and fourth, that the model of kingship therefore flows from Man to God, not from God to Man.

The essentially foreign nature of kingship (considered from the points of view outlined in the earliest Biblical narratives) is illustrated by a consideration of other Near Middle East deities. The Ammonite deity Molech is a king. *El Elyon*—the deity of city dwellers like Melchizedek, the king of Salem who invokes him—is conceived of in Syro-Palestinian mythology as a king. The roots of kingship are, in fact, bound up with the roots of cities themselves; Nimrod, the tyrant who as the first Biblical king is described by Milton as "first that hunted after faction," was also a builder of multiple cities. Babel, Erech, Accad, Calneh, Ninevah, Rehoboth, Calah, and Resen are all credited to the mighty hunter.

In direct contrast to the city-dwelling worshippers of monarchical gods, the patriarchs Abraham, Isaac, and Jacob dwell in tents, each living as "a stranger and a sojourner" (Gen. 23:4) in the land of Canaan, each worshipping a god specifically *not* conceived in terms of kingship. Significantly, though Adam names everything with which God presents him (Gen. 1:19, 2:20), he does not use the title *melekh* or king in reference to God himself. God is not yet conceived in terms of kingship at this early stage of Biblical narrative; throughout Genesis, it is only humans, and specifically humans *not* in the service of Yahweh, who make use of the term *melekh*.

It is not until after the years of Egyptian captivity that Yahweh comes to be referred to as a king. Exodus 15:18 declares that Yahweh "shall reign [*malak*] forever." In the years between Joseph and Moses, something fundamental has changed in the way Yahweh is imagined.

Baruch Halpern, in *The Constitution of the Monarchy in Israel*, explains how this imaginative change may likely have come about. Halpern maintains that Yahweh becomes "king" by delivering the Israelites from Egypt: "In return for a promise of fealty, he [Yahweh] vows to liberate the Israelites from Egypt *and* to settle them in a fruitful land."[37] Halpern suggests a parallel between Yahweh and Marduk in the way each deity achieves the rank of king: though the stories take place on different levels—Marduk's in the assembly of the Annunaki (the collected gods), and Yahweh's in the human realm of Egypt and Canaan—the parallels are striking: "the suzerain contracts to rescue the assembly; he . . . demonstrates his capacity by some sign or test; and he is enthroned on a permanent basis."[38] Both Marduk and Yahweh win their respective kingships by successfully playing the role of Divine Warrior: Marduk's victory is over Tiamat, while Yahweh's is over the Pharaoh of Egypt.

It is through this role as Divine Warrior that Yahweh's kingship is established and eventually made "universal." According to Halpern, "such poems as Judges 5:9–13, Deuteronomy 33:2–5, Exodus 15, and Psalm 44:1–5 . . . make use of the myth of the Divine Warrior in their imagery," and such use follows a typical pattern: Yahweh "rescued Israel from its foes, as the Divine Warrior rescued the world from Chaos; therefore [Yahweh] has gained kingship over Israel, as the Divine Warrior earned dominion over the cosmos."[39]

Yahweh's "kingship" emerges during the critical interval between Joseph and Moses; because the God of Israel is a successful Divine Warrior, rescuing Israel from its enemies, he is acclaimed as king, not only of Israel, but also of all the earth. Psalm 47 is a striking example of this pattern of divine acclamation: "O clap your hands, all ye people; shout unto God with the voice of triumph. For the LORD most high is terrible; he is a great King over all the earth. He shall subdue the people under us, and the nations under our feet" (1–3).

The Divine Warrior pattern, however, is (like kingship itself) a foreign import. Marduk is the god of Nimrod, not the god of Abraham, Isaac, and Jacob. While the subduing of the watery deep, the *Tehom* of Gen. 1, retains mythic echoes of the epic struggle between Marduk and Tiamat (a goddess whose name is associated in the *Enuma Elish* with the salt waters of the ocean), it has been almost completely "nativized" in a way that the elevation of the onetime Bedouin deity to universal kingship cannot be.[40]

Kingship, then, begins as an adoption of the ways of foreign nations, nations not in the service of Yahweh. Yahweh's promises to Abraham at Gen. 17:1–6 that "kings [*melekh*] shall come out of thee," along with his later promises to Jacob that kings shall descend from him (at Gen. 35:11, 12 and 36:9, 15–43), acknowledge that many of the descendants of these men (Ishmael, for example) will not be among the chosen people. Yahweh's promises are also a reflection of the thoroughly "Canaanized" monarchical regimes of David and the later kings of the northern and southern kingdoms under whom the Hebrew scriptures were written and compiled. Kingship remains a sign of the corrupting influence of living among nations not in the service of Yahweh. The provision of kingship at Deut. 17:14–20 is not a recommendation from God that the Israelites adopt a king; rather, it is an after-the-fact justification for kingship during the reign of Josiah (c. 640–609 B.C.E.).

Violence, decay, and the corrupting influence on God's people of living among the nations are nowhere more outstandingly illustrated in the Bible than in the Book of Judges,[41] the last three chapters of which are almost a straight propaganda piece for kingship. Possibly written sometime during the reign of the Judean king Josiah, Judges ends with the simple statement, "In those days, there was no king in Israel." This nearly constant refrain in the latter half of Judges lays all corruption and disorder at the feet of the failure of the Judges-period Israelites to adopt the monarchical hierarchies of the surrounding nations.

The urge to centralize is already present in the narrative, however, before this refrain appears. In Judg. 8:22–23, Gideon refuses the offer of kingship over Israel, both for himself and for his sons. In refusing kingship for himself, Gideon says to the people "I will not rule [*mashal*] over you, the Lord will rule [*mashal*] over you." Gideon's son, Abimelech—whose name means "my father is king"—did briefly attempt to reign as a king (and his name suggests that perhaps Gideon had second thoughts about the people's offer). In this early portion of the Judges narrative, a refusal of kingship is considered virtuous, a sign of a healthy and ongoing relationship with Yahweh, the true God. Even here, however, the influence of the surrounding nations with their human and divine kings can be seen taking root in Israelite soil. The primary "king" is now Yahweh. The image of God has already become corrupted, becoming like the images of deity held by the surrounding nations, and this is the first step toward the eventual adoption of human monarchy "like all the nations."

Despite Gideon's refusal of a crown, the Israelites will not be put off permanently in their quest for a centralized, king-based system of governance. 1 Sam. 8 recounts the demand of the elders of Israel that a king rule over them after the manner of the surrounding nations. Samuel tries to tell them that this is not such a good idea, listing a virtual catalog of monarchical abuses that will inevitably follow: the king will take the sons of the people to serve as charioteers and warriors; he will take the daughters of the people to serve as bakers and housekeepers; the king will take the best lands for himself, and will tax the produce of all remaining lands. Still, the people insist on having a human king. After telling Samuel that the Israelites have not rejected Samuel but the Lord God himself, Yahweh tells Samuel to grant the request of the people. Thus Saul is anointed as the first king of Israel. Saul, the first king of Israel, is set on his throne by a wrathful God who uses this first Israelite monarch to punish a people who had demanded a king.

With Israel's shift from a commonwealth (what Milton refers to in *Tenure of Kings and Magistrates* as God's "own ancient goverment" [*CPW* 3:236]) to human kingship, the practice of imagining Yahweh as a king becomes permanently entrenched. The prominence of this image of Yahweh as a king is, in fact, one of the most notable features of the Psalms. The Psalmist prays to "my King, and my God" at 5:2. Yahweh is the "Lord of hosts ... the King of glory" at 24:10, and "sitteth King for ever" at 29:10. He is "Lord of Hosts, my King, and my God" at 84:3. His "kingdom is an everlasting kingdom" at 145:13.

Nor is God dethroned by the rise of early Christianity. In fact, the image of God as king in the Greek scriptures deepens and extends the pattern seen in the preceding Hebrew examples. 1 Tim. 1:17 proclaims God *basilei ton aionon*, or king eternal. Conceiving of the Christian God as *forever* a king places him squarely alongside such king-gods as Marduk (declared king of the gods in the *Enuma Elish* prior to his defeat of Tiamat and his creation of Man), and Molech (the king-god of the Ammonites). Matt. 5:35, which describes heaven as the throne of God, refers to Jerusalem as the city of the great King (*basileus*). The adoption of the early Canaanite imagery (specifically the imagery of Molech and Nimrod as kings) and the association with Nimrod as a founder and ruler of cities are now complete. Yahweh (as well as the Christian "Father" based thereon) *as king* is in fact a portrait drawn from the "oriental" models of Molech, Marduk, and Nimrod.[42]

Arguments from recent scholarship, however, are vulnerable to the charge that Milton's contemporaries—and perhaps Milton himself—read the Bible as a unified text presenting a coherent and reliable chronology of sacred history. Such readers would naturally be unaware of modern theories that assert the influence of Near Middle East cultures on the text of the Bible, regarding Deuteronomy's provision of kingship as an expression of Yahweh's will. Two points can be raised in response to this charge. First, such a reading puts Yahweh at cross-purposes with himself—apparently establishing kingship under Moses, quietly eliminating it at some unspecified later point, then reestablishing it *as a punishment* during the latter days of Samuel—a situation that in and of itself seems to undermine any assertion of unity or coherence in the text. Second, and more important, the argument that Milton and his contemporaries read the Bible as a unified or coherent text is, at best, problematic. Christopher Hill has done valuable work in demonstrating that a view of the Bible as a unified and coherent text was far from universally held among Milton's contemporaries. Gerrard Winstanley, for example, "accepted that the text of the Bible was uncertain" and "rejected much Biblical history in favor of allegorical interpretations."[43] Winstanley also traced kingship and monarchical power to Cain's killing of Abel,[44] and characterized "Kingly government" as "the government of highwaymen."[45] Moreover, the notion that kingship was a corruption introduced into the lives of the people of the true God is current in Milton's day. Hill gives as an example of this attitude a "near-Digger pamphlet" of 1649, which argues that "'the rise of dukes was from wicked Esau,'"[46] the brother who rejected his birthright and became the founder of the Edomite people.

Heavenly and Earthly Kingship in Milton's Prose

For Milton, who writes in *De Doctrina Christiana* that "God is always described or outlined not as he really is but in such a way as will make him conceivable to us" (*CPW* 6:133), the changing portrait of God throughout the scriptures would not represent a change in God as He is, but rather a change—and a change decidedly for the worse—in the character of God's people, who clamor for a human king "like all the nations" (1 Sam. 8:5). In *Tenure of Kings and Magistrates,* Milton specifically argues that the Israelites' demand for a king reflects a generalized "oriental" tendency towards slavery: "the people of Asia, and with them the Jews also, especially since the time they chose a King against the advice and counsel of God, are noted by wise Authors much inclinable to slavery" (*CPW* 3:202–3). After lumping in Israel with the other "people of Asia," Milton goes on to characterize the giving of a king to Israel as a punishment out of God's wrath: "God was heretofore angry with the Jews who rejected him and his forme of Goverment to choose a king" (*CPW* 3:236). Milton makes his contempt for the Israelites' choice clear in *Eikonoklastes* when he refers to "those foolish *Israelites*, who depos'd God and *Samuel* to set up a King" (*CPW* 3:580). It is unsurprising that this same Milton finds grounds to refer to Englishmen who demand a king as "a race of Idiots" (*CPW* 3:542).

Milton seems to have followed a course of development that starts in the early 1640s with acceptance of kingship as the form of government most likely to be friendly to reformation of the English church, that progresses into the antipathy toward Charles I seen in the antimonarchical tracts of the late 1640s and early 1650s, and that finally develops by 1660 into a full-blown rejection of kingship in *The Ready and Easy Way*. The assumption that Milton was at least nominally royalist in his antiprelatical tracts has long been common in Milton criticism. A World War II–era royalist like G. Wilson Knight is hardly making a dramatic statement when he writes that "Milton's anti-episcopal pamphlets are the work of a fervent royalist."[47] J. H. Hanford describes Milton in his antiprelatical pamphlet period as "with the majority of his countrymen, conservative, assuming the monarchical form of government as that to which the nation is permanently committed."[48] However neatly this line may seem to connect the dots of Milton's published attitudes toward kings and kingship, I believe that this is more a tracing of what he was willing to say publicly than an accurate sketch of changing thoughts Milton may have had. This is also Christopher Hill's contention, as he argues that even before his entry into the church-government controversies of the early 1640s, "Milton [was] at least considering anti-monarchical sentiments which he did not find it expedient to express openly until 1649."[49] Rather than developing an anti-monarchical frame of mind through his career of writing prose and poetry, Milton gives clues early on about his negative attitudes towards kings, kingship, and external authority.

Early in his career as a pamphleteer, Milton reveals his predispositions on the subject of the methods of governing. In *The Reason of Church Government* (1641), he writes that "persuasion" is preferable "to keepe men in obedience than feare" (*CPW* 1:746). Nearly thirty years later, the older Milton will put similar sentiments into the mouth of the Son of God, who holds it both humane and heavenly to "Make persuasion do the work of fear" (*Paradise Regained* 1.223). I believe that this consistency lies at the heart of Milton's attitude toward externally imposed authority of all kinds—church government, secular government, and, ultimately, the human relation to the divine itself. Government must persuade, and it must do so by working with the intellects and consciences of the governed; if government does not function in this manner, then it becomes tyranny, however benevolent it may appear. Government of the "inner man" (*Paradise Regained* 2.477) is the only true government; external government— kingship both on earth and in heaven—exists only as a result of the deleterious effects of the Fall. Kingship is a daily reminder of the failure of the "inner man."

Milton's belief that this "inner man" is somehow redeemable is made clear in his 1644 treatise *Of Education*, where he outlines the ultimate purpose for human education: "The end then of learning is to repair the ruins of our first parents by regaining to know God aright, and out of that knowledge to love him, to imitate him, to be like him, as we may the neerest by possessing our souls of true vertue" (*CPW* 2:366–67).

To argue that education can "repair" the "ruins" produced by the Fall of Adam and Eve is as radical a theological statement as I can find in Milton. This verges on the territory of Pelagius, who argued that mankind was capable of, and therefore responsible for, its own spiritual regeneration. Milton here reduces everything to one simple principle: love, imitate, and be like God. This cuts to shreds notions of Milton's inconsistency on the issues of kingship and man's proper relation to God, and renders untenable the arguments that would have Milton defending in Heaven what he assailed on Earth. If Man's greatest achievement, as Milton says in *Of Education* (*CPW* 2:366) and as the Son says in *Paradise Regained* (2.475), is to know God "aright," to imitate and be like God, *and* if, as Milton argues in *Tenure of Kings and Magistrates*, human monarchy is the end result of a process of falling *away* from God, then God cannot possibly be a monarch. God is not a king; God cannot be a king, because, for Man to "love him, to imitate him, to be like him," human kingship would have to be approved by God.

Milton's "inner man" will not become like God through unquestioning obedience to any arbitrary authority intent on making equally arbitrary declarations. Authority exercised in this manner can have only negative consequences. A case in point is the proclamation made by the Father in *Paradise Lost* 5.600–615. Here, the Father (presumably without consultation) anoints the Son as a king before whom all must kneel instantly and without question or murmur. Those who fail this test of immediate and *cheerful* obedience are threatened with the direst consequences: they shall be "Cast out from God and blessed vision . . . / Into utter darkness, deep ingulft, his place / Ordain'd without redemption, without end" (5.613–15). Threats are the currency of the bully; threats are no way to govern the "inner man." Outward complicity is all that such threats will purchase, as evidenced by the consequence of the Father's threats—hypocrisy: "All seem'd well pleas'd, all seem'd, but were not all" (5.617).

That such governing techniques are doomed to abject failure is a truth all too obvious to the Son after the war in heaven. True government cannot be conducted through fear; rather, it must be undertaken through persuasion. This model of relationship between ruler and ruled, between God and Man, requires subjects capable of being persuaded, subjects educated enough to recognize the good when it is placed before them. Ironically, our ability to recognize the good requires, in the epistemology Milton outlines in *Areopagitica*, a familiarity with evil: "As therefore the state of man now is; what wisdome can there be to choose, what continence to forbeare without knowledge of evil?" (*CPW* 2:514). Milton suggests that the knowledge of evil that is necessary for the ability to recognize and choose the good is the primary benefit of "books promiscuously read" (*CPW* 2:517). Far from the "lowly wise" attitude recommended to Adam (*Paradise Lost* 8.173), Milton's suggestion reflects an attitude of aggressive knowledge and truth seeking, a model of intellectual and spiritual inquiry similar to that of the Bereans whom Paul referred to as noble because their obedience required persuasion: they "searched the scriptures daily, whether those things were so" (Acts 17:11).

Being "lowly wise"—being content to "Think only what concerns thee and thy being" (*Paradise Lost* 8.174)—is the advice not of the Father or the Son, but of Raphael, the angelic messenger sent to Adam and Eve when they are about to face an assault from Satan. Such advice does not represent any recognizably Miltonic epistemology. The "fugitive and cloister'd vertue" (*Areopagitica, CPW* 2:515) that Raphael encourages when he bids Adam to "Solicit not thy thoughts with matters hid" (*Paradise Lost* 8.167) would have left Milton himself either unwilling or unable to pursue "Things unattempted yet in Prose or Rhyme" (*Paradise Lost* 1.16), or to "see and tell / Of things invisible to mortal sight" (*Paradise Lost* 3.55). Lowly wisdom is not Miltonic wisdom, nor is it the wisdom of Milton's "fit" audience.

Far from recommending lowly wisdom, Milton spent much of his life arguing against it. From the antiprelatical tracts to the divorce tracts to the antimonarchical tracts, Milton continually struggles against human "custom"—an "everyone knows *that*" variety of lowly wisdom Milton equates with ignorance—in favor of Biblical texts and interpretations that support his arguments. As early as *The Reason of Church Government*, Milton argues for theological and political consistency on at least one level—using the Bible as the source of models for civil and religious authority:

> [T]his practice we may learn, from a better & more ancient authority, then any heathen writer hath to give us . . . how could it be but we should find it in that book, within whose sacred context all wisdome is infolded? (*CPW* 1:746–47)

Milton goes on to insist that just as Moses instructed "the Jewes . . . in a generall reason of that government to which their subjection was requir'd," so "the Gospell" should instruct Christians "in the reason of that government which the Church claimes to have over them" (*CPW* 1:747). In *The Reason of Church Government*, Milton avers that it is "custome" that is "the creator of Prelaty," and that prelaty is "lesse ancient than the government of Presbyters" (*CPW* 1:778). The hierarchy of authority inherent in this statement is a key to understanding Milton's hermeneutical stance toward both theological and political controversies; the ancient models are those that Milton "recovers," excavating them from beneath the dust and rubbish of later "custom." Milton begins his *Tenure of Kings and Magistrates* in precisely the same manner:

> If men within themselves would be govern'd by reason, and not generally give up their understanding to a double tyrannie, of Custom from without and blind affections within, they would discerne better what it is to favour and uphold the Tyrant of a Nation. (*CPW* 3:190)

Milton continues making his case by returning to original principles,[50] compared to which kingship is "less ancient":

> I shall here set downe from first beginning, the original of Kings; how and wherfore exalted to that dignitie above thir Brethren; and from thence shall prove, that turning to Tyranny they may bee as lawfully depos'd and punish'd, as they were at first elected. (*CPW* 3:198)

Originally, Milton reminds us, "all men naturally were borne free, being the image and resemblance of God himself" (*CPW* 3:198). Kings, then, in Milton's analysis, are the end result of a long chain of events set in motion by the Fall. After "*Adams* transgression, falling among themselves to doe wrong and violence," men "agreed by common league to bind each other from mutual injury, and joyntly to defend themselves against any that gave disturbance or opposition to such agreement" (*CPW* 3:199).

This history and teleology of kingship are sufficient to cast serious doubt on the idea that Milton approved of imagining God as a king. The logical, if absurd, extension of such imagining would posit a heavenly king as an angel elected by the rest to protect the angels from their own descent into "wrong and violence." This is similar to the way Satan imagines the Father in *Paradise Lost*, thinking of the Father as, in Empson's phrase, "a usurping angel."[51] However, Milton elsewhere makes his opposition to heavenly kingship clear enough that we need not rest with logical inference and reasonable doubt.

In the fifth chapter of *The Reason of Church Government*, Milton is already arguing against an identification of divinity with kingship. In refuting Bishop Andrewes's contention that Christ was foreshadowed in Hebrew scripture by both kings and priests, Milton accuses Andrewes of using this (satirically labeled) "[m]arvelous piece of divinity" to "ingage [the king's] power for them [the bishops of the Church of England] as in his own quarrell, that when they fall they may fall in a generall ruine" (*CPW* 1:769–70). Milton's pointed question to Andrewes is an early indication of his rejection of "Heav'n's king": "But where, O Bishop, doth the purpose of the law set forth Christ to us as a King?" (*CPW* 1:770). Milton's answer to his own question makes his rejection clear:

> That which never was intended in the Law, can never be abolish't as part thereof. When the Law was made, there was no King: if before the law, or under the law God by a speciall type in any king would fore-

signifie the future kingdome of Christ, which is not yet visibly come, what was that to the law? The whole ceremoniall law, and types can be in no law else, comprehends *nothing but the propitiatory office of Christs Priesthood.* (*CPW* 1:770–71)

Milton's reference to "the future kingdome of Christ" only makes his discomfort with the idea of divinity conceived in terms of kingship more obvious. "That which never was intended in the Law" (the same law that forbids graven images of the deity) was also never intended to become a part of the human imagining of the divine. Some years later, Milton will argue in *Eikonoklastes* that "*Christs Kingdom* [should] be tak'n for the true Discipline of the Church" (*CPW* 3:536). In referring to Christ as "our common King" (*CPW* 7:429), and "our true and rightfull and only to be expected King" (*CPW* 7:445) in *The Ready and Easy Way*, Milton is writing of *spiritual* kingship, not a "Heavenly" kingship that looks like an impossibly glorious version of the court of Charles I. In other words, "the future kingdome of Christ" is a spiritual arrangement of *faith* and *worship*, not a secular arrangement of politics and power (no matter whether such a "secular" arrangement is located on earth or in heaven).[52]

As the Son will later say in *Paradise Regained*, to be truly "kingly" is to exercise spiritual dominion, to govern (in the sense of discipline) the "inner man, the nobler part" (2.477). Each Christian who takes his or her obligations as a Christian in a serious and spiritual sense is thus already "kingly" in this manner and needs no other king on earth *or* in heaven. Just as Milton relies on a familiar post-Reformation formulation of the "priesthood of all believers" in his antiprelatical tracts (arguing against bishops as an unnecessary and actively deleterious hierarchical layer separating the Christian from God), so he comes to rely on an analogous construction of the "kingship of all believers" (arguing against kings and kingship in the same way) in his later antimonarchical tracts. Much as bishops stood between true Christians (who are "priestly") and a right relationship with God, so also do kings stand between true Christians (who are "kingly") and God. Worse still, *the idea of God as a king*, an external ruler who demands outward compliance delivered with promptness and ceremony, prevents the Christian from, in the Son's words, "knowing . . . God aright" (*Paradise Regained* 2.475). In the argument with Bishop Andrewes, Milton has taken his first steps, not only in arguing against the custom of picturing God and/or Christ as a king, but also in redefining what it means to be truly "kingly."

Milton does not stop here, however, but goes on in *Eikonoklastes* to a similar denigration of "custom" in relation to kingship. He refers contemptuously to those "who through custom, simplicitie, or want of better teaching, have not more seriously considerd Kings, than in the gaudy name of Majesty" (*CPW* 3:338). To seriously consider kings, Milton suggests, would be to realize that majesty, in its external, and "gaudy" trappings, is not truly kingly. Later, Milton sneers at "the easy literature of custom and opinion," declaring that "few perhaps, but . . . such of value and substantial worth" (*CPW* 3:339–40) will align themselves with Milton's own rejection of such custom. The foreshadowing of the "fit audience . . . though few" of *Paradise Lost* is unmistakable here.

In *A Defence of the People of England*, Milton briefly recalls the account he gave in *Tenure of Kings and Magistrates* of the growth of kingship, but he makes an important addition: the formation of churches. "Men first came together to form a state in order to live in safety and freedom without violence or wrong; they founded a church to live in holiness and piety" (*CPW* 4:320–21). The origin of both kings and churches, then, is the Fall. King and Church issue not from blessings but from curses, maledictions cast upon fallen mankind. This insight flowers from the seeds planted in *The Reason of Church Government*, where Milton finds the proper forms of both civil and church governments in the Bible. It is a tantalizing prospect to consider that Milton—who was, according to Thomas Newton, "a dissenter from the Church of England [and] not a professed member of any particular sect of Christians"[53]—may have rejected both King and Church, seeing them, finally, as obstacles preventing mankind from knowing God "aright."

Milton goes on in *A Defence of the People of England* to specifically and unequivocally identify the form of civil government recommended in the Bible as a commonwealth, in direct contradistinction to modern interpretations of his writings that would suggest a Miltonic longing for "ideal" or heavenly monarchy:

> A republican form of government, moreover, as being better adapted to our human circumstances than monarchy, seemed to God more advantageous for his chosen people; he set up a republic for them and

granted their request for a monarchy only after long reluctance. (*CPW* 4:344)

Furthermore, Milton argues that God gave the Israelites a king only out of anger: "God was wroth at their desire for a king, not in accordance with divine law but in imitation of the gentiles, and he was wroth furthermore that they desired a king at all" (*CPW* 4:347). In *Ready and Easy Way*, Milton flatly states that God "imputed it a sin to [the Israelites] that they sought [a king]" and further maintains that "*Christ* . . . forbids his disciples to admitt of any such heathenish government" (*CPW* 7:424).

Ample textual evidence demonstrates that Milton considers the "custom" of kingship to be a foreign imposition on God's people; kings are endured as a punishment that, but for the Fall, would never have been necessary. Thus, Milton's portrait of a monarchical Father, a character that has troubled readers and critics alike for centuries, troubles precisely because it is supposed to trouble. The Father's heavenly crown is not an exhibit of heavenly perfection; it is instead a necessary contrast to a perfect form of rule (both heavenly and earthly) that is offered by the Son, who offers the best indication of the system that had the most "obvious beauty" for Milton.

Heavenly and Earthly Kingship in Milton's Poetry

The portrait of heavenly kingship in *Paradise Lost* is a triptych; the central portion of the piece—with its somber egg tempera image of the Father as a king sitting upon the throne of heaven—cannot be understood properly without reference to the images on its right and left. The panel at the left hand of the Father depicts Satan, and the panel to the right hand of the Father pictures the Son. Each of the peripheral figures represents a balance and contrast to the middle figure; the characters portrayed on the left and right sides of Milton's triptych both offer a challenge to a Father ruling as an "absolute monarch."[54] Each character rejects the idea of the Father as an unquestioned and unquestionable ruler. For Satan and the Son, the Father will not pass unchallenged as an absolute monarch, certainly not in the terms described by Aristotle (from whom Milton learned much in preparation for his arguments against tyranny): a tyrant is "an individual which is responsible to no one, and governs all alike, whether equals or betters, with a view to its own advantage, not to that of its subjects, and therefore against their will."⁵⁵ Critics who engage in what Empson described as "the modern duty of catching Satan out wherever possible"⁵⁶ delight in emphasizing Satan's descent into tyranny while trying to avoid—at all costs—coming to grips with the uncomfortable extent to which the Father in *Paradise Lost* fits the definition of a tyrant.⁵⁷

The Father is first referred to as a "supreme King" in *Paradise Lost* at 1.735, after the demonic associations of kingship have been thoroughly rehearsed over the last three hundred lines, and in the midst of a description of the demonic architect whom men, "erring" (1.747), call Mulciber. During the debate in Hell, the fallen angels continually refer to the Father as a king: he is twice "the King of Heaven" (2.229 and 2.316), and he "first and last will Reign / Sole king" (2.325). Satan and his followers take it for granted that the Father is a king, and a tyrannical king at that. They are in this estimation, correct. A tyrant, according to Milton, is "he who regarding neither Law nor the common good, reigns onely for himself and his faction" (*Tenure of Kings and Magistrates*, *CPW* 3:212). For whom else does the Father rule, except for "himself and his faction"? The Father may very well regard "law," but it is difficult to see how he regards "the common good," especially when it is the Son who must vigorously remind him of that good in Book 3 of *Paradise Lost*. To argue that the Father gets to define the common good is particularly slippery; this is rather like the argument of Euthyphro in the Platonic dialogue of the same name—piety is piety, not of itself, but because it is dear to the gods, and impiety is impiety, not of itself, but because it is abhorrent to the gods. Variations of this same justification are made in the name of each of history's great tyrannies—the leader knows best, and what the leader defines as the good is the good.

In an argument that aims to show that Milton's "God is not a tyrant," David Norbrook writes that "the fallen angels reveal themselves as unworthy of participation in the heavenly regime as soon as they disagree with God." Furthermore, he characterizes the Father's action of "driving out from the community all who are lacking in appropriate virtue" in Book 5 as one "more likely to seem tyrannical to the modern reader than to the early modern republican who was used to limiting political participation to the virtuous or godly."[58] It is difficult, however, to see what kind of *participation* the unfallen angels are engaged in, unless by participation is meant "a continual act of praise, expressed by kneeling."[59] Unlike Milton, it seems that the unfallen angels neither ask questions, nor make suggestions; much less do they ever display the level of initiative and/or discontent required for the "Abjuration of a single person" on a throne (*A Letter to a Friend, CPW* 7:330). To use a contemporary image, the unfallen angels seem primarily to fill the role of a studio audience that dutifully responds to the applause sign, but takes not even the smallest part in writing the script that is being played. If participation is defined as round-the-clock singing of the Father's praises (while on one's knees), then there is certainly a great deal of "participating" going on in Milton's heaven. Satan's challenge changes the terms of such participation from the singing of songs to the wielding of weapons (straightening a great many knees in the process), but there is still nothing readily identifiable as political participation, which seems, perversely enough, to be limited to the rebels, as there is "no room in Heaven for deliberative rhetoric, for the arguments of the forum."[60] There are neither focus groups, nor voting booths, in Milton's heaven.

Satan's challenge to the Father is mirrored by the Son's challenge. Left and right are reversed, as in a reflection whose similitude is an illusion, a trick of technique and the manipulation of light and shade. Where Satan is shaded, the Son is light; where Satan's challenge to the Father eventually brings out what is worst in him (his desire to emulate the absolute monarchy he once rejected), the Son's challenge[61] brings out what is best in him.

Many Milton scholars will object to the notion that the Son challenges the Father, holding instead that the Father and the Son speak with one voice, or express the essence of a Trinitarian—or quasi-Trinitarian—"Godhead" in a celestial dialogue. Albert Labriola, for instance, describes the scene between the Father and the Son in Book 3 as "the celestial dialogue that elaborates on the process leading to the consummate union of the faithful and the Godhead."[62] Rather than seeing them as two aspects of the same whole—a state that is *promised* by the repeated invocations of the idea that God will be "All in All," but not yet achieved in the time frame of the poem— I argue that the Father and the Son are *different* and *separate* entities.

In both his poetic and his theological representations of the Father and the Son, Milton opens up a space in which the Son may be considered as not merely subordinate to, but ontologically separate from the Father: in *De Doctrina Christiana,* Milton argues that "the Son is a different person from the Father" (*CPW* 6:205); "It does not follow, however, that the Son is of the same essence as the Father. For a real son is not of the same age as his father, still less of the same numerical essence: otherwise father and son would be one person" (*CPW* 6:209). In *Paradise Lost,* Milton clearly presents the Father and Son as separate persons. The demands of dramatic structure and dialogue require such a presentation, but the separation is more profound than that necessitated by simple dramatic exigency; while the Son reinforces the Father's ire in Book 6, he acts as a check on the Father's ire in Book 3. The Son (like Abraham, Moses, and Israel standing before Yahweh) *struggles* with the Father. In brief (previewing a point to which I will return in chapter 4), behind the Son's words in *Paradise Lost* 3.144–66 are the words of Abraham and Moses. The Son's "that far be from thee" is an almost direct quotation of Abraham's "that be far from thee" during his challenge to Yahweh over the planned destruction of Sodom and Gomorrah at Gen. 18:25.[63]

It should come as no surprise that the often irascible Yahweh looms behind the figure of a poetic character that Milton is careful to identify as Jehovah: "Great are thy works, *Jehovah,* infinite / Thy power" (*Paradise Lost* 7.602–3). What may surprise is the use to which Milton puts the Biblical character in the celestial dialogue of Book 3. Casting the Son in the position of Abraham emphasizes the confrontational nature of the Son's approach to the Father in this scene. Abraham's verbal struggle with Yahweh is no mere polite disagreement. Abraham takes a potentially fantastic risk by challenging the righteousness of his God. Another Biblical confrontation scene with which Milton works is that between Moses and Yahweh in Exod. 32. Yahweh tells Moses to leave him alone so that he may destroy the very people whom he has only recently led out of slavery in Egypt. Just as Moses pleads with God to "repent of this evil against thy people" (Exod. 32:12), so the Son implores the Father not to take an action that will allow Satan to question and blaspheme "without defense."

In the context of such challenges, the Son's confrontation of the Father is a demonstration of the passibility, the Yahweh-like emotional volatility and moral ambiguity of the Father. Michael Lieb has argued that Milton "not only intensifies the idea of passibility, but bestows upon it a new significance" in his portrait of the Father.[64] Lieb concludes, "the figure of God in *Paradise Lost* is portrayed as a fully passible being."[65] Such a being, passible and morally ambiguous, is what the Son confronts in Book 3 of *Paradise Lost*.

The Son begins his public career in a manner much less confrontational toward the Father than the stance he adopts in the debate of Book 3. When the Father announces his begetting in Book 5, the Son seems little more than an extension of the Father; the Father's ever-present concern with his "Omnipotence," "Arms," "Deity," and "Empire" (721–24) are echoed by the Son, who describes the controversy in heaven as "Matter to mee of Glory" (737). As the War in heaven is being fought and won, when "War wearied hath perform'd what War can do" (6.695), the Son still speaks of his own glory, but is beginning also to speak in terms of relinquishing the very power he has recently assumed: "Sceptre and Power, thy giving, I assume, / And gladlier shall resign" (6.730–31). After the war and the expulsion of the vanquished, the Son no longer seems so impressed with "Sceptre and Power" as he may have been previously. Mercy is now the Son's focus, not Power, not Sceptre, not even the Justice about which the Father rails (at 3.210) in what Empson describes as "the stage villain's hiss of 'Die he or Justice must.'"[66]

The Son's concern with "Glory" and "Sceptre and Power" has completely faded by the time he embarks on the fulfillment of the fatal bargain he made with the Father in Book 3 of *Paradise Lost*. In *Paradise Regained*, the Son's expressed contempt for the idea of kingship is devastating in its power. Government, to avoid being tyranny, must be internal, a self-government of each individual guided only by truth, and by "knowing . . . God aright" (2.475). The Son's contention is that existing forms of rule have not enabled most to properly know God. Kingship, Churches, external rule, threats, and the demand for outward compliance—all of these things have not only *not* enabled mankind to know God "aright," but have actively led mankind astray.

However, this is the kind of external regime that the Son has come to bring to an end, replacing it with a rule of "the inner man" (*Paradise Regained* 2.477). The Son has nothing to do with either oriental despotism or feudalism; nor is the Son's rule a "self-renouncing monarchy."[67] The Son promises, and delivers, something entirely different: *monarchy-renouncing monarchy*. Milton creates a Son for whom to be truly kingly is to "lay down" a kingdom, an action the Son considers "Far more magnanimous than to assume" (2.483). The Son's entire message, if he can be said to have a message in Milton, is that to know God "aright" is to know God as the Son himself knows God, to know that the rule of heaven is not external, but *internal*. The regime of the Son is not "o'er the body only," but of the "nobler part," a rule where there is no first, but only equality. To know God "aright" is to know that God is not a king.

Like the Son, Satan begins with concern for glory, but his progression is one designed, albeit unsuccessfully, to recover what he feels to be his own lost glory and to accrue more glory through battle, a quest that results in an ascension to a hellish throne. Satan's "ambition" is to "reign" (*Paradise Lost* 1.262), a concern similar to that the Father expresses in Book 5: "Nearly it concerns us to be sure / Of our Omnipotence, and with what Arms / We mean to hold what anciently we claim / Of Deity or Empire" (721–24). Both the Father and Satan seem primarily concerned with the consolidation, maintenance, or acquisition of power. Satan was, in this sense, right to claim that the Father held "the Tyranny of Heav'n" (1.124). However, Satan's mistake is not his challenge of the Father, but his method. Where Satan chooses military force in an attempt to cause the Father to doubt "his empire" from "terror of this arm" (1.113–14)—a strategy that proves an abject failure—the Son chooses to "make persuasion do the work of fear" (*Paradise Regained* 1.223), a preference Milton expresses as early as 1642, when in *The Reason of Church Government* he writes that "persuasion certainly is a more winning, and more manlike way to keepe men in obedience than feare" (*CPW* 1:746).

Through the contrasting challenges offered by Satan and the Son, Milton's rejection of the very idea of earthly *and* heavenly kingship comes sharply into focus. Milton's use of Satan and his rebellion against an absolute monarch in heaven also helps answer the perennial question of why Satan seems to overwhelm the reader's senses with the scope of his Achillean heroism. Satan is supposed to seem heroic—and not in Fish's sense of misleading the unwary reader line by line. Satan's heroism is real, and therefore his slow degeneration from Book 1 to Book 10 is not, as C. S. Lewis would have it, farcical, but legitimately tragic. Satan rises against an absolute monarch. So far, so good, Miltonically speaking. The complex of reasons for which he rises comprises both the failure and the wrong-headedness of his rebellion. Satan's sense of "injur'd merit" (1.98), according to his own admission to his closest compatriot, Beelzebub, is what raised him to contend with the Father. As Satan sees it, the issue is simple: Who has the right to reign in heaven? Satan proclaims that in preparation for battle he had "brought along / Innumerable force of Spirits arm'd / That durst dislike his reign, and mee preferring" (1.100–102). Thinking along similar lines, the Father, through his concern with "Deity" and "Empire" (revealed, not in spite of, but through what the Son glosses as "derision" [5.736]), seems to indicate that Satan may be more like the Father than many Milton critics would care to admit.

What drives the Son to contend with the Father in Book 3 is not a concern with his own merit—injured or rewarded—but mercy for the as-yet unfallen human race. Readings of this scene, like Fish's, that insist on the merely rhetorical character of the Father's conversation with the Son in the celestial dialogue deliberately puncture and deflate the swelling drama of what are perhaps the most important passages in all of *Paradise Lost.* If the Father is "determinedly non-affective" and is not talking "to anyone in particular,"[68] then Milton's great poetic triptych has its right hand panel lopped off, and is rendered less an artistic marvel of an earlier age than a damaged, but historically significant, curiosity. If denied the emotional weight of speaking back to power *in his own voice,* the Son is denied the great dignity of Abraham (a frail and mortal man contending with the Almighty over the fate of any righteous men who may live in Sodom and Gomorrah). The Son is also denied the heroism through which, by pleading for mercy to be shown to humanity and offering to die to satisfy the implacable "Justice" of the Father, he displays the greatest bravery imaginable. In a reading that denies him an active and crucial agency in Book 3, the Son is rendered a figure merely ridiculous and sycophantic, the worst—because the most powerful—of the "Minstrelsy of Heav'n" (6.168). Such a Son makes a villain of the Father who creates him. Such a Son hands the moral high ground to Satan.

In contrast to the tripartite structure of Milton's picture of heavenly kingship, earthly kingship in Milton's epics is portrayed rather more simply, nearly always associated either with tyranny or with estrangement from God, or in some combination thereof. Solomon, the "uxorious king" of *Paradise Lost* 1.444, is an example of kings alienated from the true God. A particularly instructive example is Jeroboam, the "rebel king" of 1.472–89, whose Miltonic portrait in *Paradise Lost* is one of apostasy, wickedness, and rebellion against God. However, as Davies has pointed out,[69] Milton, in his polemical argument with Salmasius (in *A Defence of the People of England*), finds himself forced to defend Jeroboam. Milton argues rather weakly: Jeroboam had overthrown his brother Rehoboam (the heir to the throne by birthright), and turned out to be exceedingly pagan and wicked; nevertheless, though Jeroboam and his successors were offenders against the true worship of God, they were not rebels (*CPW* 4:405–6). Davies takes from this seeming inconsistency on Milton's part a most apposite maxim: "This apparent contradiction between prose and poetry may serve as a warning to the reader to modify his expectations of the manner in which the former will elucidate the latter."[70]

Milton's prose and poetry are certainly written in different contexts and for different purposes, and the immediate polemical squeeze into which Salmasius had been able to catch Milton over the rather embarrassing failure of the successors to the Solomonic throne to live up to seventeenth-century English antimonarchical principles was tense and, doubtless, exquisitely uncomfortable. Milton had used Jeroboam as an example of justified rebellion against a wicked king, equating Jeroboam (who deposed Rehoboam) and the English revolutionaries (who deposed Charles I) as "Brethren, not Rebels" in his *Tenure of Kings and Magistrates* (*CPW* 3:209); Salmasius had Milton dead to rights, because Jeroboam turned out to be an idolatrous and tyrannical ruler.

Years after his controversy with Salmasius, however, Milton vigorously attacks in poetry what he previously defended in prose because he is no longer faced with a rhetorical situation that demands that he defend an exposed and nearly indefensible flank. I suggest that the characterization of Jeroboam in *Paradise Lost* is the one to be given the most weight, because it is more consistent with Milton's view of kingship as a curse, a malediction, a punishment wrought by Sin and the Fall. If readers are to modify *any* expectations regarding the relationship between the attitudes toward kingship expressed in Milton's poetry and prose, let them look to the teleology of kingship expressed in *Tenure of Kings and Magistrates*, the characterization of kingship in *The Ready and Easy Way* as "heathenish" and forbidden by Christ to those who would follow him, and the impulse of the Son, both in *Paradise Lost* and *Paradise Regained*, to lay down the scepter, step away from the throne, focus on the inner man, and to finish his poetic sojourn "Home to his Mother's house private return'd" (*Paradise Regained* 4.639).

Readerly expectations should be further informed by the fact that elsewhere in *Paradise Lost* kings are described as having demonic origins or associations: the "Memphian kings" of 1.694 and the Babylonian kings of 1.721 are entangled in a web of demonic rebellion and rejection of God. Satan's throne in hell is associated with Eastern kings of "Ormus and of Ind" (2.2), while Moloch, the "Sceptr'd king" (2.43) is described in a manner no different from the "Sceptr'd Angels" (1.734) who in Heaven rule "Each in his Hierarchy, the Orders bright" (1.737). Thus, Milton tars the hierarchy of Heaven with the blackened palette of Hell. By first presenting us with kings and kingship in Hell (Satan, Moloch, and Death are all described in the language of kingship), and then in the "dark / Illimitable Ocean" (2.891–92) in which Chaos reigns with "the Sceptre of old Night" (2.1002), Milton lays the groundwork for his portrayal of a heaven gone horribly wrong. Milton has not shown us first the kingships of Satan, Death, and Chaos in order to "create a King of Heaven so glorious and a court so splendid that it put his idolatrous imitators to shame";[71] rather, he creates a King of Heaven so unworthy of the idea of God as to put his fellow post-Restoration Englishmen to shame.[72]

Only in Book 12 of *Paradise Lost* is there any glimmer of hope. King David of Israel is mentioned with approbation, but he is the all-too-rare exception to the rule of earthly kingship. David, a deeply flawed ruler who used his power to steal another man's wife while simultaneously having the cuckolded victim killed in battle, has much more in common with his earthly and demonic predecessors than he does with the figure who follows him, the Son, "of Kings / The last" (329–30). His reign—the reign of the "inner man"—shall have "no end" (330). Kingship, heavenly and earthly, looks forward to this solitary figure, the Son who in *Paradise Lost* accepts regal power only to lay it down in *Paradise Regained*, who spurns deeds of glory and the pomp and circumstance of the earthly kingships Satan shows him, but who also rejects any form of rule—*earthly and heavenly*—that does not cause the ruled to know God aright: to know his virtue, patience, and love. Thus for Milton, the purpose of government, just as the purpose of education, is to repair the ruins of the Fall and to restore the original relationship of humanity and divinity.

If we pull back for a moment from the monumental canvases of Milton's epics, and look briefly at an early poem like Sonnet 19, it might seem that such opinions on kingship as Milton expresses therein are relatively conventional, but they only seem so until they are placed in relation to the opinions Milton places in the mouth of the Son in *Paradise Regained*. Milton's brief epic is a textbook of antimonarchical attitudes. From Book 1's portrait of Satan's continuing obsession with monarchies—earthly and heavenly—to Book 2 and 3's depiction of the Son's thoroughgoing rejection of earthly monarchy (including, significantly, *Davidic* monarchy), and, finally, to the Son's radical redefinition of what it means to be truly "kingly" in heavenly and spiritual terms, *Paradise Regained* seems to represent a significant ideological shift from the terms of Sonnet 19. Both works, however, focus on what it means to be "kingly," not what it means to be an actual monarch. "Kingly" is a term that need not necessarily be limited to its most literal sense—being, or partaking of, the nature of an actual monarch; it can also refer to traits of character such as nobility, dignity, passion governed by wisdom, justice tempered by mercy, confidence without arrogance, intellectual weight, empathy, and patience.

Sonnet 19 makes reference to a God who has just such traits, an equable deity who does not need the labors and talents of humans in his service. This God, whose "State / Is Kingly," imposes only a "mild yoke" (11); and while "Thousands at his bidding speed" (11), those who serve him best are those who bear the mild yoke, including those who "stand and wait" (14) if that is their lot. This is not the military monarch of *Paradise Lost*, a glowering and derisive Father who makes it his business either to create dissent, or to drive it into the open (in Book 5). Sonnet 19's "Kingly" God is a king in the sense of having a "kingly" *character*. The tolerance and mild yoke of a God who demands nothing more than patience from his blinded and wounded servant Milton are "kingly" in much the same way that the Son's concern with the "inner man, the nobler part" is "kingly" in *Paradise Regained* (2.477). To be "kingly" is not to be either an earthly or a heavenly monarch. To be truly "kingly" is a *spiritual*, not a *political* achievement; neither Satan nor the Father, the two characters in Milton's epics most visibly concerned with achieving or maintaining *power*, gives any evidence of real spirituality of such a "kingly" nature.

I contend that Milton hoped his "fit" audience would recognize that it was the Son, and not the Father, whom he was offering as a lamp to guide their footsteps in the dark world of the restored Stuart monarchy. Challenges to the Father offered by both Satan and the Son show each defying the received opinion of heaven: Satan's challenge is to a position that Abdiel represents in Book 5 as a variation of the classic "I brought you into this world, and I'll take you out" threat of an angry father. Abdiel's retort can be read in everyday terms as *He'll show you, and you'll be sorry—he brought you into this world, and he'll take you out*: "Then who created thee lamenting learn, / When who can uncreate thee thou shalt know" (5.894–95).

Abdiel's behavior in this scene is often portrayed as that of a faithful angel who is bearing solitary witness, under severe duress, to the requirements of true obedience; for example, Stella Revard contends that it is Abdiel, despite his arguments from force, who is being bullied in his argument with Satan.[73] I find it difficult to concur with Revard's assessment of Abdiel's position in this scene, given the fact that he is in no way subjected to reprisal. I am closer to the position of Empson here, who sees Satan as displaying a certain nobility in allowing Abdiel to leave unmolested: "we do not find Milton's God being content to differ from someone who contradicts him."[74] Rather than being assaulted, or even seriously threatened, Abdiel is told to leave, told, in fact, to take a message to "the Anointed King" (5.870). The warning that evil might intercept his flight if he does not leave quickly is merely a goad to get him to *go* and *go now*. In fact, in this debate, although Satan also argues from force—declaring that "our own right hand / Shall teach us highest deeds, by proof to try / Who is our equal" (5.864–66)—it is Abdiel, rather than Satan, who introduces the theme of uncreation, or death.

Abdiel seems to believe—and significantly, no one contradicts his belief—that the proper heavenly response to serious dissent is lethal force. Satan is given no immediate verbal response to this dark truism of heaven's monarchical regime, responding instead to this threat as he has responded to the Father's, by demanding proof through the force of deeds. Satan, it would seem, has learned his lessons rather too well; the way to resolve a serious dispute is through violence. Thus, it is entirely predictable that Satan's challenge to the Father is one of military force.

The Son challenges both received opinion and the Father rather differently; in a sense, he challenges the Father's received opinion of himself. Are you, the Son asks, really concerned only with strict, retributive justice? What, then, separates you from your adversary, who is concerned with strict retributive revenge? In another sense, however, the Son is also challenging the Father with the violent terms of Abdiel in mind. Are you really going to uncreate your human creation? "[W]ilt thou thyself / Abolish thy Creation" asks the Son (3.163). Are you actually the sort of parent who would kill his own children? Are you, in fact, exactly the sort of tyrant that the rebels accuse you of being? If the answer is yes, then "So should thy goodness and thy greatness both / Be question'd and blasphem'd without defense" (3.166). Michael Lieb has argued, not only that the Son is *challenging* the Father, but also that the Son is *warning* the Father: "One senses in the challenge that the Son himself would be the foremost among the reprobate in excoriating the Father, should the Father fail to heed the Son's warning."[75] In other words, there will be no defense to be made of a "goodness" and a "greatness" that the Father himself will have proven to be lies. If there is no defense that can be mounted against charges that initially seem to be blasphemous, then there is, strictly speaking, no blasphemy. Truth is not blasphemous, and truth is the basis of the Son's challenge.

Finally, what lies at the heart of the challenges of Satan and the Son is the question of what it means to be truly "kingly"; for Satan, to be "kingly" is to be a monarch, the sense in which most Milton critics today seem to read the term, while for the Son, to be "kingly" is specifically *not* to be a power-wielding monarch, but to be of noble and virtuous character, "to know God aright, and out of that knowledge to love him, to imitate him, to be like him, as we may the neerest by possessing our souls of true vertue" (*Of Education, CPW* 2:367). Thus do the kingliness of the Son and Milton's definition of the purpose of education meet: for the Son, to be "kingly" is to have "repair[ed] the ruins of our first parents" (*CPW* 2:366–67). To be "kingly" is to know God and to be like God, a God imagined *not* as a wielder of power and a giver of orders, but as a soul "of true vertue" (*CPW* 2:367).

Being like God is the promise the serpent makes to Eve in Genesis, and it is the promise Satan makes to Eve in *Paradise Lost.* Raphael's continual suggestions that Adam and Eve may ascend to heaven "under long obedience tri'd" (7.159), and that their "bodies may at last turn all to spirit" (5.497), are variations of the theme of being like God. Ultimately, the question of what it takes to be like God depends upon the answer to a far more fundamental question: *what is God like?* If God cannot be directly apprehended, if the divine is, as Augustine maintained, "unspeakable,"[76] or if, as Milton argued, "God, as he really is, is far beyond man's imagination, let alone his understanding" (*CPW* 6:133), then an even more fundamental question must be asked. *How is God to be imagined?*

Competing definitions offered by Satan and the Son of what it means to be "kingly" are also competing answers to the question of how God is to be imagined. The competition between these definitions and these imaginings, pursued in contrasting challenges to the Father, is the core of Milton's attempt to reject kingship and to re-imagine God. Milton wishes to seriously consider kings and kingship and re-imagine God in terms other than "the gaudy name of Majesty" (*CPW* 3:338). In so doing, Milton is rejecting the Father and his concern with "Empire" as a proper image of God, and is instead elevating the Son, whose focus is "true vertue."

Satan imagines the Father as a king, while the Son imagines the Father as "kingly." There is all the difference in the world between the two conceptions, and in this last great effort of his life, Milton is England's poetic John the Baptist, a voice crying out in the wilderness of "the easy literature of custom and opinion" to teach his "fit audience . . . though few" to recognize that difference.

3
"Who durst defy th' Omnipotent to Arms": Satan's Fall from Hero to King

> Who can in reason then or right assume / Monarchy over such as live by right / His equals, if in power and splendor less, / In freedom equal?
> —John Milton, *Paradise Lost*

SATAN AS TRAGIC HERO

SATAN IS, OF COURSE, A GREAT VILLAIN (WITH EMPHASIS ON THE WORD *great*, not *villain:* villains are inexpensive, common, and often uninteresting—Satan is none of these things). By far the most interesting non-human character in *Paradise Lost*, and Milton's most brilliantly Shakespearian creation,[1] Satan is a hero-villain, or, to use a modern cinematic phrase, an *antihero*: were Satan a human character, Iago and Lady Macbeth could very well be Satan's father and mother. Harold Bloom goes further:

> Satan is *both* Iago and the ruined Othello, *both* Edmund and the maddened Lear, *both* the exalted and the debased Hamlet, *both* Macbeth poised on the verge of regicide and Macbeth lost in the ensuing web of murder.[2]

Bloom's claim is apt. Milton, like Shakespeare, is writing secular literature, not sacred texts. Milton's Satan is not a religious figure, but a literary character whose family tree is as much Shakespearean as Biblical. A Shakespearan view of Milton's Satan necessarily opposes the idea that Milton is, as John Carey suggests, attempting to "encapsulate evil in Satan." What Carey describes as "the mentality we think of as Shakespearean, [one] which accepts the fact that evil is inextricably meshed in collective human experience,"[3] is Miltonic as well. Milton's Heaven, the place in which Satan learned all of his habits of thought and action, is a place where evil—both in terms of the Father's capacity to create evil (2.622–23), and in terms of Satan's capacity to promulgate war and rebellion at the Father's instigation—is inextricably meshed in collective angelic experience. Satan is not the "single Evil One"[4] that Carey claims Milton is presenting in *Paradise Lost*—such a description would better fit the Father, who is not only evil in himself, but the cause that evil is in others.

Satan's "sense of injur'd merit" (1.98) is Iago's resentment at being passed over for promotion by Othello, and Satan's struggle with the Father is part Edmund's rage against Gloucester (the father who prefers son Edgar to son Edmund), part Hamlet's disdain for the questionably legitimate king (his murderous uncle Claudius), a dash of Lady Macbeth's ambition, all mixed with the Thane of Cawdor's public determination and private doubts that drive him to the edge of madness. Satan is filled with the rage of a brilliant son who cannot, for whatever reason or combination of reasons, ever be quite brilliant enough to hear his parent say, "Thou art my beloved Son, in whom I am well pleased" (Mark 1:11).

Satan is not, despite S. Musgrove, an "Ass."[5] He is no more an ass than is Iago. Like Iago, Satan is a *tragic* figure, not a fool, a clown, or a simpleton, as many critical portrayals have insisted over the years. Satan is also no more "real" in a non-literary sense than is Iago, so to prepare to read *Paradise Lost* by indulging in a good morning's hatred of Satan, as C. S. Lewis once suggested, is no less ridiculous than reading *Othello* only after a good morning's hatred of Iago.[6] Lewis's admonishment is fundamentally pious in nature, suited more to a sacred than a secular text. Reading a literary work like *Othello* however, is different from reading a sacred text in at least one crucial way: no organized social, political, and moral structures have been built around the characters, words, actions, and settings of Shakespeare's drama. In this way, reading *Paradise Lost* is no different from reading *Othello*. Reading Milton's epic poem is not the same as reading the sacred texts of the Judeo-Christian tradition (or any other tradition). Reading Milton is more akin to reading Shakespeare or Homer than to reading the Bible (when the latter is read through the lenses of faith), and reading *Paradise Lost* only after reminding oneself to *hate Satan* is a pious act, not a literary endeavor.[7]

Just as Satan is not an ass, neither is he, strictly speaking, "the Devil." What, after all, is "the Devil" except the various ideas of him that have been promulgated through the millennia? In one guise, he is the prosecutor in Yahweh's heavenly court, the accuser a reader may meet in the biblical book of Job. He is also a trickster figure named Asmodeus, who livens up the action in the apocryphal book of Tobit. He appears once again in the synoptic gospels as Beelzebub or Belial. The earliest portions of Hebrew scripture suggest that he may also have been a part of Yahweh himself. The *malak*, often translated from the Septuagint Greek *aggelos* and the Vulgate's Latin *angelos* into the modern English "angel" or "messenger," is perhaps more accurately understood as "the voice of the God, the spirit of the God, the God himself."[8] Understood in this way, the *malak* represents the destructive side of Yahweh seen at Exod. 12:23 (the killing of the first-born of Egypt), and 2 Sam. 24:13–16 (the destroyer who punishes Israel with pestilence for having taken a census of the people). The *malak* can also represent a spirit in service of Yahweh, but one still devoted to a dark and destructive function, as in the example of the "lying spirit" of 1 Kings 22:20–23. Other cultures and religious traditions imagine similar, and perhaps even more imposing Devilish figures: the Iblis of the Koran and the Angra Mainyu or Ahriman of the Zoarastrian Zend Avesta. Which of all these creations of the human imagination might be the "real" personification or principle of evil?

Leaving aside the question of whether or not one believes in the actual existence of Satan or Ahriman or any other personification of evil, the issue of literary representation and its relation to "reality" remains. Just as Milton's literary God is not "God," so also is Milton's literary Satan not "Satan" or any other "actual" personification of the principle of evil. Milton's Satan is not a medieval Prince of Darkness, a Faustian Spirit who Negates, or a Jaggeresque Man of Wealth and Taste. Despite the influences of earlier literary Satans created by Andreini, Dante, Du Bartas, Tasso, or Vondel, the Satan of *Paradise Lost* is a creation of Milton's own, a prince, a warrior, a hero, and finally, a tragic figure who aspires to be, and finally becomes, the very thing he claimed to despise.

Milton's Satan, who brings a "mind not to be chang'd by Place or Time" (*Paradise Lost* 1.253) carries, as Blake recognized, much of his creator within him wherever he goes: each combined "courage never to submit or yield" (1.108) with a sometimes misguided but nevertheless awesome determination to resist the irresistible, to stand up in the face of greater power and say *no*. Had Milton not escaped the executions that overtook many of his colleagues in rebellion upon the return of the Stuart monarchy, King Charles II might soon have found that Milton's international reputation would have ensured that he "who overcomes / By force, hath overcome but half his foe" (1.648–49).

Milton's Satan more closely resembles a character from Greek drama or Homeric epic than one from the Bible. Stella Revard calls Milton's Satan a "classical battle hero,"[9] arguing that he is "in demeanor like Agamemmnon, in tactics like Odysseus."[10] Although Revard makes these remarks in the context of an argument that positions Satan more as a manipulative coward than a battle-hardened hero, she makes a thorough and convincing case for reading Milton's Satan as a figure drawn from a Renaissance tradition that looked back to Homer, Aeschylus, and Virgil as at least as much as it did to the Bible.

Such classical heroes themselves thought in terms of military prowess: those who had it were noble (Achilles, Odysseus, etc.), while those who did not were barely worthy of contempt (much less notice). Greek heroes equated honor with the ability to conquer one's enemy or suffer gracefully in defeat. To suffer defeat was not, in and of itself, a disgrace; however, to go to down in defeat begging, weeping, abasing oneself before the enemy—this was the worst of shames. Growing out of this rich literary context, Milton's Satan is a classical hero, much closer in spirit to Prometheus or Achilles than he is to the prosecutorial figure of the Book of Job or the Lucifer of Isai. 14:12. Like his classical literary predecessors, Satan's concern is for honor, for victory in battle, or at least for defiance in defeat. Like Aeschylus' Prometheus, Satan fights against what he perceives to be the arbitrary injustices of the divine, and like Achilles, is deeply wounded by slights—real or perceived—to his honor and position.

Both Prometheus and Achilles are read as tragic characters, ultimately defeated, but no less heroic for having failed to overthrow Zeus, or to achieve both long life and lasting fame. Readings such as

Musgrove's and Lewis's reduce Satan to a figure of fun, a butt of jokes, a thoroughly pathetic creature with whom it is difficult to see Milton wasting precious time and poetic energy. Rather than viewing Satan in so derisive a light, it is more helpful to view him with the sympathy and awe afforded the greatest characters of classical epic and tragedy. Milton's poetic and political use of Satan requires understanding and acknowledging what is admirable about the rebel angel in order to set the stage for an analysis of where, exactly, he eventually goes wrong.

Milton gives his Satan numerous strengths: he is a gifted leader both in word and by example of deeds; he is courageous; he is not afraid to show emotion when appropriate, nor is he so insecure that he is unwilling to let others have their say, whether or not the others in question are in agreement with Satan's position. Satan's most admirable quality, however, is one he shares with the author who gave him being: he is determined to stand up and fight for what he believes in. That Satan is fighting for something wrong (or against something self-evidently good) is neither obvious to a literary character without the benefit of thousands of years of mythological hindsight, nor to a literary reader who does not share the assumptions of a neo-Christian interpretive tradition. For Satan, the war against God is not an allegory of good and evil, but a real and present struggle against a tyrant.[11]

The argument that it is Satan, and not God, who is a tyrant in *Paradise Lost* rather determinedly ignores both Milton's own definition of tyranny and his ideas regarding the relation of external commands to true government. Milton's well-known description of the tyrant as "he who, regarding neither Law nor the common good, reigns onely for himself and his faction" (*Tenure of Kings and Magistrates, CPW* 3:212) can equally well be applied to the Father and to Satan. Both reign for themselves and those who follow them. Milton's definition of tyranny was designed to throw into sharp contrast the kind of politics in which power comes from, and is exercised for the benefit of, those who are governed. In neither Milton's Heaven nor his Hell is this the case. Instead, in each realm, the ruler reigns by virtue of having greater power and/or greater courage, intelligence, and determination than those whom he rules. The Father's rule is challenged, and he upholds his throne through overwhelming force. Satan's hold on his newly acquired throne is solidified through bravery and intellect that is beyond those of his followers. In neither case is the throne consciously given over to the ruler by the ruled. In neither case is the power of the ruler given him by the ruled. In the Miltonic sense, therefore, both monarchs, Satan and the Father, are tyrants.

Milton is at pains to make clear that both monarchs operate under a fundamental misunderstanding of what government means and what true government is. When Satan claims, in his argument with Abdiel in Book 5, that the "Imperial Titles" the angels possess in heaven "assert / Our being ordain'd to govern, not to serve" (5.802) he sounds very much like Milton, who argued in *Tenure of Kings and Magistrates* that human beings were "born to command, and not to obey" (*CPW* 3:197–98). But Satan has missed the point entirely. So also has the Father, when out of nowhere he imperiously announces that he has declared the Son his "Vice-gerent" and demands that "to him shall bow / All knees in Heav'n" (5.607–8). Both Satan and the Father equate command and government with external shows of dominance and submission, with "Imperial Titles" and imperious decrees, with demands for knee-crooking, cringing, and grateful, eternal deference given by the weaker to the stronger. Nowhere is self-government, the quiet reign of the "inner man, the nobler part" (*Paradise Regained* 2.477) to be seen in either ruler's theory or practice of government. Nowhere is tyranny more perfectly illustrated in all of Milton's work.

Satan's moral advantage is that he does not begin as a tyrant; Satan's moral tragedy is that in the process of trying, and failing, to overthrow a tyrant, he becomes one himself. That is both the paradox and point of Satan as a character. He serves as a warning of how rebellion against a tyrant can itself sink into tyranny. Satan's is the charisma that exudes from such modern figures as Che Guevara and V. I. Lenin, rebels against tyranny who themselves descend into tyrannical attitudes and practices. The rebel is eternally exciting, but his dark side seems always to be the same tyranny he fought against.

Yet, Satan is a hero. Satan's decision to resist tyranny places him in the ranks of the great mythological heroes of world literature. From the tale of Prometheus's defiance of Zeus; to the first recitation of the *Mahabharata* and its tale of the war between Yudhisthira and a man, the tyrant Duryodhana; to the Anglo-Saxon *Beowulf* with its hero who dies fighting the tyranny of a beast, the struggle against tyranny has stirred bards, poets, audiences, and readers for thousands of years. Milton's Satan is a hero who struggles against the greatest and most terrifying tyranny of all—the tyranny of God himself. Satan's downfall is not that he opposes God, but that he opposes God on God's own terms, matching threats with threats and violence with violence. Satan is a hero who chooses to fight the right battle in the wrong way. His heroism is not undone by the fact that he is weaker than his enemy. His heroism is undone by the fact that he tries to become the thing he despises. The God of *Paradise Lost* is a top–down leader inclined to dictatorial pronouncements, war, and destruction, and in resisting this God, Satan becomes just like him. That paradox is the crux of Satan's character.

Satan seems heroic because he *is* heroic. If Satan is not heroic, *Paradise Lost* becomes a farce, not an epic whose literary and emotional roots lie in tragedy. *Paradise Lost* is, of course, no more a farce than is the *Iliad*. In fact, it is much more serious and elevated a story than is the Greek battle epic. *Paradise Lost* begins with Satan, just as the *Iliad* begins with Achilles. But the wrath of Satan, much more so than the wrath of Achilles, is serious, elevated, and quite literally superhuman. What decision could possibly be more serious than Satan's to declare war on God? Satan's wrath is engendered by no mere stealing of a battle prize with an attendant loss of honor: Satan's wrath grows from a sudden demand for total, unquestioning, and eternal submission to someone who gives every appearance of having been plucked out of relative obscurity and suddenly elevated to a position of near-absolute power. The Father suddenly and arbitrarily elevates one angel over the others, declares the newly exalted angel his "only Son" (5.604), and imperiously demands that all other angels serve the "Son" and "confess him Lord" (5.608). As Satan puts it, "by Decree / Another now hath to himself ingross't / All power, and us eclipst under the name / Of King anointed" (5.774–77), using the word "Another" in the sense of "one of us," implying that the figure now known as the Son was, until the Father's sudden decree, known as an angel. This is why Satan regards the elevation of the Son as such a grievous affront: Satan's is a "who does this 'Son' think he is, anyway?" reaction.

Satan has an entirely different reaction to the Father's role in the affair, seeming to assume that the Father is Other, apart from the angels, though whether through absolute power, or merely through "old repute, / Consent, or custom" (1.639–40) is not clear. What is clear, however, is that when Satan refers to the Father, he speaks in language that suggests the Father is regarded as not "one of us"—the Father is "him who reigns" (5.680), and Satan (as Lucifer) seems to have accepted—though with difficulty—that apartness, that otherness, that reign coming from the Father. It is only when another angel is both declared Son and raised to the level of King and Lord of the angels that Lucifer cracks, and Satan is born. The very language of Satan's resentment implies that the Son had been previously another angel, an equal, not a superior: "Who can in reason then or right assume / Monarchy over such as live by right / His equals, if in power and splendor less, In freedom equal?" (5.794–97). Evidently, it is not at all obvious to Satan that this "Son" is a superior. Empson argues that Satan's response to the Father's decree is one of genuine shock at the demand for total, uncompromising, and immediate worship of the Son by the angels:

> [Satan] does not revolt directly against God, but against God's appointment of a "regent" described in detail as a King; and at the climax of his speech . . . he claims that to submit here would be worse than submitting to a tyrant, because the Son actually demands worship, the full ancient barbarism . . . [12]

It is not the Son, however, but the Father who makes the demand that all bow down before the Son and confess him to be their "Head" and "Lord." The Father, who in Raphael's oxymoronic construction, "voluntary service . . . requires" (5.529), makes the demand for worship on behalf of the Son. Satan's pique is such, however, that he either does not notice or chooses to ignore this distinction. His outrage is focused on the sudden elevation of the one, and the concomitant demotion of the many. His language makes it clear that he regards the one to be in no way inherently superior to the many: who can assume the right to rule over his equals, asks Satan, "much less for this to be our Lord, / And look for adoration . . . ?" (5.799–800). The words *for this* carry the full weight of Satan's assumption that the angel newly declared "Son" is, or was, no superior.

Stella Revard writes that Milton "chose to make Satan rebellious at the advancement of a superior rather than an inferior . . . Milton's Satan evokes less sympathy from the reader with his refusal to bow the knee to *the Son* (newly appointed king) than does . . . Vondel's with the parallel refusal to bow to Adam."[13] Given the language in which Satan expresses his resentment over the exalting of the Son, however, it seems apparent that the elevation of the Son over the angels in Book 5 has more in common with the elevation of Man over the angels in Vondel than Revard suggests. Vondel's Lucifer objects to the raising of Man because he is unable to accept the idea that "Spirits once consecrate / To service in empyreal palaces / Shall serve an earth-worm that from out the dust / Hath crawled and grown."[14] In Lucifer's view, Man is demonstrably inferior to the rank and file angels, much more so to Lucifer, the "Stadtholder" or Governor of Heaven.

In *Paradise Lost*, the Son is newly begotten (anointed, not created)[15] and raised to a rank unprecedented in heaven except in the figure of the Father himself. There is no indication, however, that this Son—who is only declared "Son" on the day he is raised—was always, or even ever, a "superior" as Revard argues. Satan objects to the raising of the Son because he cannot stand the thought of "Knee-tribute yet unpaid, prostration vile, / Too much to one, but double how endur'd, / To one and to his image now proclaim'd?" (5.782–84). We have only Abdiel's word for the idea that the Son to whom this knee-tribute must now be paid was always a superior, the Word by whom "the mighty Father made / All things" (5.836–37). Although neo-Christian critics delight in ridiculing Satan's retort, the fact remains that within the poem itself, this is, as Satan says, a "strange point and new" (5.855), an idea never before brought up and only once more referred to, long *after* this argument takes place, by the chorus of angels who sing of the Son, "He Heaven of Heavens and all the Powers therein / By thee created; and by thee threw down / The aspiring Dominations" (3.390–92). In discussing this passage, William Empson makes a similar point: "Nobody has mentioned the doctrine in the poem before; God does not say it in his pronouncement giving power to the Son. It was the only argument which could have satisfied the mind of Satan, but God preferred to issue a bare challenge."[16]

It is often argued, of course, that Satan admits his created status in his soliloquy of Book 4. Is there, then, a significant split between a "public" Satan—a schemer and liar who knowingly misleads those who follow him—and a "private" Satan—a pathetic, even cowardly, figure who admits the unpleasant truth only when he is sure of not being overheard? Such a conclusion disregards the difference between the epic *in medias res* narrative structure *Paradise Lost* adopts, and the chronology of events *Paradise Lost* portrays. Satan's response to Abdiel in Book 5 comes *before* the trial of arms in which he puts so much faith. Satan can admit no superior, much less any creator before such a trial is concluded. Only *after* losing, *after* seeing the force of his "right arm" repulsed, does the idea of being a created being becomes thinkable—if still abhorrent—for Satan, and not before. The "admission" of Book 4 comes after the failure of that in which Satan had put his faith. In essence, Satan is adrift in a universe he had never before even considered—one in which his own strength has been bested by that of another. After such a defeat, Satan's confident public demeanor in Book 2 is not only demanded by the situation, but is an act of amazing fortitude. What kind of leader would Satan be were he to choose that moment to give in to doubts and fears, the "pale, ire, envy, and despair" of his soliloquy in 4.115? Satan's stunned and defeated troops "lay intrans't / Thick as Autumnal Leaves" (1.301–2) on the "inflamed Sea" (1.300) of Hell. This is neither the moment, nor is this "furnace of fire" the place, for indulging in "wailing and gnashing of teeth," *pace* Matthew 13:42. A leader who has doubts may, or may not, express them to trusted members of an inner circle, but no leader worth the name expresses such doubts, in a crisis situation, before the rank and file. Satan's soliloquy in Book 4 is, in crucial ways, the beginning of his real and permanent Fall, his confirmation of himself in the path that will lead to his own tyranny, but it is neither hypocritical, nor is it cowardly. It is tragic. On a more human scale, it is sad. But the fact that he keeps these private fears *private* is entirely consistent with the demands of the military and political position he is in.

Before the trial of battle that leads him to doubt, Satan responds to Abdiel with wrath that is personal but also political: what good, after all, are titles and privileges in a hierarchical order if these can all be superceded by monarchical fiat? This is Satan's question in *Paradise Lost,* much as it is Lucifer's question in Vondel's play. In each case, the answer seems at first to be self-evident: the titles and privileges are, in fact, no good at all in such circumstances. At the point where he questions the legitimacy of monarchical fiat, Satan seems about to make a major Miltonic breakthrough, one that the Son himself will not make until after the war in heaven, and perhaps not even until his rejection of Satan's temptations in *Paradise Regained.*

After realizing that titles and privileges are inherently worthless in a regime ruled by an absolute monarch, the critical next steps for Satan would have been to reject titles and privileges altogether, and then to cast aside the notion of external authority, pomp, circumstance, and ceremony in favor of the notion that all are "In freedom equal" (*Paradise Lost* 5.797). Were he a successful hero and not a tragic one, Satan *could* have understood "freedom" in terms of the inner government of "the inner man, the nobler part" (*Paradise Regained* 2.477), as the Son will come to realize and express thousands of years later. But Satan remains stuck in the patterns of thought he has learned all too well in the rigidly hierarchical heaven Milton presents.

Satan assumes that freedom is linked, not to the inner, nobler part, but to "Imperial Titles which assert / Our being ordain'd to govern, not to serve" (*Paradise Lost* 5.801–2). Satan's fall is at least partially due to the fact that he cannot make the imaginative leap beyond the concepts and categories of the military regime in which he lives, moves, and has his being. In large part, Satan's predicament in *Paradise Lost* is a result of the way he thinks. The character who famously brings "A mind not to be changed by place or time" (1.253), believes that his way of thinking determines his reality: "The mind is its own place, and in itself / Can make a Heaven of Hell, a Hell of Heaven" (1.254–55). He is by no means wrong, or even alone, in coming to this conclusion. Hamlet, to whom Milton's Satan owes much of his brooding energy, thinks along much the same lines: "there is nothing either good or bad, but thinking makes it so" (*Hamlet* 2.2.249–50).[17] To get at the heart of who Satan is, it is necessary to be clear about what and how he thinks.

Satan's thoughts revolve around issues of power and position within a hierarchical order. Although Satan is a commanding speaker, a natural leader, and the possessor of a potent intellect, his references to power—both his own and that of others—are most often made in a military context. Satan views power as something that flows from military techniques and arms: in essence, for Satan, power grows out of the barrel of a gun. When he asks his gathered forces "Who can in reason then, or right, assume / Monarchy over such as live by right / His equals, if in power and splendour less, / In freedom equal?" (5.794–97), the power he refers to is not the power of "reason" or "right," not intellectual, moral, or personal power, but *military* power. The proof lies in his response to Abdiel's retort in the debate scene of Book 5: "Our puissance is our own; our own right hand / Shall teach us highest deeds, by proof to try / Who is our equal" (5.864–66). After appealing to the *moral* equality of all angels in his argument against submitting to the "Monarchy" of the Son, Satan ultimately brings the debate back to the level of power (puissance), framing that power in military terms: the strength of his "right hand" will determine who is "equal" and who is not.[18]

Satan's view of hierarchy flows naturally from his view of power: those with the greatest military prowess are entitled to the highest positions. Satan makes his position clear after the defeat in Heaven through his appeal to "just right and the fixt Laws of Heav'n / [That] Did first create [me] your Leader / With what besides in council or in fight / Hath been achieved of merit" (2.18–21). Essentially, Satan says, he is the leader of the fallen angels because he is their most powerful warrior and most eloquent battlefield orator, linking "merit" with military prowess, just as he finally links equality with such prowess.

Satan's view of the Father is colored by his views of power and hierarchical order. However, there is a serious question regarding causes and effects. Does Satan see the Father as a warrior king because of his own views on power and hierarchical order? Or has Satan developed those views from the example set in Heaven? Clearly, Satan views the Father as a military monarch, a king who commands legions into battle, but he does not adopt this view out of sheer perversity, creating the Father in his own battlefield image. Satan in fact sees the Father as a military king because the Father *is* a military king, and Satan is not alone; in fact, this view is one that *no one* in Heaven questions—least of all the Son, whose earliest moments chronologically in *Paradise Lost* are a brief study in military swagger and machismo, as he speaks of the dangerous discontent in Heaven as:

> Matter to me of glory, whom their hate
> Illustrates, when they see all regal power
> Given me to quell their pride, and in event
> Know whether I be dextrous to subdue
> Thy rebels, or be found the worst in Heav'n.
>
> (5.738–42)

At this early point in his career, the Son thinks in the same way that Satan thinks. Power is about force, not persuasion, external compulsion, not internal government. For the Son, the war about to break out in Heaven is a matter of "glory," and "regal power" has been given him to "quell" the "pride" of those who until now had never given any evidence of being either "vain," rebellious, or in need of subduing. In fact, the Son seems to view the imminent conflict as a big joke, as he shares in the Father's derisive laughter. If the Son has been raised to his position through any merit other than military prowess, he gives little or no sign of it here.

Satan's Challenge to the Father

Why does Satan set himself the task of defying "the Omnipotent to arms"? The question of Satan's motivation has long been a source of contentious debate, ever since Dryden publicly suspected that Satan was the hero of Milton's poem, and since Shelley's open declaration that Satan is the hero of *Paradise Lost*. Between "Satanists" (those critics of Milton who assume that he was "of the Devil's party") and "anti-Satanists" (those who assume that Milton was, if not orthodox, at least vigorously pious) Satan's motivation tends to be interpreted in two ways: anti-Satanists generally present one variation or another on the patristic notion that Satan fell due to an overweening pride that rendered him unwilling to submit to anyone or anything; Satanists, on the other hand, find this argument less than convincing, locating the source of Satan's decision to rebel in the dramatic situation of the poem rather than in traditional theological arguments.

The two camps remain unreconciled, and are perhaps irreconcilable. Although Stanley Fish maintains that his is an argument designed to "reconcile the two camps,"[19] it seems that what his argument actually accomplished in this regard was merely to drive the subject of Satan's motivation and the Father's provocation underground, to make it somehow gauche to discuss the topic at polite Miltonist dinner tables. The sheer amount of critical energy that has been expended over the last two centuries to prove that Milton was not "of the Devil's party" stands as a curious testament to the power of the "Satanist" position. To be sure, a naively held "Satanist" position has its own excesses: Satan is by no means a pure, uncomplicated or uncompromised hero. Shelley—one of the most prominent of the so-called "Satanists"—recognized that fact, emphasizing that Satan, unlike Prometheus, was not "exempt from the taints of ambition, envy, revenge, and a desire for personal aggrandizement."[20] But the "anti-Satanist" position has its own troubles: in the rush to place all blame for the events of *Paradise Lost* on its singular rebel, the "pernicious casuistry" that Shelley once described as the cause that leads readers to "weigh [Satan's] faults with his wrongs and to excuse the former because the latter exceed all measure"[21] is reversed. The pernicious casuistry becomes the cause of neo-Christian attempts to excuse the Father, becoming the "something worse" that Shelley argued was engendered by reading *Paradise Lost* with "a religious feeling."[22]

That "something worse," as Kenneth Gross has eloquently contended, can say more about the "anti-Satanist" critic than it does about either *Paradise Lost* or the character of Satan. Gross describes "something worse" as "that self-perpetuating system of tyranny, revolution, and revenge which Shelley saw as built into the morality of both tyrant *and* rebel, both punitive father and violent, devouring child," and further argues that "we might also read that 'something worse' as whatever can lead us so happily to slander certain sympathies or do violence to the serious ambivalence of our moral judgments by forcing a text to take on completely the cast of orthodoxy."[23] "The worst such 'something' might come through in the shrewd, nasty finesse with which a critic like C. S. Lewis reads Satan," Gross writes, wondering whether Satan, or Lewis's reading of Satan, is the more "subtly degrading."[24]

An evenhanded instance of thorough critical engagement with the question of Satan's motivation, neither recognizably "Satanist" nor "anti-Satanist," is Arnold Williams's 1945 article on the subject,[25] in which he traces the history of the conflicting theological, biblical, and pseudo-biblical accounts of Satan's rebellion. Beginning with the pseudepigraphical Book of Enoch, with its explanation that rebel angels fell due to lust for human women, Williams moves on to medieval Latin versions of the life of Adam and Eve that depict Satan refusing to worship the newly created man despite God's explicit command to do so. Williams also considers the first-century C.E. *Book of the Secrets of Enoch*, with its account of an angel who plans to set his throne higher than the clouds so as to equal or exceed God in rank and power. The motives of Milton's Satan are barely touched upon by any of these accounts. Satan displays what might be interpreted as lust in his relations with Sin (at least if her account of matters in Book 2 is to be wholly credited), but sexual lust is hardly a factor in his decision to fight against God. Unlike Vondel, who makes the issue of the relative rank of angel and man an explicit issue in his *Lucifer*, Milton does not put his Satan in the position of refusing an order to worship mankind—whether as the incarnation of God or not. Milton's Satan does, however, aim to set his throne against the throne of God, just as does the rebel angel in the *Book of the Secrets of Enoch*.

Having outlined the various ways in which angelic rebellion has been portrayed and explained, Williams finally alights upon the traditional Augustinian explanation: Satan fell through pride, ambition, and the refusal to submit his will to that of the Almighty. The question remains, however, of why *Milton's* Satan "falls." Williams rejects the Augustinian explanation as insufficient to account for the action of *Paradise Lost*, saying "Milton has little to work with if he takes the standard motivation from pride."[26] Williams also rejects as a form of begging the question Augustine's idea that Satan was evil from the first moment of his existence. The "motivation from pride" solution essentially claims that Satan's impetus to evil is the fact that he is evil. This explanation, if applied to Milton's literary creation, would reduce Satan to a kind of Coleridgean misreading of Iago—a character whose motiveless malignity is all the more inexplicable as it grows more virulent and determined.

Yet Shakespeare's Iago is given both malignity and a clear motive for that malignity in the first lines of *Othello*—he has been passed over for promotion to a position he had coveted passionately, and the man who gets the promotion instead is raised to the position of second-in-command, seemingly without warning. Milton's Satan is in almost the same situation. Like Iago, he had long served his master in a highly placed military role. Also like Iago, Satan bitterly resents the sudden promotion of another, with the attendant loss of personal stature, and quite possibly, the loss of intimate access to the central figure that the extra layer of command brings. Milton provides his Satan with much more than simple pride as a motive for rebellion: he provides betrayal, rejection, and emotional hurt; furthermore, he gives his Satan much more than mere pride—"Envy and Revenge" (1.35) rouse Satan to rebellion. Pride is there, yes, but explanations that rely on pride alone have as part of their agenda an inversion of the kind of "pernicious casuistry" that Shelley once described as the reader's reaction to Satan. Reading Milton's "magnificent fiction" with a religious eye changes the source of a reader's casuistry from Satan to God, leading to a determination to try, at all costs, to excuse the God of *Paradise Lost,* to relieve him from any blame for Satan's rebellion and the subsequent fall of Adam and Eve.

Rather than merely relying on the old warhorse, pride, Milton carefully goes out of his way to give Satan a motive that is both credible and forceful: the Father's raising of the Son in Book 5. It is not only *that* the Father does it, but *how* he does it that provides the crucial impetus for the events that follow:

> Hear all ye Angels, Progeny of Light,
> Thrones, Dominations, Princedoms, Virtues, Powers,
> Hear my Decree, which unrevok't shall stand.
> This day have I begot whom I declare
> My only Son, and on this holy Hill
> Him have anointed, whom ye now behold
> At my right hand; your Head I him appoint;
> And by my Self have sworn to him shall bow
> All knees in Heav'n, and shall confess him Lord:
> Under his great Vice-gerent Reign abide
> United as one individual Soul
> For ever happy: him who disobeys
> Mee disobeys, breaks union, and that day
> Cast out from God and blessed vision, falls
> Into utter darkness, deep ingulft, his place
> Ordain'ed without redemption, without end.
>
> (5.600–615)

The first thing this decree is, is *unnecessary*. The second thing it is, is *necessary*. It is unnecessary if the aim of Milton's God is to make a peaceful announcement, one that he does not expect to cause any trouble. "Here is my Son, and today I am raising him to the rank of heir to the throne." This would hardly be an unexpected move, and by itself would be highly unlikely to create the kind of stir needed for the development of a large-scale rebellion. This decree is necessary, however, for Milton to make credible why Satan rebels, and why one-third of the angels seem to require little or no convincing to join him in rejecting and warring upon God.

3 / "WHO DURST DEFY TH' OMNIPOTENT TO ARMS"

The primary problem with God's decree—or the primary power of it, depending upon one's point of view—is its belligerent tone: the Father seems to be *daring* any and all to object, to utter the slightest squeak of protest, to cast eyes down in the smallest way, to let faces permanently frozen into expressions of joy melt into the slightest signs of discontent. The Father tells the assembled audience that 1) they have a new "Head"; 2) everyone has to get down on one knee and "confess him Lord"; 3) everyone will do this—no one is exempt; 4) everyone has to be happy about it—forever; and 5) anyone who doesn't provide instant and cheerful compliance to items 1–4 will be cast out without any appeal. This is hardly the kind of announcement that can be expected to engender warm, cooperative feelings and best wishes for the Son as he embarks upon the duties and responsibilities of his new position. What the decree must be intended to do is drive dissent out into the open, to create dissent in the first place, or both.

That Milton had in mind the idea of uncovering and/or causing rebellion is made apparent in his somewhat loose translation of Psalm 2, the biblical text on which the Father's decree in Book 5 is based. As Milton translates the lines, "I, saith hee, / Annointed have my King (though ye rebel) / On Sion my holi' hill" (11–13). The phrase "though ye rebel" appears nowhere in the original Hebrew text. Milton includes this phrase in 1653, sketching in miniature what he will years later paint in the broad strokes of *Paradise Lost*. The added phrase in Milton's translation of the Psalm seems to assume that the raising of the King will engender rebellion, and that God is fully aware of that fact. The anointing of the king both creates dissent and drives it out into the open as active rebellion, and this is exactly what happens in Book 5 of *Paradise Lost*. The Father's decree creates animosity where none existed before; it is only *after* the Father's announcement that "All seem'd well pleas'd, all seem'd, but were not all" (617).

The background of the original Psalm 2 seems to imply that animosity already exists at the time of the anointing of the King who sits upon the "holy hill of Zion" (2:6):

> Why do the heathen rage, and the people imagine a vain thing? The kings of the earth set themselves, and the rulers take counsel together, against the LORD, and against his anointed, saying, Let us break their

bands asunder, and cast away their cords from us. He that sitteth in the heavens shall laugh: the LORD shall have them in derision. Then shall he speak unto them in his wrath, and vex them in his sore displeasure. (Psa. 2:1–5)

However, in Milton's heaven, the Hamlet-like *seeming* that follows the Father's imperious decree is something new, a time-buying strategy adopted in reaction to the new and dangerous order of things. "That day, as other solemn days, they spent / In song and dance about the sacred Hill" (5.618–19). No reference is made to *seeming* in relation to these "other solemn days." Unlike Psalm 2, in which the Israelite king is anointed and "begotten" as the official human vice-regent of Yahweh amidst the hostile and non-Yahwist nations, the coronation scene taking place in *Paradise Lost* not only takes place in a previously non-hostile context, but it takes place in an entirely "monotheist" or "Fatherist" context. There are no "heathen" raging, or "people imagin[ing] a vain thing." There are no earthly kings who worship non-Israelite gods at work here. There are no other gods, period. Absent the geographic and henotheistic rivalries at work in the original context of Psalm 2, Milton's borrowing of the basic dramatic structure of the Psalm serves to highlight the violently and deliberately confrontational nature of the Father's decree. In *Paradise Lost*, Milton's Father deliberately creates hostility where none had previously existed, in order to replicate the conflicts, tensions, and jealousies with which Psalm 2 begins.

More than creating *hostility*, however, what the Father replicates in Book 5 is the economy of dominance and submission, of mutual resentment, hatred, and violence that plays out even now in the geographic region in which Psalm 2 had its origin. The Israelite king David—traditionally regarded as the author of Psalm 2—is anointed as the king of a nation of invaders and conquerors, the vice-regent of a god who, as Regina Schwartz writes, establishes a system in which "to be 'a people' is to be God's people is to inherit his land, and if they are not the people of God, they will not be a people, and they will lose the land."[27] The people who "will not be a people" are the Philistines, as well as other residents of the area, such as the Jebusites, the residents of the walled city—Jebus—that is conquered by David, and transformed into his capital, Jerusalem. Most alarmingly, perhaps, to modern sensibilities, the Philistines are as close an analogue to the present-day Palestinians as the Bible has to offer. What does this make of Milton's God? From the point of view of the Philistines, David and his god are usurpers who have taken what is not rightfully theirs. From Satan's point of view, the Father is "a usurping angel,"[28] one who has arrogated to himself powers that are rightfully those of *all* the angels, not just those who, like Henry Bolingbroke in *Richard II*, "know the strong'st and surest way to get."

In laying the groundwork for Satan's challenge, Milton also leaves deliberately vague any notions of who Satan was, or what he was doing before the Father's decree. Where Vondel portrays his pre-fall Lucifer as possessing great dignity, rank, and respect, Milton gives us Satan fully formed and already fallen. Even in Book 5, which gives us the earliest glimpse of Satan, he is already Satan, and already "his former name / Is heard no more in Heav'n" (5.658–59). It is as though, on the day that the Father begets the Son, he also begets Satan. The Father creates the hostility of Psalm 2, hitherto absent in heaven, by "creating" a resistor, effecting the transformation of Lucifer into Satan.[29] Satan resists the Father, foments rebellion and declares war in heaven, not because he thinks it might be a good idea, but because he is, in a sense, made for the job. Just as Lucifer was a servant of God, so also is Satan such a servant. Just as the Son is moved into a new position, so also is Lucifer moved into a new position.

Thus it is not true that all of those who fall in *Paradise Lost* are "Authors to themselves in all" (3.122), nor is it accurate to claim, as the Father does, that Satan (or those who followed him) by his "own suggestion fell, / Self-tempted, self-deprav'd" (3.129-30). Nor is Satan right in accepting the full share of blame for his fall when he bemoans his fate at the beginning of Book 4:

> pride and worse ambition threw me down
> Warring in Heaven against Heaven's matchless King:
> Ah, wherefore! he deserved no such return
> From me, whom he created what I was
> In that bright eminence, and with his good
> Upbraided none; nor was his service hard.
> What could be less than to afford him praise,
> The easiest recompence, and pay him thanks,
> How due! yet all his good proved ill in me,
> And wrought but malice . . .
>
> (4.40–49)

Satan's momentary, grief-filled, and soon-rejected entertaining of the Augustinian fall-through-pride hypothesis notwithstanding, Satan is not self-tempted any more than he is "self-begot, self-raised," as he claimed in his heated debate with the angel Abdiel (5.860). Just as the Father literally created Lucifer "In that bright eminence," the Father, through "his good" which "wrought but malice," figuratively creates Satan, malice from "good," and at the same time he brings forth "Infinite goodness" (1.218) from Satan's malice (the malice that the Father himself has created).

In *Paradise Lost*, the Father is, much like Yahweh in the Hebrew Scriptures, the ultimate generative source of both good *and* evil, of creation *and* destruction. That the Father can and does create evil is a point that is reinforced early in the poem: the regions of Hell are created by the Father as "A universe of death, which God by curse / Created evil, for evil only good" (2.622–23). It can be no surprise then, that the Father who creates also destroys, as Raphael mentions in an oddly offhanded way to Adam. On the day the Earth was created, Raphael was unable to watch:

> For I that day was absent, as befel,
> Bound on a voyage uncouth and obscure,
> Far on excursion toward the gates of Hell;
> Squared in full legion (such command we had)
> To see that none thence issued forth a spy,
> Or enemy, while God was in his work;
> Lest he, incensed at such eruption bold,
> Destruction with creation might have mixed.
>
> (8.229–36)

Not only is the Father perfectly capable of creating "A universe of death," and of mixing "Destruction with creation," he is also capable of begetting a Satan at the same time that he begets a Son. Satan is, because the Father makes him. Satan was no more "Sufficient to have stood" (3.99), than was the "universe of death, which God by curse / Created evil" sufficient to have been a garden of delights. Lucifer *may* have been "Sufficient to have stood," against ordinary temptation. But there is no temptation (ordinary or otherwise), no opportunity for rebellion, or reason to rebel, until the Father introduces temptation, opportunity, and reason in the form of his imperious, taunting, and willfully inflammatory decree. In a universe where temptation comes from God, no one is truly "Sufficient to have stood."

It is the Father who tempts Lucifer and begets Satan. Satan is not twisting the truth when he claims that the Father "tempted our attempt, and wrought our fall" (1.642). Neither is Satan inaccurate in his interpretation of how the Father "tempted" the rebellion. Satan assumes that it is a matter of sheer power:

> ... he who reigns
> Monarch in Heaven till then as one secure
> Sat on his throne, upheld by old repute,
> Consent or custom, and his regal state
> Put forth at full, but still his strength concealed.
> (1.637–41)

Where Satan falls short is in failing to come to grips with *why* the Father "tempted" the rebellion. His reduction of the issue to its mechanics without its motives, to strength without the reasons that strength is used, is symptomatic of how Satan miscalculates throughout the poem. From the military monarch who sits on heaven's throne Satan has learned how to recognize power, but he has underestimated the sheer perversity of a King whose expressed concerns are for his pleasure in others' obedience (3.107), his omnipotence, deity, and empire (5.722–24), and who surrounds himself with a vast coterie of servants who bow "lowly reverent" (3.349) before him as they sing his praises with "loud hosannas" (3.348) day in and day out.

Satan is certainly given to perversity of his own, particularly in displays of almost laughable vanity, but when he is at his absolute worst, most vainglorious, even most ridiculous, he is also most attempting to emulate the Father. Satan approaches Heaven's battlefield "exalted as a god" (6.99), an "Idol of majesty divine" (6.101). As an *idol* of majesty, Satan is an image of majesty, an imitation of the Father. Carrying the baggage of thousands of years of Biblical and theological discourse along with its Greek roots, the word idol suggests a false, illusory, or phantom image, necessarily removed from that which it imitates just as the physical manifestation of a Platonic form is removed from, and an inferior copy of, the form itself. More interesting than the inferior quality of Satan's imitation of the Father, however, is what characteristic of the Father he chooses to imitate: military and monarchical power. In retrospect, Satan frames the entire rebellion as a struggle over who has the right to wield monarchical power in the universe. Satan proclaims after his defeat that those who had fought with him had been an "Innumerable force of Spirits arm'd / That durst dislike his reign, and mee preferring" (1.100–102). In other words, Satan never imagines the conflict in any terms other than the monarchical and military terms that are the Father's own. The Father's expressed concern with "Omnipotence," "Deity," and "Empire" (5.736) are the terms in which Satan thinks from beginning to end. In a sense, what Satan never does, despite his violent and heroic attempt to live up to his boast that he had been "self-begot, self-raised" (5.860), is grow up. Despite his rebellion against the Father, Satan never steps out of the Father's shadow. Satan never achieves self-government, the quiet reign of the "inner man, the nobler part," because he never makes the imaginative leap beyond the notion of externally wielded kingship to the notion of internally realized kingliness.

Satan's basic position boils down to a series of questions. By what right does the Father rule? Does the Father rule merely on the basis of greater power? If so, what kind of right is that? Does might makes right? Does the Father rule because he's *bigger* than everyone else? Satan challenges all of these ideas in his debate with Abdiel in Book 5, where Abdiel argues for the Father's supremacy on the basis of power:

> Canst thou with impious obloquy condemn
> The just decree of God, pronounced and sworn,
> That to his only Son, by right endued
> With regal scepter, every soul in Heaven
> Shall bend the knee, and in that honour due
> Confess him rightful King?
>
> (5.813–18)

Abdiel's strategy is to argue for the Father's supremacy by asserting it: the Father's decree is just because it is just. Everyone must bow before the Son and acknowledge his right to have the "regal scepter" because he has the "regal scepter." For Abdiel, power is its own justification: he seems unwilling or unable to consider the relation of might and right. God is simply right, no questions asked. *Why* is God right? Because he is the one who made Abdiel (and everyone else). Abdiel argues by once again asserting God's might:

3 / "WHO DURST DEFY TH' OMNIPOTENT TO ARMS"

> Shalt thou give law to God? shalt thou dispute
> With him the points of liberty, who made
> Thee what thou art, and formed the Powers of Heaven
> Such as he pleased, and circumscribed their being?
> (5.822–25)

Satan's responds to Abdiel by drawing a distinction between power and freedom, arguing that greater power and greater formal rank (not the same thing) do not necessitate differences in degree of freedom. For Satan, all of heaven's citizens are equal in freedom: he rallies the crowd gathered at his stronghold in "The quarters of the north" (5.689) by challenging them to "know yourselves / Natives and sons of Heaven possessed before / By none; and if not equal all, yet free, / Equally free" (5.789–92). Satan here makes a classically Miltonic argument: all angels are free because they are "Natives and sons of Heaven." In *Tenure of Kings and Magistrates* Milton argues that all men are free because "all men naturally were borne free, being the image and resemblance of God himself" (*CPW* 3:198). In the strife-filled heaven of *Paradise Lost*, however, what it means to be "Natives and sons of Heaven," or "the image and resemblance of God himself" is a matter of considerable disagreement for Satan, for the angels who do not rebel, and even for the Son and the Father. Abdiel sees the Father as an unquestioned and unquestionable monarch, a king of severe and forbidding power and majesty. Satan sees the Father as a monarch as well, but is no longer so sure that his power and majesty are unquestionable and unchallengeable.

One thing that none of heaven's residents disagree on is the idea that the Father reigns as heaven's king. Being a king puts the Father in a curious and Miltonically indefensible position. The Father does not raise monarchy to an impossibly glorious standard; rather, monarchy lowers the Father to a dangerously debased level. Years before the God of his epic poem sees the light of day, in his *Defence of the People of England* Milton offers a telling response to Salmasius. The French scholar had insinuated that in defending the execution of Charles I, Milton had become caught up in a logic that implies that "we must call God the king of tyrants and indeed the greatest of tyrants himself" (*CPW* 4:367). Milton's reply is swift and blunt:

> We spit out your second point and would have your blasphemous mouth stopped for calling God the greatest of tyrants because, as you keep saying, he is spoken of as king and lord of tyrants.
>
> (*CPW* 4:367)

For Milton, Salmasius's assertion that "we must call God the king of tyrants" depends on the single assumption that God is properly to be imagined as a heavenly version of Charles I. That assumption is what Milton spits at, angrily throwing Salmasius's charge back at him. In many ways, the Father of *Paradise Lost* is the God that the French scholar had once accused Milton of creating. The Father is the model of divinity that Salmasius—the defender of kings and kingship—might have imagined. In Miltonic terms, the Father is "king of tyrants."

Elsewhere in his work, Milton is at pains to situate the development of the very idea of kingship within a narrative of sin and the fall. Kings result from "*Adams* transgression" (*Tenure of Kings and Magistrates, CPW* 3:199), and the resulting failure of mankind to govern themselves from within, according to the dictates of the "inner man." William Empson is thus not entirely incorrect to place the Father, as the king of heaven, in the position of a "usurping angel,"[30] because Milton describes a king as one appointed by those "who agreed by common league to bind each other from mutual injury, and joyntly to defend themselves against any that gave disturbance or opposition to such agreement" (*Tenure of Kings and Magistrates, CPW* 3:199). As a heavenly king, the Father could very well have been an angel elected by the rest to protect the angels from their own descent into "wrong and violence." At least this is how the pre-war Satan imagines the Father in *Paradise Lost*.

Satan imagines himself as a noble, prince, or magistrate in heaven's court, one entitled to defend his own interests and the interests of his peers by resisting, and if necessary, overthrowing heaven's king if that king turns to tyranny. Both before and after the war in heaven Satan's view of himself and of the Father is rooted in Reformation-era "Protestant" theories of princes and magistrates, and a feudal *primus inter pares* theory of heaven and its king. Such a view of heaven's politics and power structures provides the framework for Satan's arguments against the Father's rule, and the justification for his rebellion.

Satan's Protestant Rhetoric and Descent Into Tyranny

In his own days as a rebel against a king, John Milton defended not only the overthrow but also the execution of tyrants. Taking an approach much like his Satan's, Milton, in *Tenure of Kings and Magistrates*, marshals a variety of arguments derived from Reformation-era Protestant political theories to bolster his case. Protestant theologians—from the Swiss theologian John Calvin, to the Anabaptist revolutionary preacher Thomas Müntzer, to Milton's contemporary, the English Presbyterian Stephen Marshall—had long argued over what rights magistrates (the *pares* in the *primus inter pares* formula) had to take up arms against a king. The crux of the argument is this: *Who may resist a king, and under what circumstances?* In summary terms, the conclusions of the above-mentioned figures are these: while so-called "private-persons" may themselves take no action whatsoever against either a king, a prince, or an inferior magistrate, such magistrates and/or princes may themselves resist, and may even depose, a king or other superior ruler, if that ruler is behaving in a grossly unjust and violent way toward his subjects.

Milton puts many of these very same arguments in the mouth of his Satan. Satan uses the Protestant rhetoric of legitimate rebellion by "princes" or "inferior magistrates" against a king and transforms it into a rallying cry for the overthrow of the Father. Satan continually refers to his compatriots as "Princes," as "Powers," as "Potentates." Even the poem's narrator gets in on the act: in referring to Mammon in his pre-fall role as Heaven's architect, the narrator gives readers an image of "Scepter'd Angels" who viewed "many a Tow'red structure high," angels who "sat as Princes, whom the supreme King / Exalted to such power, and gave to rule, / Each in his hierarchy, the Orders bright" (1.733–37). The political structure of Heaven itself is drawn on a model of a King and his princely magistrates, the very magistrates by whom, according to the aforementioned Protestant thinkers, resistance, rebellion, and overthrow could be carried out under the right circumstances.

In making Satan the mouthpiece for Protestant theories of rebellion that spell out the "proper" relation of the subject to a king, Milton critiques not only the theories themselves (which tended to uphold secular tyranny so long as it was decent enough to refrain from intruding into the realm of Christian religion), but also notions of magistracy and kingship contained therein. Through Satan, Milton takes the arguments of Protestant theologians like Calvin, Müntzer, and Marshall into much more radical territory than those men were willing to enter. According to these men, the power of princes is from God. Satan goes even further, implying that the power of (heavenly) princes is "self-begot, self-rais'd," before he finally claims, of himself and his fellow princes, that "Our puissance is our own" (5.860, 864). Milton the political writer comes dangerously close to making the same claim for the people. For Milton, the people, in the sense of "private persons," do not need a representative body of magistrates to rid them of a tyrannical king. The people may rid themselves of such a king directly, because, according to Milton, "the power of Kings and Magistrates is nothing else, but what is . . . committed to them in trust from the People" (*Tenure of Kings and Magistrates*, CPW 3:202). In his *A Defence of the People of England*, Milton writes that "kings . . . [owe] their rule to the people alone, to whom therefore they are accountable" (*CPW* 5:358).

The idea that a king receives his kingship from the people is one that Satan relies upon in his characterization of the Father as he who holds "the tyranny of Heaven" (1.124). If the Father is the "usurping angel" that Empson suggests he is, then Satan is as justified in his decision to rebel as are those who overthrew King Charles I of England. In this line of thinking, the Father would have received his kingship from the "people" of heaven—from the angels, both those who rebel and those who do not. However, Milton is careful to include God in his theory of power, writing that "all human power . . . be of God" (*CPW* 3:197–98), and that the "rights of the people, then, just as those of the king, whatever they are, are derived from God" (*CPW* 5:359). Keeping in mind the important distinction between "God" and the Father in *Paradise Lost*, the important issue that must be confronted at this point is what it means to say that the power of the people is from God. At first this making of the *vox populi* into an image of, or conduit for, the *vox dei*, seems, paradoxically, to threaten God with erasure. If the people may with this power appoint and depose kings and princes on earth, why may they not, as Satan does, turn this power against God? But Milton uses this conflation of the voice of the people with the voice of God, not to argue against God, but to argue against an image: God imagined as a king, a wielder of external authority. Making the voice of the people come from God is tantamount to arguing that the people themselves are, in an important sense, God. It is the "inner man, the nobler part" of the people through whom God as Milton imagines him lives, moves, and has his being in the world. Poetically and politically, the implications of this connection between God and the people are crucial for an understanding of *Paradise Lost.* Milton argues in prose (the writing, as he says of his "left hand") that the power of a king or a magistrate comes from, and may be revoked by, the people ruled by that same king or magistrate. Milton also consistently portrays God as a king in his great epic (the work of his right hand). Milton, of all poets, is one whose left hand knew what the right hand was doing: through this powerful dialectic of prose and poetry, left and right hands, Milton stakes out a position that enables him to use his Satan as a powerful critique of the Father's monarchical authority.

Milton gives Satan a politics that are an eclectic patchwork of Reformation-era Protestant thought: from Calvin come the seeds of the idea that magistrates have a divine right (or as Satan would put it, the right of "Natives and sons of Heaven") to overthrow a tyrannical ruler; from the Anabaptist radical Thomas Müntzer comes the suggestion that force, even lethal force, is just and right in the service of ridding the world of a tyrant, as long as it is a magistrate and not a private person who is applying such force; and from Stephen Marshall, a contemporary of Milton, comes the idea that true power— power that is not lawful to resist under any circumstances—is only to be found in the union of a prince (or king) *and* his magistrates. The hodge-podge of theology and politics upon which Satan draws in justifying his rebellion against "Heaven's king" leads him to identify himself as a magistrate entitled to take up arms against the throne of Heaven if and when its occupant turns to tyranny. Far from thinking he is doing wrong, Satan is sure that he is doing right in marshalling his forces against he who "holds the tyranny of Heaven" (1.124).[31]

Satan's idea of himself and his position is not without support. According to Calvin, "Those who serve as magistrates are called 'gods.'"[32] The scriptural passages he cites in support of this point (Exod. 22:8, and Psa. 82:1,6) use the word *elohim*, which may be translated variously as God, gods, and even magistrates or judges. Calvin takes full advantage of this word and its possible translations to suggest that magistrates are in some way divine due to the divine nature of their positions.[33] Satan consistently refers to the "Natives and sons of Heaven" as gods: in bemoaning their defeat in heaven, Satan wonders aloud "How such united force of gods, how such / As stood like these, could ever know repulse?" (1.629–30). Satan also refers to his followers after the debate in Book 2 as a "Synod of Gods" (2.391).

For Thomas Müntzer, rebellion against a tyrant is to be carried out by the "elect," specifically, princes who take seriously their duty to God's church, as opposed to those "godless rulers who should *be killed.*"[34] The fact that Müntzer grounds his theory of rebellion in a defense of God parallels, rather than opposes, Satan's characterization of his rebellion as a defense of the rights of the heavenly nobility, the body of princes that make up the "Natives and sons of Heaven." In each case, the argument for the right to overthrow a ruler is grounded in a conception of the highest rights, duties, and ultimate goods. Müntzer and Milton's Satan define these rights, duties, and ultimate goods differently, but the structure of the defense of rebellion is the same. Overthrowing a ruler is done in the name of a value that is higher than the ruler.

Stephen Marshall makes his argument using much the same structure: rebellion is justified if it is done in the name of a higher good. For Marshall, the power to rebel against a king lies with the "representative body of a State."[35] While this representative body may only rebel against the king when the question is one of "defence against unlawfull violence,"[36] Marshall clearly asserts that magistrates may be resisted if they are unjust:

> although they may not take from the Magistrate that power which God hath given him; yet may they defend themselves against such unjust violences, as God never gave the magistrate power to commit.[37]

Inferior magistrates may take up defensive arms against an unjust and violent king because they are, according to Marshall's interpretation of Romans 13, the "higher power" or "governing authority." Marshall goes on to outline a tripartite system of power consisting of 1) "The power of making and repealing Lawes," 2) "The power of making Warre and Peace," and 3) "The power of judging Causes and Crimes." It is this system that represents power that may not be resisted:

Where these three meet, and make their residence, whether in one person, as in absolute Monarchs; or in many, as in mixed Monarchies or Aristocracies; or in the body of the people, as in the ancient Roman Government, there is the highest power which every soule is forbidden to resist.[38]

Satan conceives of himself and his angelic compatriots as being a crucial part of that higher power. In justifying his, and his faction's, rebellion against heaven's king, Satan portrays himself as a prince *entitled* and even *required* to resist an unjust monarch who is grasping for absolute power and thereby attempting to usurp that portion of the "higher power" or "governing authority" that belongs to the lower magistrates. Among those who follow Satan's lead, the picture of heaven's king as a grasper, a usurper of powers not rightfully his own is common. Nisroch, "of Principalities the prime," addresses Satan as "Deliverer from new Lords, leader to free / Enjoyment of our right as Gods" (6.451–52). Satan himself characterizes the pronouncement of the Son as the great Vice-gerent as a usurpation of power rightfully belonging to others: "Thrones, Dominations, Princedoms, Virtues, Powers, / If these magnific Titles yet remain / Not merely titular, since by Decree / Another now hath to himself ingross't / All Power, and us eclipst under the name / Of King anointed . . . " (5.772–77).[39] Satan goes on to characterize this shift in heavenly politics as a demand for "Knee-tribute yet unpaid, prostration vile, / too much to one, but double how endur'd, / To one and to his image now proclaim'd?" (5.782–84), and asserts that, as magistrates, he and his followers cannot allow such usurpation of power: "A third part of the Gods [read "Gods" as *elohim* in Calvin's sense of gods, magistrates, or judges], in Synod met / Thir Deities to assert, who while they feel / Vigor Divine within them, can allow / Omnipotence to none" (6.156–59).

The political balance of Stephen Marshall's "Letter" is at work here in two ways: Satan characterizes the heavenly system as one in which (until the usurpation) the threefold power of enacting laws, making wars, and judging "causes and crimes" had been shared by the king and his princes and magistrates; the "Father infinite" of 5.596 characterizes the heavenly system as one in which the threefold power is contained in one ruler, the king. By claiming to defend their right to rule, to defend "those Imperial Titles which assert / Our being ordain'd to govern, not to serve" (5.801–2), Satan and his followers are claiming their rights under a system of government which holds that it is the duty of lesser magistrates to hold the king in check. This fits with Calvin's insistence that it is the sacred *duty* of lower magistrates to resist the tyranny of a king:

> I am so far from forbidding them to withstand, in accordance with their duty, the fierce licentiousness of kings, that, if they wink at kings who violently fall upon and assault the lowly common folk, I declare that their dissimulation involves nefarious perfidy, because they dishonestly betray the freedom of the people, of which they know that they have been appointed protectors by God's ordinance.[40]

That Satan claims to be fighting against tyranny is made clear by his numerous references to the Father as a tyrant: Hell is the "Prison of his Tyranny who Reigns / By our delay"; the Father is "our grand Foe, / Who now triumphs, and in th' excess of joy / Sole reigning holds the Tyranny of Heav'n" (1.122–24). The key here is the phrase "Sole reigning." In a system in which lesser magistrates or princes had real power, the monarch would not be in a position of exclusive and absolute reign. Satan justifies his rebellion in Heaven and maintains his power in Hell by appeal to what he and his followers represent as the king-in-parliament model of an ideal (if not actual) heavenly government: the system of "Orders and Degrees" that "Jar not with liberty" (5.792–93) to which Satan refers when he tells his fellow fallen angels that the "just right and the fixt Laws of Heav'n / Did first create your Leader" (2.18–19). However, Satan appeals to this system precisely in order that he may *establish* a tyrannical rule over his fallen compatriots, imposing a top-down system in Hell after having explicitly rejected and rebelled against such a system in Heaven.

What is distinctly missing from Satan's political rhetoric is any mention of those who are ruled. Over whom, after all, do all of these "Thrones, Dominations, Princedoms, Virtues, [and] Powers" reign? If "those Imperial Titles" indicate that the angels were "ordain'd to govern, not to serve" (5.801–2), whom are the angels governing? Each other? William Empson somewhat whimsically suggests a solution to this problem by postulating the existence of what he calls "the vast dim class of proletarian angels who are needed so that angels with titles may issue orders."[41] Before the creation of Adam and Eve on a new-made Earth, one might ask the same question about the reign of the Father. Over whom, besides these "Thrones, Dominations, Princedoms, Virtues, [and] Powers" does the Father reign? *Does* the Father reign if there are no subjects but angelic princes and magistrates?

Protestant political theory, at least as it appears in Calvin, Müntzer, and Marshall, assumes as a given that magistracy and the power thereof is designed for the good of those who are ruled, basing this claim on Rom. 13:4, where the magistrate is described as "the minister of God to thee for good." Marshall describes a proper Magistracy as one set up "with a sufficiencie of power and authority to rule for the publicke good."[42] However, in *Paradise Lost*, there appears to be no *public*, much less a public good, until the rebellion by Satan, and the subsequent creation of Adam and Eve on Earth. Until this radical break, heaven appears to have been little more than a gigantic parade with only Party members in attendance. There is only dictatorship, no proletariat in Milton's prelapsarian heaven.

All of this, of course, is from Satan's point of view, and Satan is mouthing the very Protestant political formulas that Milton tears down in *Tenure of Kings and Magistrates*, his justification of the ways of the regicides to men. Why does Milton write his Satan to sound so much like Calvin, so much like Stephen Marshall, in his descriptions of the roles of princes and magistrates in relation to a king? Because Milton wants to ground his theory of political power in the very private persons whom Calvin so despised, and whom Satan never mentions: the ruled (who do not themselves rule) who are conspicuously absent from pre-rebellion heaven. For Milton, it is "all men" who are "born to command, and not to obey" (*CPW* 3:198–99), not merely those who possess "Imperial Titles" as it is for Satan, or special "magistrates of the people, appointed to restrain the willfulness of kings" as it is for Calvin, or the "representative body of a State" as it is for Marshall. Milton casts the people in the role of Müntzer's "elect," those "true friends of God" who take seriously their duty to God's church, and themselves have the power to oppose those "godless rulers who should *be killed*."

Milton is far more radical than his own Satan. Next to Satan's relatively mainstream rhetoric of "justified" rebellion against a tyrant, Milton's arguments glow white-hot by comparison. Where Satan grouses in reference to heaven's king, "Whom reason hath equall'd, force hath made supreme / Above his equals" (1.248–49), Milton brooks no use of the word *equals*. Much less than being the *equal* of the people, the king or magistrate is the *servant* of the people:

> since the King or Magistrate holds his autoritie of the people, both originaly and naturally for their good in the first place, and not his own, then may the people as oft as they shall judge it for the best, either choose him or reject him, retaine him or depose him, though no Tyrant, meerly by the liberty and right of free born Men to be govern'd as seems to them best. (*Tenure of Kings And Magistrates*, CPW 3:206)

Ultimately, Milton's attempt to ground the source of political power in the people (with God as the granter or giver of such power) undermines the entire top-down structure of political power relied upon not only by Calvin, Müntzer, and Marshall, but by Satan and the Father in *Paradise Lost*. If the people may choose or reject, retain or depose a ruler, "though no Tyrant, meerly by the liberty and right of free born Men to be govern'd as seems to them best," why may not, by the same logic, the people choose or reject, retain or depose an unsatisfactory God, *whether or not that God is conceived of as a tyrant?* In the epic universe of *Paradise Lost*, the question is analogous: why may not Satan and his followers choose or reject, retain or (attempt to) depose the Father? The argument that God gives and God can take away is an argument for tyranny: once such a power is given, it cannot be taken back again without tyrannical force or deception.

Furthermore, what is to prevent Hell's legions from choosing or rejecting, retaining or deposing Satan himself? Satan seems to realize that this possibility has now been made available since the rebellion in heaven, which is why he appeals immediately to the system of "Orders and Degrees" that "Jar not with liberty" (5.792–93) when he tells his fellow fallen angels that the "just right and the fixt Laws of Heav'n / Did first create [me] your Leader" (2.18–19). This may also explain the speed with which Satan moves to cut off the opportunity for any of the other fallen angels to step forth as his rival in the debate in Book 2, as he "prevented all reply, / Prudent, lest from his resolution rais'd / Others among the chief might offer now / (Certain to be refus'd) what erst they fear'd; / And so refus'd might in opinion stand / His Rivals, winning cheap the high repute / Which he through hazard huge must earn" (2.467–73). The reference to "opinion" is crucial: in a truly top-down system of political power, a system in which magistratical power was truly from God (God taken here in the sense of an unquestioned and unchallenged power, neither of which the Father of *Paradise Lost* has proven to be), "opinion" would be irrelevant. So also would be any question of earning "high repute." In a sense, Satan is trying, through appeals to the pre-rebellion system of top-down power and through quick action, to prevent anyone else from taking advantage of what he realizes is a bottom-up political order, and to stuff the genie of that realization—loosed through rebellion in heaven—back into a hopelessly smashed bottle.[43] Satan's political rhetoric is an attempt to preserve for himself the very system of power the Father had claimed, and against which he had rebelled, a political and rhetorical move that merely serves as a justification for his own growing tyranny.

Milton uses Satan to critique tyranny; that much is commonplace. However, it is the way in which Milton uses Satan that is the interesting point. Milton suggests that Satan's critical error is not the rebellion in heaven, but the *reasons* for that rebellion. Satan's railing against the "Tyranny of Heav'n" is not the problem. The problem is that Satan *does not go far enough*. Satan does not go on from rejecting the "Tyranny of Heav'n" to rejecting all tyranny, in fact, to rejecting *kingship itself*; Satan merely sets himself up as an alternate monarch, another tyrant, another king.

Satan becomes a tyrant because in establishing his infernal monarchy, he appeals to the very system of power that he once rejected. He appeals to this system of power in the language of sixteenth- and seventeenth-century Protestant political theories that emphasize the political rights of princes while denying such rights to "private persons." Satan fits in with those "dancing divines" Milton criticizes so harshly in *Tenure of Kings and Magistrates*, hypocrites who use the "same quotations to charge others, which in the same case they made serve to justifie themselves" (*CPW* 3:196).

The trouble with Satan's defense of his rebellion is that it follows the lead of the "dancing divines," taking as a given the idea that kingship is legitimate. For instance, Satan never questions a formulation of power like Calvin's: "Authority over all things on earth is in the hands of kings . . . by divine providence and holy ordinance."[44] Satan would merely argue that *his* is the "divine providence" by which monarchical power should be established. This *a priori* assumption of the unimpeachable legitimacy of kingship is exactly what Milton struggles against, both in *Tenure of Kings and Magistrates* and in *Paradise Lost*. Satan starts out at precisely the political and theological point Milton is at pains to argue must be left behind if the English are ever to grow beyond being a nation "worthie . . . to be for ever slaves" (*The Ready and Easy Way*, CPW 7:428).

Satan differs from Calvin, Müntzer, and Marshall about the *source* of kingship, "magnific titles" (5.773), and "imperial titles" (5.801), arguing that such things come from the inherent majesty of "Natives and sons of Heaven" (5.790), rather than from God. But he is in firm concord with these men on the question of the *legitimacy* of kingship, "magnific titles," and "imperial titles." Satan's rebellion—as well as those earthly rebellions sanctioned, strongly or tepidly, by Calvin, Müntzer, and Marshall—is aimed at the wrong target. Rather than overturning a single king, the goal should be to overturn kingship itself, both as an institution and as a way of thinking about governance, authority, and power.

It is not Satan (his or anyone else's) that Milton is holding up for criticism. Why bother with such an easy target? Nor is his primary target the "dancing divines" and the tradition out of which they have sprung and from which they argue. Milton's primary target here, as elsewhere in *Paradise Lost*, is the image of God that such "dancing divines" promulgate through their theological and political ideas, an image of God as a king. For Milton, the Protestant rhetoric of legitimate rebellion (which outlined the course many revolutionaries believed God wanted the English people to take during the civil wars of the 1640s), much like Satan, does not go far enough, does not reject the notion of kingship itself, and that is why Milton puts that rhetoric in the mouth of a character whom he is at great pains to make heroic in the beginning, only later to tear down. For the Milton who is writing *Paradise Lost*, such rhetoric was a crashing failure because it is not merely one king, Charles I, who must be overthrown, but all kings, and especially, the source of all tyranny on earth: the erroneous image of God as a heavenly king. With his poetic portrayals of Satan and the Father, Milton insists that only when God is no longer imagined as an external authority figure, as a monarch who wields destructive military power, will the promise of the Reformation be realized.

Satan is Milton's indictment of the failures of Protestant thought up to his day, both in terms of its earthly politics and its imaginative constructions of God. Satan's story—his rejection of kingship in heaven, and his subsequent rise to monarchy and tyranny punctuated by his infamous declaration that it is "Better to reign in Hell, than serve in Heav'n"—forms a curious and compelling metaphor for the Protestant Reformation, a rejection of Papacy that set up Prelates and Presbyters in the places of Bishops, Cardinals, and Popes. *New Presbyter is but Old Priest writ Large.* It also serves as a scathing critique of the English people and its slow but steady backsliding into the political habits of a nation long used to living under the yoke of kingship, a nation that maintained throughout its brief period of liberty the image of God as a heavenly king, and finally welcomed with open arms the return of a human king, Charles II. Milton uses Satan, his rebellion, and his rhetoric, as an indictment of everything that had, in his view, gone wrong with the attempt to reform England, to reform Christianity, and to reform the image of God.

The Romantics were right—to a point. Satan's railings against the "Tyranny of Heav'n" are stirring, even devastating criticisms, which no amount of apologism will fully deflect. In the end, however, Satan becomes, like many rebels, a hypocrite. He rejects the Son as king, only to aspire to be a king himself—aspiring to be like God in the wrong way. The desire to be a king is Satan's error; not the desire to overthrow a king. Satan's assertion that the angels were born to "govern, not to serve" (5.802) is not wrong; in fact it is perfectly Miltonic. Milton describes mankind in *Tenure of Kings and Magistrates* as "born to command, and not to obey" (*CPW* 3:198–99). Satan's mistake is to assume that command and obedience are external, where, for Milton, they are internal. The mistake is natural, however, because of the exaggerated externality of governance in the hierarchical heaven of *Paradise Lost*. This is the sense in which Satan's claim that God "tempted our attempt and wrought our fall" rings true—not in Empson's sense of concealed power, but in the sense that the very hierarchy of heaven serves to conceal the central truth that only the Son discovers: *command and obedience are internal, and the one who governs himself serves no one.*

4

"That far be from thee": Divine Evil, Justification, and the Evolution of the Son from Warrior-King to Hero

> When we talk about knowing God, it must be understood
> in terms of man's limited powers of comprehension.
> God, as he really is, is far beyond man's imagination,
> let alone his understanding
> —John Milton, *De Doctrina Christiana*

THE FATHER: DIVINE EVIL AND JUSTIFICATION

NONE OF MILTON'S CHARACTERS, NOT EVEN HIS GRANDILOQUENT AND bellicose Satan, has proven more disturbing for readers than the Father. Both characters read their critics as much as their critics read them. Reveal what you think of Satan and/or the Father, and you reveal something important about yourself.

Although critical discourse on *Paradise Lost* has often focused on the question of Satan and his heroism (or lack thereof), the Father provokes equally dichotomous reactions; curiously, however, there are no clearly identified "Fatherist" or "antiFatherist" camps, no labeling analogous to that which identifies the participants in the long-running debates over Milton's Satan. Empson is not so much anti-Father as he is anti-God (or anti *Christian* God); likewise, C. S. Lewis is not so much a Fatherist as he is a booster for an Anglican concept of the Christian God. Regardless of the religious leanings of the critic, the Father in *Paradise Lost* presents a significant interpretive problem.

A particularly thorny dilemma is why angelic and human characters alike express anxiety regarding the Father's capacity for good and evil.[1] Raphael, the messenger angel whose discourse takes up most of Books 5–8, expresses misgivings about the Father's capacity for evil when he casually mentions the possibility of the Father mixing evil with good during the creation of Earth (8.233–36). To Adam and Eve, who pray that the Father will "be bounteous still / To give us only good" (5.205–6), the assumption that evil might originate in the Father does not appear to be an unreasonable one, should his bounty and his good one day run out. This nervous prayer follows Adam's apprehensive declaration to Eve that "Evil into the mind of God or Man / May come and go" as long as it is "unapprov'd" (5.117–18)—a disturbingly thin thread upon which to hang the idea that one's creator is wholly good. Adam here is attempting to comfort Eve after a disturbing dream (in which she rehearses the scene of eating from the forbidden tree) given her by Satan, who uses "his Devilish art to reach / The Organs of her Fancy, and with them forge / Illusions as he list, Phantasms and Dreams" (4.801–3). But Satan does what he does at the Father's sufferance, by the "sufferance of supernal Power," (1.241) and as part of the Father's determination that Satan's attempts at "desperate revenge" will "redound / Upon his own rebellious head" (3.85–86). In essence, therefore, the evil that comes into the mind of Eve, through the dream suggested by Satan, has its ultimate source and sanction in the Father.

The apprehension expressed by characters in *Paradise Lost* mirrors reader reactions to the Father that have often ranged from anxiety to outright distaste. Alexander Pope provided an early example, blasting Milton in 1737 for writing a scenario in which "God the Father turns a School-divine."[2] Pious critics like Pope have often faulted Milton for portraying the Father as less than spotlessly good and immediately sympathetic, while less pious readers have seen in the Father all manner of criticisms of God or a particular *idea* of God. Blake, in his poem "Milton," describes the Father of *Paradise Lost* as the worst sort of tyrant he could personally imagine, "Urizen . . . in chains of the mind lock'd up,"[3] while Shelley described the Father of *Paradise Lost* in Satanic terms: "one who in the cold security of undoubted triumph inflicts the most horrible revenge on his enemy, not from any mistaken notion of inducing him to repent of a perseverance in enmity, but with the alleged design of exasperating him to deserve new torments."[4]

Much twentieth-century criticism has been engaged in a defense of the Father, arguing that the Father is, in fact, the model of kingly deity and government that Milton is recommending to his fit audience. The mid-century critic George Wilson Knight is perhaps typical in this regard, constructing a royalist Milton, arguing that Milton was a defender of constitutional monarchy, and claiming that Milton's attitude, even during the height of the Republican years, was "sympathetic to the idea of royalty."[5] Such present-day critics as Robert Fallon and Stevie Davies construct a Milton who, though not royalist on earth, is certainly royalist regarding heaven. Such readings take as an axiom the idea that the Father's words not only positively express Milton's deepest and most cherished opinions on order and hierarchy, but also delineate the proper moral center of *Paradise Lost*. William Empson, thirty-eight years after publishing *Milton's God*, is still regarded as somehow "anti-Milton" for having suggested otherwise. Empson was insightful; however, Milton is not, as the estimable critic suggested, struggling to use his poem and poetic characterization of the Father to graft a good and just appearance onto an irredeemably wicked God. The Father's words cannot be relied upon as simple statements of truth in the light of which all other utterances must be interpreted. In Book 3 for instance, when after a confrontation by the Son the Father replies "All hast thou spok'n as my thoughts are, all / As my Eternal purpose hath decreed" (171–72), the Father's words cannot be taken literally any more than the words of Satan in the famous Council scenes of Book 2.

Of course, Satan will not do as a model for Milton's fit audience either. As compelling a character as Satan is, he is no more the moral center of *Paradise Lost* than is the Father, and he is ultimately a secondary element in Milton's grand project to "justify the ways of God to men." Satan is a portrait of rebellion gone wrong, but *not* of the wrongs of rebellion. Satan is too conservative in his aims and too blunt in his methods for Milton to have been of his party, knowingly or otherwise: Milton's party, like Blake's, was far more radical than that of Satan, who looks to the very ruler he despises for his model of government. Only the Son offers a thoroughly Miltonic radicalism, a point of view that insists, as Christopher Hill writes, "the true fight is fought first in the hearts of men."⁶ Hill describes the Son's radicalism in compelling terms:

> True glory comes from renunciation of glory—a conclusion to which Milton returned in *Paradise Regained*, whose truly heroic theme is 'one man's obedience fully tried', and in *Samson Agonistes*, where Samson achieves true heroism when he stops wanting to be a hero.⁷

Satan represents an entirely different perspective, one that insists that war is its own glory, and power is its own reward; for Milton, this misses the point entirely. As Hill puts it, war, "so far from being glorious, defeats its own ends because it produces the wrong virtues,"⁸ virtues that are embodied in Milton's Heaven by the Father (whose concern with "Omnipotence," "Arms," "Deity," and "Empire" [5.722–24] is about as unMiltonic as it is possible to get). In sharing the Father's obsessions with rank and power, Satan reflects the Father's image in a way that the Son ultimately refuses to. Whereas Satan means to overthrow the Father and take him down from a heavenly throne, the Son adopts an end more radical than Satan's (and closer to Milton's) while employing means hitherto unseen in Milton's Heaven: he fights—through reason, self-sacrifice, and self-denial—to overturn heavenly kingship, to refuse thrones both earthly and heavenly, and to abolish kingship itself by reclaiming a Miltonic, internal definition of glory, heroism, and true government.

Using the Son in this way, Milton concurrently creates a Father who is profoundly disturbing, an illustration of what can and will go wrong with deity imagined in absolutist and monarchical terms. The Father that Milton portrays in *Paradise Lost* reigns through application of a justice code so rigid that to call it draconian would be an insult to the liberality of Draco.⁹ Milton portrays the Father in such a harsh light, *not* to say to his "fit audience . . . though few" that this is how God really *is*, but that this is how God has been *wickedly imagined*. Milton's great poems are in this sense a variation on Meister Eckhart's famous prayer to be able to "for God's sake . . . take leave of god,"¹⁰ to abandon a slave's image of God as a military monarch who rules often recalcitrant subjects through force and fear, and to adopt a free man's image of God as one who prefers to "make persuasion do the work of fear" (*Paradise Regained* 1.223).

It must be noted that a cornerstone of literary study is the recognition of a distinction between representation and represented. Poetic characters are not, in any absolute sense, identical with what they represent. In writing a poem, Milton works with *images* of God. The difference between poetry and systematic theology (a form that also works with *images* or *conceptions* of God) is wide enough that responsible readers must be cautious about assuming that poetic representations of God are necessarily intended to be synonymous with whatever "presence" or "absence" is pointed to with the word "God." There may be a wide difference between a poet's representation of the divine and whatever private beliefs about the divine that poet may hold. To wit, Dennis Danielson asks what is perhaps the prototypically orthodox question of modern Milton studies: "Does Milton worship, and present, a good God?"[11] The unspoken assumption seems to be that the character known as the Father in *Paradise Lost* is somehow the same God that Milton may have worshipped. But "present" and "worship" are not synonymous, and a poetic character is not God. A poetic character is created in the human imagination; the figures that emerge therefrom cannot be any less human and fallible than their creators. The seemingly instinctive tendency to conflate the character Milton creates with the divine itself should not excuse his readers and critics from considering the legitimate difficulties of that character. Concretizing the metaphor only blinds us to the richness of Milton's work,[12] leading to readings arguing that any flaws in Milton's poetic portrayal of God necessarily mar the poem itself: "If Milton presents a God who is wicked, or untruthful, or manipulative, or feeble, or unwise, then his epic poem must suffer accordingly."[13]

To counter the argument that a "wicked" presentation of God in *Paradise Lost* makes the poem suffer, it is necessary to take a closer look at the words of the Son in Book 3 of *Paradise Lost*, words chosen with painstaking care in the face of the highest possible stakes, not only for humankind, but for the Son *and* the Father. In one of the finest and most compelling sections of Milton's entire poem, the Father is presented as "wicked, . . . untruthful, . . . manipulative, [and] unwise," but rather than marring the poem by darkening the Father's character, Milton's presentation raises his work to heights truly "invisible to mortal sight" (3.55) by presenting the emerging glory and heroism of the Son.

Working with carefully constructed images of God, Milton deliberately builds the Son's monologue at 3.144–66 on the twin foundations of Abraham and Moses. The Son's "that far be from thee" is a direct reference to Abraham's ethical challenge to Yahweh at Gen. 18:25 over the planned destruction of Sodom and Gomorrah. When the Son pursues this confrontation with the Father, inquiring "wilt thou thyself / Abolish thy Creation" (162–64), his challenge is an echo of Moses at Exod. 32, pleading with a Yahweh determined to destroy his own people.

Casting the Son in the position of Abraham serves to demonstrate clearly how courageous is the Son's action in this situation. Abraham's bargaining is no simple mediatorship, no mere intercession over a metaphysical bargaining table between equals (or near-equals). Abraham is a fantastically puny human being standing toe to toe with Yahweh himself. His action is a challenge that requires astounding courage. Abraham not only asks for mercy for the residents of the cities of the plain, he asks *repeatedly*, bargaining with Yahweh in a way that seems to be testing both the limits of the deity's ability to control his temper and also the extent to which mercy and righteousness can lessen the deity's wrath. Will fifty "righteous" be enough to avoid wholesale slaughter? How about forty-five? Forty? Thirty? Twenty? Ten? As it turns out, there are only four (or three, depending on how one takes the story of Lot's wife), and four apparently are not enough. God is not testing Man here; Man is testing God. Similarly, in Book 3 of *Paradise Lost*, the Father is not testing the Son; the Son is testing the Father.

Even a veteran reader of the Bible may still experience a moment's shock on re-reading the distressingly numerous accounts of a fast-talking Moses trying desperately to cool off a furious and hotheaded Yahweh. By an informal reckoning, Moses finds himself in this position four different times, while these instances are themselves recounted repeatedly through the rest of the Hebrew scriptures.

Of all of these instances of Mosaic intervention, by far the most interesting is found in Exod. 32. Here, a newly released people find themselves left to their own devices, far away from any homes they have ever known, while their charismatic—if somewhat bizarre and difficult—leader has gone off to communicate with the strange new god in whose name and by whose power the leader has brought them out of Egypt. These are people who have never known gods they could not see, gods of whom they could not form images for daily devotion, and so they (understandably) form an image of this strange new god to whom they owe their freedom. Old habits, ingrained through centuries of myth, ritual, religion, and all of the seasonal and social patterns thereof, are not easy to break, and the people backslide, having been insufficiently re-educated into the new ritual and religious order of things; by way of response, this strange new god gets murderously angry.

Yahweh tells Moses to go away and leave him alone while he destroys the people: "let me alone, that my wrath may wax hot against them, and that I may consume them" (32:10). Moses, however, will have none of this. He tells Yahweh to watch out that the Egyptians do not get the opportunity to gloat over the destruction of the people: "Wherefore should the Egyptians speak, and say, For mischief did he bring them out, to slay them in the mountains, and to consume them from the face of the earth?" (32:12). This call to remember what the enemy will make of the destruction—by God—of God's people is precisely the call that Milton ascribes to the Son in his confrontation with the Father in Book 3 of *Paradise Lost*. Both the Son and Moses are pleading with God not to take an action that will allow the enemy to question and blaspheme "without defense."

What both the Son and Moses are trying to forestall is *divine evil*. Moses, with what will become his characteristic bluntness toward Yahweh, tells the deity outright to "repent of this evil against thy people" (32:12), and Yahweh "repented of the evil which he thought to do unto his people" (32:14). The Hebrew word here (translated in the King James Bible as "evil") is *ra*. This word—which can be translated variously as evil, wickedness, displeasure, or wrong—comes from the root *rawah*, which means literally to break to pieces. If, as any Bible reader learns in Gen. 1, creation is literally *good*—from the Hebrew *tov*—then to "Abolish . . . Creation," to break it to pieces, is literally *evil*.[14]

Related to the notion of divine evil is the question of the passibility or impassibility of Milton's God. Can Milton's God be moved emotionally, to anger, joy, rage, even fear, so that he is capable of acting on impulse for good or for evil? Yahweh's capacity for evil is a fact so often emphasized in the Hebrew scriptures as to be almost monotonous, and the concept of Yahweh as the source of *all* things, both of good and of evil, is repeated frequently. Job asks his wife, "Shall we receive good at the hand of God, and shall we not receive evil?" (2:10). Lam. 3:38 asks, "Out of the mouth of the most High proceedeth not evil and good?" At Isa. 45:7, Yahweh tells Cyrus "I form the light, and create darkness: I make peace, and create evil: I the Lord do all these things." Each of these instances (as well as numerous others that could be employed in their place) reaffirms the aforementioned synergy between divine good (creation, *tov*) and divine evil (destruction, *rawah*). By placing his character of the Father in an unmistakably Yahwistic role in Book 3, Milton is quite openly presenting the Father both as capable of good *and* evil, and as passible, capable of being moved. Michael Lieb has done notable work in this area, arguing that Milton "not only intensifies the idea of passibility, but bestows upon it a new significance" in his portrait of the Father.[15] Lieb concludes, "the figure of God in *Paradise Lost* is portrayed as a fully passible being."[16] Milton creates a passible and morally ambiguous character in the Father, a character with the rich personality of Yahweh as a model.

The possibility of divine evil may explain why an old, blind, disgraced poet would feel it necessary to "assert eternal providence and justify the ways of God to men." But what exactly does it mean to "justify" God? Curiously, in most editions of Milton, this word—in the midst of a stunningly grandiose statement of ambition—is treated as if its meaning were concrete and self-evident. Editors often give no note whatsoever. Hughes gives no note. Fowler gives no note. Shawcross gives no note. Flannagan gives no note. One of the few editions I have seen that *does* give a note is that of Christopher Ricks. The note he gives is "bear witness to the justice of."[17] Such a comment, while certainly valid as far as it goes, seems to be straining to maintain an "orthodox" reading of Milton. What such a gloss does not mention—in fact, what it seems to be assiduously avoiding in relation to Milton's phrase—is the theological doctrine of "justification." Milton's use of the word "justify" brings with it (and in fact depends on) the theological issues involved in the Protestant reformulation of the justification doctrine. The full implications of this doctrine, when understood in relation to Milton's phrase, might lead a reader to have to consider—willingly or unwillingly—the possibility that an equally valid gloss might be "explain the injustice of."

An idea as old as the Bible itself, justification is the process through which fallen mankind is either made or declared righteous in the sight of God. "Protestant" theologies in the traditions of Luther and Calvin interpret justification as God imputing righteousness to mankind through its faith in the sacrifice of Christ. The older Augustinian view held that justification was the process through which God *made* unrighteous humanity righteous. Protestant theologies departed from this view of justification as involving a shift in humanity's *being*, preferring to define justification as a change in humanity's *status*. Being *declared* righteous in the sight of God implies that one is not *really* or *ontologically* changed, but that one is merely credited with something one does not actually have. (In this way, justification might be seen as a kind of spiritual line of credit extended to a bankrupt and essentially uncreditworthy humanity.)

However, this view of justification also necessitates a certain legalistic dualism. The imputation of righteousness is at once an *accusation* of unrighteousness and a simultaneous *acquittal* from the same. Milton's contemporary, the Kidderminster curate Richard Baxter, defines justification in his *Aphorismes of Justification* (1649) as "the acquitting of us from the charge of breaking the Law,"[18] and further argues that "Justification implyeth accusation."[19] Milton's reversal of this definition, therefore, is dramatic: when he declares that he will attempt to justify the ways of God to men, Milton is actually declaring his intent to accuse God in order to acquit God.

In announcing his intention to "justify the ways of God to men," Milton is appropriating and reversing the process through which Man is reconciled to God.[20] Rather than reconciling Man to God, Milton is reconciling God to Man.[21] Milton places God in a position similar to that in which "sinful" and "fallen" humanity is put by the theological doctrine of justification, which focuses on the inability of humanity to redeem itself—even to defend itself—without the intercession of Christ. In *Paradise Lost*, Milton turns the tables; for Milton, the Son is the poetic figure through whom the justification of God (the Father) is made possible.

Justification can be traced back to the earliest portions of the Hebrew scriptures. The Hebrew word translated as "justice" is *sedaqa*, whose root is *sdq*; this root, according to the historian and theologian Alister McGrath, has as its most likely core meaning "conformity to a norm."[22] *Sedaqa* then, is behavior that conforms to, reinforces, and supports the norm. The *sedaqa* of Yahweh and the *sedaqa* of Israel are each bound up in the covenant relationship between Yahweh and Israel. For Yahweh to threaten to destroy his people (as he does at Exod. 32:10) is to break *sedaqa*; for the Israelites to forsake Yahweh (as they do repeatedly) is also to break *sedaqa*.

To "justify" in the sense of *sedaqa* is to restore the norm, to restore a covenant relationship, to make things *saddiq*, or as they should be. The need to make things *saddiq* carries the sense that something has been broken, that someone has done wrong, that someone has broken *sedaqa*. One in need of "justification" is one who has failed to conform to the norm, one who has broken a covenant.

This sense of wrongdoing is carried over into the Greek verb *dikaioun*, which the translators of the Septuagint used to render the Hebrew *hasdiq*, a term meaning "to make right," or "to restore *sedaqa*." According to McGrath, *dikaioun* "in its classical usage . . . with a *personal* object almost invariably seems to be applied to someone whose cause is *unjust*."[23] In this usage *dikaioun* takes on a punitive aspect—to do justice to. However, in the Septuagint, *dikaioun* takes on a completely different character. Still used in the context of someone whose cause in *unjust*, *dikaioun* takes on a positive aspect— to justify, to acquit, to declare to be in the right. When Israel is invited to confess her sins at Isa. 43:26, it is "in order that she may be acquitted of them."[24]

The idea of justification moves then, from a bedrock sense of justice as conformity to a norm, of behavior that reinforces and supports a covenant relationship, to a sense of the *in*justice of the breaker(s) of that norm or relationship and the concomitant necessity of rapprochement.

By the time of the Vulgate, in which *dikaioun* is rendered as *iustificare*, another important shift has occurred. Most Latin-speaking theologians followed Augustine in interpreting *iustificare* as *iustum facere* (making just or making righteous). The idea of justification has shifted from "declaring to be in the right" to "making right." The emphasis of justification has shifted from a sense of restoring an abandoned conformity to a norm and returning to a covenantal relationship in which that norm is embodied, to an ontological change in the one who is "justified." The Hebrew and Greek senses of justification emphasize *status*, while the Latin (Augustinian) sense of justification emphasizes *being*. The difference is explained by McGrath as one between a "Greek verb [that] has the primary sense of being *considered* or *estimated* as righteous," and a "Latin verb [that] denotes *being* righteous."²⁵ It is the Latin sense of justification as being *made righteous* that is dominant in "orthodox" theology from the time of Augustine until the Reformation; after the Reformation the earlier sense—the sense inherent in the Hebrew *hasdiq* and the Greek *dikaioun*—is once again asserted.

Luther, by way of illustration, who insisted that man was entirely passive in the face of divine justification, regarded justification as a "healing process which permits God to overlook the remaining sin on account of its pending eradication."²⁶ Overlooking sin *pending eradication* is not *making righteous*; overlooking sin is closer to the sense of *dikaioun* (declaring just or righteous) than to *iustificare* (according to Augustine, making just or righteous). Fallen man, in Luther's formulation, is considered as if he were just, as if he were righteous, when he is in fact no such thing. The sense is not of making man sinless, but of returning man and God to a covenant relationship, restoring *sedaqa*. It is justification in Luther's sense that enables man—whose cause is essentially *unjust*—to be "declared to be in the right," to be "acquitted."

In raising the issue of justification in his famous declaration of intent, Milton is not working with the Augustinian sense, but with the earlier Septuagintal and Hebrew sense of justification—restoring *sedaqa* between God and man. In declaring that the "ways of God" are the object of justification, Milton is declaring that the "ways of God" stand in the place of that object of *dikaioun* whose cause is *unjust*. However, it is important to keep in mind the difference between the formulations of justification as either *declaring* or *making* righteous when analyzing the implications of Milton's appropriation and reversal of the justification doctrine. What Milton says he will "justify" is not God itself—God as an ontological essence—but the "ways of God": the observable, conceivable, categorizable aspects and actions of God in the world. Milton is not trying to *make* God righteous, but to *declare* God righteous. In essence, Milton is turning justification around in the only way possible for a mere mortal: not by changing God's *being*, but by changing God's *status*, changing the way in which God is conceived of by human beings.²⁷

Milton was not only keenly aware of the justification doctrine and the controversy surrounding it in 1650s England, but he was in this instance—as in so many others—on the minority or quasi-heretical side of the controversy.²⁸ It becomes difficult then, given the implications of a poetic justification of God, to conceive of Milton's purpose being, as Fish has argued, to confront the reader "with evidence of his own corruption," or to make the reader "aware of his inability to respond adequately to spiritual conceptions."[29] The reader is being confronted with nothing quite so commonplace as *his own* corruption, or "his inability to respond adequately to spiritual conceptions;" rather, the reader is being confronted with—and only a "fit audience . . . though few" will be able to see—evidence of the corruption and inadequacy of a particular "spiritual conception:" the conception of God as a military monarch.

Ultimately, for Milton, God desperately needs a defense attorney. Milton serves as God's advocate by setting in motion a poetic process of justification through accusation and acquittal that uses the Son as its main instrument. Milton at once accuses and acquits the Father by putting the Son in the position of patient, quiet, yet firm petitioner before the Father. In so doing, Milton provides a model of confrontation with the Father that serves as a poetic negative image of the confrontations of Satan. Both Satan and the Son reject a model of arbitrary and unquestioned rule by the Father; however, each chooses a radically different style of confrontation. Satan's attempt—military conquest—fails. The Son's challenge to the Father, by contrast, succeeds so dramatically that the Father claims that the bold words of the Son were, in fact, merely an expression of the Father's already-established purpose. Where Satan chooses to use military might against a heavenly king who commands a vast angelic military, thus in a real sense *adopting the tactics of the very ruler he rejects*, the Son instead uses language, diplomacy, persuasion, and argument to confront the Father, thus adopting the tactics of Milton the poet and pamphleteer.

In Book 3, the Father has just finished a lengthy monologue on the subject of just who is to blame for the human fall, a tragedy that—in human time—has not yet happened. After focusing on such noteworthy things as the freedom to stand or fall of those who fell, his lack of pleasure in any obedience that is one iota less than entirely freely willed, his desire that his creature serve him rather than "necessity," his defensive insistence that he cannot be "justly accuse[d]," and his ever-present concern with his "glory," the Father at last comes around to a mention of mercy for the as-yet unfallen first human pair, saying "Mercy first and last shall brightest shine" (134).

After several lines from the narrator about how wonderful this monologue was, and how joyful were the "blessed Spirits elect" (136) to hear the Father's legalistic self-defense, the Son responds. What is especially interesting about the Son's response is that he completely ignores the Father's legalistic arguments, vitriol, and self-defense, choosing instead to focus on, and attempt to reinforce, the Father's afterthought of mercy: "O Father, gracious was that word which clos'd / Thy sovran sentence, that Man should find grace" (144–45).[30]

Even more interesting than what the Son does *not* respond to is what the Son *does* respond to. In urging mercy, the Son responds to something that has only been *directly* uttered, not by the Father, but by Satan. The Son asks, "shall the Adversary thus obtain / His end, and frustrate thine, shall he fulfill / His malice, and thy goodness bring to naught / . . . and to Hell / Draw after him the whole Race of mankind, / By him corrupted?" (156–59, 162). In Book 2, it is Satan who proposes the attempt to "seduce" Adam and Eve "to our Party, that thir God / May prove thir foe, and with repenting hand / Abolish his own works" (368–70). It is in reference to this destructive—hence, *evil*—aim of *Satan* that the Son directs his "that far be from thee" in Book 3 (154). In essence, the Son is pleading with the Father to be as far from evil as he can manage to be. "That far be from thee" to fulfill the ambitions of Satan: "That far be from thee" to lose control of yourself to such an extent that you become Satan's accomplice.[31]

Despite the parallels, there are important differences between the accounts of Yahweh in Gen. 18 and Exod. 32 and that of the Father in Book 3 of *Paradise Lost.* The Father never, for instance, threatens to destroy his people—but he doesn't have to, because his own messenger makes the threat for him (however obliquely). Raphael, in relating to Adam the story of the war in heaven and the creation of Earth, refers to having served sentry duty against the new inhabitants of Hell while the Earth was in production. The sentries were "To see that none thence issu'd forth a spy, / Or enemy, while God was in his work, / Lest hee incenst at such eruption bold, / Destruction with Creation might have mixt" (8.233–36). For the Father to mix destruction with creation, to literally mix *evil* with *good*, is not considered unusual enough as a possibility to even merit an ironically raised eyebrow from the garrulous messenger. Adam himself intuited this possibility of evil in the Father when he told Eve—in reference to her Satan-inspired dream—that "Evil into the mind of God or Man / May come and go, so unapprov'd, and leave / No spot or blame behind" (5.117–19). The key phrase in Adam's speech, however, is "so unapprov'd." Evil may come into the mind of God or Man and leave no spot *only if that evil is not acted upon*. Eve does eventually act on evil that comes into her mind, and Raphael seems to take for granted that the Father is also quite capable of acting on such evil.

THE FATHER OF LIES

There is another important difference between the Yahweh of Exod. 32 and the Father of *Paradise Lost*: Yahweh *repents*. Yahweh does not simply claim, after having been justly and courageously confronted by Moses, that he was planning to be merciful all along and only exterminate *some* of the Israelites over the matter of the golden calf. In *Paradise Lost*, the Father, having been confronted by the Son, claims that the Son was merely speaking aloud what he, the Father, had in mind the whole time. The Son is *cajoling* the Father, saying, in effect, "you can't destroy Man utterly, or else the adversary will have defeated you." The Father vacillates between mercy and wrath; one minute he declares that "Mercy first and last shall brightest shine" (3.134), and the next minute he reverts to rage and bluster, announcing that Man "with his whole posterity must die" (3.209). The Son pleads consistently for mercy; nowhere does he entertain the thought that destroying mankind would be a good idea. After this intercession by the Son, for the Father to come back and say, "All hast thou spok'n as my thoughts are, all / As my Eternal purpose hath decreed" is a deliberately jarring note played against the carefully composed background that Milton provides for the Son's action. *The Father has been caught out*, and he has had neither the courage nor the honesty to admit it. The Father, in short, *lies*.[32]

A God who lies is not a comforting prospect. The easy response would be to reject the notion altogether. After all, received wisdom, along with a literal interpretation of John 8:44, tells us that it is Satan who is "the father of the lie." Milton writes in *Paradise Lost* of the fallen angels corrupting "the greatest part / Of mankind" by "falsities and lies" (1.367–68). Milton also has the Father speak in the future tense of Satan's "glozing lies" (3.93), lies that will contribute to the Fall. Gabriel refers to Satan as a "liar traced" in their confrontation at 4.949. The Father tells Raphael that Satan plans to assault the first human pair with "deceit and lies" (5.243). Raphael then tells Adam of the "lies" of Satan in heaven (5.709). The Father again, at the beginning of Book 10, speaks of Satan's "lies / Against his Maker" (42–43).

Plainly, Milton is at great pains to create a portrait of Satan as a liar. This is a truism as banal as it is well known. This truism, however, does not necessarily preclude the possibility that the Father may also lie. In carefully constructing his Father/Son dialogue in Book 3 on the twin pillars of Abraham and Moses, Milton bases his poetic character on an unmistakable model—Yahweh.

Yahweh, though he is described at Num. 23:19 as "not a man, that he should lie," *does* lie. The story of the "lying spirit" at 1 Kings 22:20–23 paints a portrait of a deity who is not at all adverse to generating lies and then punishing others for the lies generated. "The Lord hath put a lying spirit in the mouth of all these thy prophets, and the Lord hath spoken evil concerning thee."

The "lying spirit" sent forth in 1 Kings 22:20–23 is the *malak* of Yahweh. If, rather than being translated as "messenger," *malak* is here understood—as Jeffrey Burton Russell suggests—as "the voice of the God, the spirit of the God, the God himself,"[33] then it is Yahweh *himself* who lies in order to achieve his ends. Yahweh, the model upon which Milton bases so much of the Father, can and does lie, both directly, and through the words and actions of his servants. Examples of Yahweh's lies, half-truths, and manipulations abound in the scriptures. It is Yahweh who, at 2 Sam. 24:1 "moved David" to take a census of the people of Israel, and it is Yahweh who savagely punishes David and Israel for this census by "a pestilence" that kills "seventy thousand men" (2 Sam. 24:15). Yahweh serves as his own "lying spirit" here, moving David to take the very action for which Yahweh will inflict horrible punishment. It is also Yahweh whose "hand shall be upon the prophets that see vanity, and that divine lies," or, in the translation of the NRSV, "If a prophet is deceived and speaks a word, I, the Lord, have deceived that prophet, and will stretch out my hand against him" (Ezek. 13:9).

The curious story of the lying prophet in 1 Kings 13 brings the *malak* of Yahweh into the arena of lies and deception once again. It is the "word of the Lord" delivered by the lying prophet that causes another prophet to break his oath and to be killed and eaten by a lion as punishment. No mention is made of the lying prophet being punished for his role in this grotesque affair; therefore, despite the fact that 13:18 says that "he lied unto him," it is by no means clear that the lie was not, in fact, instigated by Yahweh himself.

Even by the time of the Pauline epistles, the Hebrew god had not lost this reputation for using deception to accomplish his purposes. Although he is universalized as *theos*, or "God," the figure of whom Paul writes to the Thessalonians acts much like the Yahweh of Job, working hand in hand with Satan to ensure that the "Wicked" shall be revealed: "And for this cause God shall send them a strong delusion, that they should believe a lie" (2 Thess. 2:11). A god pictured as a liar, as a punisher of actions he has initiated, as an oracular figure who puts false words in the mouths of prophets and then punishes both the prophets and those unfortunates who believe in them, is a portrait of divine evil, even if that god—in a Machiavellian ends-justify-the-means manner—seems to act for good purposes. Such a god is a figure found in the books of Job, Lamentations, and Isaiah, a capricious and unpredictable deity from whom people expect evil. Milton is keen to reject such a conception of the divine. In *De Doctrina Christiana*, he affirms that "God's will is the first cause of everything" (*CPW* 6:163), but he is at great pains to prevent God from being portrayed as "the cause and author of sin" (*CPW* 6:166). In prose, Milton defends God from such a charge by arguing against its verity, by arguing forcefully against Calvinist notions of predestination that insist that "all future events must happen by necessity because God has foreknown them" (*CPW* 6:165). In poetry, however, Milton takes a different tack, inventing a "long argument to prove that God is not the Devil" (*CPW* 6:166), by embodying the concept of God he wishes to undermine in a poetic character. In so doing, Milton is able to illustrate into what kinds of "error" those who "do not hesitate to assert that God is, in himself, the cause and author of sin" (*CPW* 6:166) are falling.

In order to see clearly how Milton subtly weaves Yahweh's manipulations, half-truths, and "divine lies" into the whole cloth of the Father, a reader must take a closer look at the narrator's descriptions. The Father is described at 3.77–78 as "beholding from his prospect high, / Wherein past, present, future he beholds." This seems to make it impossible for the Father to be "lying" at 3.171–72, since it seems that he knew in advance what the Son was going to say. However, one of a reader's primary sources of information that the Father sees "past, present, future" is the fact that the narrator says so. The verity of this assertion should not simply be taken for granted. Milton criticism, by and large, is suspicious of those descriptions of the Father emerging from the mouths of "Satanic" forces. In fact, the assumption that Satan's words must be viewed with unceasing suspicion is a severely overworked commonplace of Milton criticism—what Empson once referred to as "the modern duty of catching Satan out wherever possible."[34] However, an equally overworked commonplace seems to be the tendency to take the words of heaven, and the presumably pro-heaven narrator, as always and completely truthful and accurate. The assumption that the narrator, after the trepidation expressed in his invocation to Book 3, is always in possession of a complete and perfect understanding of the events being narrated, is questionable. The narrator is not always entirely reliable; an example of this unreliability is the matter of ire.

Uriel, having initially failed to recognize Satan at the end of Book 3, finally does recognize him in Book 4. Uriel is able to recognize Satan because of the latter's emotional state: Satan's "borrow'd visage" was "marr'd" by "pale, ire, envy, and despair." The narrator then goes on to assure the reader that "heav'nly minds from such distempers foul / Are ever clear" (115–19), but this turns out to be not quite true. "Ire" is quite at home in "heav'nly minds." The "ire" of the Son (presumably a character in possession of a "heav'nly mind") is referred to by Raphael at 6.843. The "just avenging ire" of the Almighty is celebrated by the unfallen angels at 7.184. Michael speaks of how "willingly God doth remit his Ire" at 11.885. The "ire" of the Father is spoken of numerous times by the infernal forces, and this, perhaps, is one time when they just might be trusted after all.

The issue is not whether or not the Father's ire is justified (a point many will no doubt wish to argue), but just how much reliance can be placed on the descriptions of a narrator who cannot seem to keep his "heav'nly" and not-so-"heav'nly" minds straight. A narrator wrong about ire might be wrong about other things. In eagerly assigning every moral negative to Satan, while excusing the Father from every appearance of similar moral negatives, the narrator of *Paradise Lost* functions as a type of orthodox apologist, carrying all of the ideological baggage that such apologism brings. Additionally, though the narrator does not always fully understand the nature of what he is describing—this is made clear by the tentative quality of the invocation to Book 3—he is nonetheless quite wrong about the issue of ire and "heav'nly minds." Given this error on the part of the narrator, readers may legitimately hold some doubt about the narrative contention that the Father "past, present, [and] future . . . beholds." The Father may not have known exactly what the Son was going to say. The Father may very well be lying—or, at the very least, quickly shifting his rhetorical position—when he says to the Son, "All hast thou spok'n as my thoughts are, all / As my Eternal purpose hath decreed." The Father has been taken aback.

With this picture in mind of the Father and Satan, both of whom resort to lies and shifting rhetorical stances when pressed, it becomes clear that such a similarity between the Father and Satan is what seems to worry the Son so much in Book 3.[35] Michael Lieb has argued along similar lines, outlining a list of questions that the Son seems to be asking the Father, among which are the following:

1) Shall Satan triumph?
2) Will you allow your goodness to be undermined?
3) Will you abolish your creation?

Lieb writes of a warning from the Son to the Father, "a warning that if the answer is indeed 'yes' (the very real possibility is implied here) then God's 'goodness and . . . greatness both' would be justifiably 'questioned.' "[36] Lieb goes on to write, "One senses in the challenge that the Son himself would be the foremost among the reprobate in excoriating the Father, should the Father fail to heed the Son's warning."[37]

With divine evil, divine lies, and divine passibility all at work, Milton is not establishing anything like an orthodox scenario that insists on the impassibility and absolute goodness of the Father. Were Milton insisting on such a scenario, one that he notoriously fails or refuses to create, then his use of the Father in his attempt to "justify the ways of God to men" would be an abject failure.

Such an orthodox defense, however, is not part of Milton's scheme. Milton has the Father and Son play out long-familiar roles, not of mere *mediation*, but of open and high-stakes *confrontation* between a developing nation and its likewise-developing God, in order to accuse the Father. God, in order to have his ways "justified," is depicted by Milton in two aspects: Father and Son. Milton *accuses* God in the image of the Father so that he may then *acquit* God in the image of the Son. This combination of accusation and acquittal is part of a larger scheme of movement by Milton away from the model of divinity inhabited by the Father (a heavenly *dux bellorum,* leader of angelic troops and occupant of a heavenly throne) and toward an alternate model of divinity, embodied by Milton in the form of the Son (a heavenly—and later earthly—destroyer of kings and kingship, both on earth and in heaven).

It is in this tension between two images of God, Father and Son, that Milton's search for a "fit audience . . . though few" resides. The Father of *Paradise Lost* is not synonymous with God in any absolute or ontological sense. The Father may therefore be portrayed (and analyzed) without finally submitting such portrayal (and analysis) to the demands of theological orthodoxy. As is clear from the context of the Father–Son dialogue in Book 3 of *Paradise Lost*, the Father is plainly based on another famous character who also is not synonymous with God in any absolute or ontological sense—Yahweh as he is presented in the Hebrew scriptures. Just as Yahweh is passible, so the Father is passible. Just as Yahweh lies, so the Father also lies. Just as Yahweh must be dissuaded from evil, so must the Father be dissuaded from evil.

With Yahweh firmly entrenched as part of his character, the Father is, in a sense, trapped in the role of a divine military tyrant, unable to escape from it, or lay down the power and trappings of his heavenly throne. However, the Father is aware of his position, and his plans for the Son indicate his desire to relinquish power. As Empson observed, "Milton did expect God to abdicate."[38] While not going so far as Empson, David Norbrook raises the issue of divine abdication when he refers to the episode at 3.312–19 as being "closely parallel to a king's abdicating and showing solidarity with his people."[39] Empson makes an interesting point when he compares Oliver Cromwell to the Father. In describing Cromwell's "admitted and genuine bother" as being a desire to "find some way of establishing a Parliament under which he could feel himself justified in stopping being a dictator,"[40] Empson has anticipated an important part of the point this essay is trying to drive home. Milton's dilemma is how to create a poetic God who is a dictator, but who can "feel himself justified in stopping being a dictator."

Milton effects this transformation by having the Father hand over power to the Son, for all intents and purposes stepping down from the heavenly throne. In so doing, however, Milton puts a strongly antimonarchical and antihierarchical spin on the scriptural source from which he borrows his language. Milton *deliberately* alters the terms of 1 Cor. 15:28 in his descriptions of the Son's assumption and subsequent renunciation of power. 1 Corinthians clearly spells out that the Son shall "himself be subject unto him that put all things under him, that God may be all in all." This is neither a rejection of monarchy nor an erasing of hierarchical distinctions in a union of all creation with God. Milton's rendering of this passage into his poetic speech of the Father to the Son is both of those things: "All Power / I give thee, reign forever . . . / Then thou thy regal Sceptre shalt lay by, / For regal Sceptre then no more shall need, / God shall be All in All" (3.317–18, 339–41). The Father relinquishes power to the Son. The Son then lays down the "regal Sceptre," putting aside the final symbol of the external rule that is passing away forever. In so doing, the Son shatters the image of divine kingship, and no provision remains for renewed submission by the Son, or anyone else, to the Father. God (no longer imagined as a king) is simply All in All.

Given Milton's use of the Son, those passages in which the Father claims that the Son has anticipated his own thoughts or expressed his own will are somewhat misleading. The Father's claim (after the Son has just finished pleading for mercy to be shown to mankind in Book 3) that the Son has "spok'n as my thoughts are" is true, but only in the sense that it is the Son who will show such mercy, because the Son is the one to whom and through whom the "Tyranny of heav'n" will be given and finally eliminated. The Son is to be what the Father could not be: a divinity imagined in non-monarchical terms. Furthermore, although the narrator of *Paradise Lost* describes the Son as if he were somehow an *expression* of the Father ("the Son of God . . . in [whom] all his Father shown / Substantially express'd" [3.139–40]), the Son is much more than that: the Son is a character instrumental in the *development* of the Father. The Son challenges the Father to be better, more merciful, and less destructively violent than he has been. The Son's challenges allow a poetic character, the Father, to escape from the immutability into which a theological concept, God, is often confined. The Son is both Milton's critique of the monarchical Father and the Father's avenue for growth and change. The monarchical Father cannot become the God who "shall be All in All" (3.341) except through means of the Son.

The Evolution of the Son from Warrior to Hero

Just as the Father should not be mistaken for God, neither should the character of the Son be mistaken for God in an absolute or ontological sense. The Son is also merely an image of God. The Son's challenges to the Father in *Paradise Lost* are cornerstones of Milton's extended poetic attempt to destroy the no-longer-tenable image of God as an arbitrary figure of military might and monarchical power. Milton's great epic comprises a poetic *Eikonoklastes* in response to an *Eikon Theios* (God as a military king) that had made the English people "worthie . . . to be for ever slaves" (*The Ready and Easy Way*, *CPW* 7:428). In replacing this disastrous image, Milton offers the Son, a figure through whom the process of justification—in its full theological sense—begins in *Paradise Lost* and eventually is completed in *Paradise Regained*.

The Son as he first appears to the reader in Book 3 is already well on the way to accomplishing Milton's goal. His discourse with the Father over the salvation of humankind shows him valuing mercy and forgiveness over punishment and power. The Son, at this point, takes a significant turn away from the models offered by the Father and Satan, mirror-image monarchs whose concerns are for power, glory, and reign. The Son's concern is not for himself, but for *others*, the relatively defenseless human race, caught between two implacably hostile kings who use their respective militaries to shoot first and ask questions later—if ever.

In order better to understand how Milton portrays the Son, it is important to note that two different ways of reading *Paradise Lost* are possible in terms of time. Reading the poem as it is presented, with crucial events of the past held back until the middle of the poem, gives a different picture of both the Son and Satan than does a reading that considers these characters in terms of chronological development from their earliest to their latest appearances in the time span referred to in Milton's universe. *Paradise Lost* begins, as do the epics of Homer, Virgil, and the later Renaissance Italians Boiardo, Ariosto, and Tasso, *in medias res*. Past events which led up to the current situation are presented in conversational or monologic narrative "flashbacks." Presenting his narrative in this fashion allows Milton to heighten the contrast between his greatest superhuman characters by showing each of them first at crucial and defining moments.

In the earliest books of *Paradise Lost*, the Son and Satan are each presented in a heroic light. Each is rhetorically brilliant, emotionally stirring, and, in different ways, courageous and self-sacrificing. However, each has changed from what he once was; no longer is either figure what he was in Books 5 and 6, the time of rebellion and war in Heaven. By showing the reader what these characters now are, and then showing what they once were, Milton presents their narratives in a way that illustrates in each character profound changes that have followed opposing trajectories. Each seems noble the first time he appears on the narrative stage, but the similarity of their appearance is deceiving, as the Son and Satan are headed in different directions: the Son is becoming nobler just as Satan is falling further into tyranny and degradation. Satan is still heroically impressive in Books 1 and 2, but he is less than he was, and his arguments have more of the flavor of tyranny than they did in Book 5, the earliest *chronological* point at which Satan appears. The Son appears in his strongest and most noble light in Book 3, the earliest *narrative* point at which he appears, but the Son does not start out this way. The Son of Book 3, whose arguments are those of mercy, and of persuasion rather than fear, is a stunning maturation of the Son of Book 5, whose "sentence," much like Moloch's, is for "open War" (2.51), and whose concern, much like the Father's, is for "Glory" (5.738).

Taking a chronological view of *Paradise Lost* creates a picture of the Son as a rapidly developing character, a preternaturally bright child who learns through painful experience to transcend his upbringing, to become more than his environment might have suggested it would be possible to become. The Son's earliest moments are spent in an atmosphere of hostility, threats, and resentment. When he is raised to the position of "Vice-gerent" (5.609), rebellion and war break out immediately. Had the Son already been at a later stage of development, his approach to the situation might have been one of diplomacy, discourse, and reasoned attempts at conciliation and rapprochement. The Son of Book 3 might very well have been able to smooth ruffled feathers, and likely would have wanted no part of a scheme to *create* resentment and rebellion where none previously existed. But the Son of Book 5 is not yet what he will become. In fact, at this point, the Son is still a warrior eager for a military victory.

For the Son of Book 5, the uproar and uprising in Heaven is a matter of personal "Glory" (5.738), not, as Satan argues, a matter of the disastrous and not-to-be-tolerated arrogation of all power to one ruler, nor even as Abdiel argues, a matter of the Son's rights as the Father's agent in the creation of everything that exists (a "strange doctrine and new" according to Satan). Raw power is what the entire matter seems to boil down to for the adolescent Son, as he casts the issue in remarkably Satanic terms:

> Mighty Father, thou thy foes
> Justly hast in derision, and, secure,
> Laugh'st at thir vain designs and tumults vain,
> Matter to mee of Glory, whom thir hate
> Illustrates, when they see all Regal Power
> Given me to quell thir pride, and in event
> Know whether I be dext'rous to subdue
> Thy Rebels, or be found the worst in Heav'n.
>
> (5.735–42)

Several interesting points come to light in the Son's brief speech. The Father has "foes," and the Son gives a clear indication that he understands those foes to have been of recent—and therefore, of the Father's—creation. The Son indicates this understanding by celebrating the Father's derision and laughter, as both he and the Father are *amused* by the "vain designs" of "Thy Rebels," rebels created and, in a sense, owned by the Father. Finally, power and merit are directly related for the Son at this point: he will subdue the Father's rebels, *or* he will be "the worst in Heav'n." This is precisely how Satan views power—as an indication of the merit of the one possessing power. Satan makes this abundantly clear in his argument with Abdiel in Book 5: "Our puissance is our own; our own right hand / Shall teach us highest deeds, by proof to try / Who is our equal" (5.864–66). What is different about Satan's and the Son's appeal to power as a measure of merit is that the Son takes an even more extreme view than does Satan. Where Satan views his power as a means by which to measure who is equal to him in nobility and merit, for the adolescent Son, his power is an all-or-nothing proposition: he is either powerful enough to subdue the rebellion or he is *nothing*, "the worst in Heav'n."

Thus the Son starts out, much like Satan, in the vein of a classical battle hero, a warrior prince whose "puissance" comes from his "right hand." Strength is what finally decides the outcome of the war in Heaven, not righteousness or merit defined in terms of goodness. Merit, if it is to be insisted upon as the deciding factor in both the Son's elevation and his victory over Satan's angelic army, is the merit of Achilles, the merit of strength and skill in battle. The Son does not defeat Satan because he is more righteous than Satan; the Son defeats Satan because he is *stronger* than Satan. The developing nobility and righteousness of the Son makes the outcome a fortunate one for humankind, but it does not decide the outcome. Might, not right, wins the war in Heaven.

Just before entering—and finishing—the battle, the Son takes a significant step away from his hardened rhetoric of battle and glory from Book 5. He announces that he will resign power, gladly returning to a state of union and peace:

> Sceptre and Power, thy giving, I assume,
> And gladlier shall resign, when in the end
> Thou shalt be All in All, and I in thee
> For ever, and in mee all whom thou lov'st.
>
> (6.730–33)

This is an almost identical statement to that which the Father makes regarding power in Book 3. Just as in that speech, the background text of 1 Corinthians is manipulated in such a way that the idea of *subjection* is no longer present. Milton's adaptation of 1 Cor. 15:28, whether spoken by the Son—*chronologically* the first to express the idea of relinquishing monarchical power in *Paradise Lost*—or by the Father, emphasizes inwardness and union in favor of external authority, subjection, and hierarchical order.

Stressing inwardness and union at this point shows the Son already progressing toward a Miltonic ideal. The Son expresses his dawning awareness of what it is to favor and uphold the tyrant of a nation (much as Milton does in the first paragraph of *Tenure of Kings and Magistrates*), while his ruminations reflect Milton's pairing of the internal government of individuals with the external government of states. The worst kind of tyranny involves both internal and external circumstances, "a double tyrannie, of Custom from without, and blind affections within" (*CPW* 3:190). In Milton's view, the internal serves as the base and root cause of the external; slavish people beget tyrannous regimes: "being slaves within doors, no wonder that they strive so much to have the public State conformably govern'd to the inward vitious rule by which they govern themselves" (*CPW* 3:190). In announcing his intention to relinquish "Sceptre and Power," the Son has done what Satan could not do—abolish tyranny by freeing himself *internally*. No longer a "slave within doors," the Son can now strive to "have the public State . . . govern'd to the inward [Miltonic and truly liberated] rule" by which he has begun to govern himself.

Despite the momentous import of this first step, the Son's maturation is neither complete nor manifest to all at this point. As he enters the battle, the Son seems to revert to his battle-hardened rhetoric, placing blame exclusively, and unfairly, on the rebels for reducing Heaven to a contest of strength:

> they may have thir wish, to try with mee
> In Battle which the stronger proves, they all,
> Or I alone against them, since by strength
> They measure all, of other excellence
> Not emulous, nor care who them excels;
>
> (6.881–85)

What "other excellence" the Son might be referring to at this point is a mystery—in a *chronological* reading of the poem. Though he has announced his plans to relinquish his recently acquired monarchical power, the Son who "full of wrath bent on his Enemies" (6.826) is not yet the patient petitioner in whose face "Divine compassion visibly appear'd, / Love without end, and without measure Grace" (3.141–42), and he is not yet the figure who argues with the Father for mercy to be shown to as-yet unfallen humanity. What "other excellence" the Son *will* show is already clear to a reader by this point in the poem, but it is not yet clear to the Son (unless one sees a touch of Prince Hal's "herein will I imitate the sun" speech from *1 Henry IV*).

It is true that the rebels measure everything by strength, just as the Son maintains. But this is not a characteristic exclusive to the rebels: Abdiel shares it in abundance. His arguments against Satan in Book 5 are rife with references to the strength and power of the Father and the Son. The Father has given the "regal scepter" to the Son, and that's the end of the matter: discussion is neither necessary nor allowed. To those who insist upon resisting the elevation of the Son, destruction awaits: "Then who created thee lamenting learn, / When who can uncreate thee thou shalt know" (5.894–95). The basis for all of Abdiel's assertions and unpleasant threats, however, is not righteousness or justice, but *power*. Abdiel is no different from Satan in measuring all by strength, because strength is the foundation of everything until the Son changes both the foundation and the universe built upon it in Book 3.

What the Son does is redefine merit, changing the terms in which merit is conceived from the classical to the Miltonic. Merit is no longer the puissance of a warrior's right hand, but the persuasion of the mediator's voice and moral courage. Though the Father tells the Son in Book 6 that "War wearied hath perform'd what War can do" (695), he does so in the context of telling the Son to end the war by using overwhelming force. What the Son does in Book 3 is to shift the emphasis of the Father's words, taking the attitude that *justice and punishment wearied have performed what justice and punishment can do*, and calling for mercy and forgiveness from a Father who has heretofore displayed no inclination to either quality.

The Son changes the terms of conflict in Heaven from force to persuasion. Milton's own attitude toward force is clear: it is to be used as a last resort, only when absolutely unavoidable, and always in the defense of liberty. Milton, in his desperation to avoid a return of kingship to England in the early months of 1660, does argue that force may be used to defend and retain freedom: "More just it is, doubtless, if it come to force, that a less number compel a greater to retain (which can be no wrong to them) their liberty, than that a greater number, for the pleasure of their baseness, compel a less most injuriously to be their fellow slaves" (*The Ready and Easy Way*, *CPW* 7:895). But this argument can easily be twisted, as Milton came to realize and dramatize in *Paradise Lost*. Though the narrator describes "necessity" as "the tyrant's plea" (4.393–94), it seems that liberty is the "plea" of both the tyrant and the libertine. "License they mean when they cry liberty," the insight Milton put into his Sonnet 12, is one he seems to have momentarily forgotten—or merely suppressed—in the last days of his struggle against the Restoration. It sums up, however, the abuses to which Milton's allowance of force in *The Ready and Easy Way* can lead.

Both Satan and Abdiel claim to be arguing on behalf of true liberty in Book 5 of *Paradise Lost*. Satan asserts his, and his faction's, right to reject the reign of the Son, to "cast off this Yoke" (5.786) by taking up arms. Abdiel asserts that true liberty is to be found in the dictates of the Father, "who made / Thee what thou art, and form'd the Pow'rs of Heav'n / Such as he pleased" (5.824–26). Abdiel, like Satan, backs up his claim to know, and defend, true liberty with threats of force. The Father will "uncreate thee" (5.895), rages Abdiel as he leaves. Each angel can claim to be that "less number [who can] compel a greater" to which Milton refers in *The Ready and Easy Way*. Each is right, from a certain point of view, and each is wrong, from a different point of view. Abdiel, as has been pointed out by such critics as Stella Revard, is a solitary figure arguing against what appears to be the will and animus of the majority present.[41] However, once Abdiel makes his way back to "the Mount of God" (6.5), he is among the two-thirds majority of Heaven. The war in Heaven takes place between a "less number" and "a greater," but it is *Satan's* force that is the "less number [who is trying to] compel a greater," while it is the side on which Abdiel fights that is the majority. Who is right? Satan certainly claims to be defending liberty: in fact his entire program in Book 5 is one of defending the liberty of Heaven's "Thrones, Dominations, Princedoms, Virtues, Powers" (5.772) against what he sees as a usurpation of power. Satan's followers see things through a similar lens: Nisroch refers to Satan as "Deliverer from new Lords, leader to free / Enjoyment of our right as Gods" (6.451–52). But Abdiel also claims to be defending liberty—the liberty of the Father to elevate whom he will, when he will, to what position he will. If Milton's 1660 prescription for the use of force by a minority to compel a majority to retain freedom is taken to extremes, the result is a chaos in which tyrants and those who resist them become indistinguishable. The Son comes to this insight only after using force himself, realizing that Satan is right: he "who overcomes / By force, hath overcome but half his foe" (1.648–49).

Milton himself, though in desperate times he suggested the possibility of force in the case of political liberty, had long since rejected the use of force in matters of religion and conscience. He refers, in the mid-1640s, to the religious authorities who held sway under the Long Parliament as those who "force our Consciences that Christ set free,"[42] and held them up to a scathing comparison to the recently overthrown bishops: *New Presbyter is but Old Priest writ Large*.[43] In 1659, Milton writes *A Treatise of Civil Power*, with the thesis that no earthly power has the right or the lawful power to force matters of religion and conscience: "force" is the first mentioned factor that has "bin ever found working much mischief to the church of God, and the advancement of truth" (*CPW* 7:241). Not only can "church-governors [not] use force in religion," but "civil magistrates [have no] autoritie to use force" in matters of religion either (*CPW* 7:245–46). In his 1673 tract *Of True Religion*, Milton—though he specifically excludes Catholics—argues that no Christian should force another's conscience: "no true Protestant can persecute, or not tolerate his fellow Protestant, though dissenting from him in som opinions, but he must flatly deny and Renounce . . . his own main Principles, whereon true Religion is founded" (*CPW* 8:420–21). However, despite his 1660 flirtation with force as a way to defend and retain liberty against the onrushing return of the Stuart dynasty, Milton had also long resisted the idea that force made for good civil government. In *The Reason of Church Government* (1641), he cites Plato in writing that "persuasion" in civil society "is a more winning, and more manlike way to keepe men in obedience than fear" (*CPW* 1:746). Nearly thirty years later, the older Milton puts these sentiments into the mouth of the Son, who argues that it is both humane and heavenly to "Make persuasion do the work of fear" (*Paradise Regained* 1.223).

The Son encountered by readers in *Paradise Lost* has not quite reached the point in his Miltonic progression that he will reach in *Paradise Regained*. He does, however, grow weary of the use of force, and take up the persuasive arms of his creator, the words, phrases, and arguments of Milton himself. In Book 3, the Son engages the Father on the Father's own terms, much like Satan in Books 5 and 6. The difference, however, is that the Son plays on the Father's sense of grandeur, importance, and even vanity, while Satan challenges the Father's strength. Where the Son once relied upon military power, now he uses subtlety, and he has rich material with which to work.

The Father, in the speech he delivers announcing the redemption of as-yet unfallen humanity, refers to himself or his possessions six times before he mentions humanity even once:

> O Son, in whom *my* Soul hath chief delight,
> Son of *my* bosom, Son who art alone
> *My* word, *my* wisdom, and effectual might,
> All hast thou spoken as *my* thoughts are, all
> As *my* Eternal purpose hath decreed:
> Man shall not quite be lost, but sav'd who will
> (3.168–73, emphasis added)

The Father here is certainly no less syntactically self-obsessed than Satan is at any point in the poem. Even when he is menacingly fuming over being discovered by two angels in Eden who fail to recognize him in his fallen state, Satan does not manage to work six references to himself into a mere five lines of poetry (he manages three references in seven lines):

> Know ye not then said Satan, fill'd with scorn,
> Know ye not *mee*? Ye knew *me* once no mate
> For you, there siting where ye durst not soar;
> Not to know *mee* argues yourselves unknown,
> The lowest of your throng; or if ye know,
> Why ask ye, and superfluous begin
> Your message, like to end as much in vain?
> (4.827–33, emphasis added)[44]

The Son, knowing with whom he is dealing, refers to the Father nine times in a speech asking for mercy for humanity (3.144–66). *Thy* word, *thy* sovran sentence, *thy* praises, are just some of the constructions used by the Son as he works hard to convince the Father that what he is suggesting—that Man should not "finally be lost" (3.150)—is actually the Father's own idea. It works: the Father claims that the Son's speech had been expressing "my Eternal purpose" (3.172). The Father, as a result of the Son's arguments, announces that Man shall be saved, and none but those who "neglect and scorn" (3.199) his "day of grace" (3.198) shall be excluded from mercy. But just as soon as he says this, the Father changes his tone, reverting back to the destructive anger out of which the Son had just cajoled him:

> But yet all is not done; Man disobeying,
> Disloyal breaks his fealty, and sins
> Against the high Supremacy of Heav'n,
> Affecting God-head, and so losing all,
> To expiate his Treason hath naught left,
> But to destruction sacred and devote,
> He with his whole posterity must die,
> Die hee or Justice must; unless for his
> Some other able, and as willing, pay
> The rigid satisfaction, death for death.
>
> (3.203–12)

Here it becomes obvious to the Son that persuasion will not be enough: the Father demands death and destruction as his "rigid satisfaction." Empson's speculative characterization of this scene as a representation of Milton's thoughts is unusually apt, *if* its application is limited to the Father of *Paradise Lost*: "What Milton is thinking has to be: 'God . . . could only have been satisfied by torturing somebody else to death.' "[45] The very language in which the Father expresses himself in this speech is filled with allusions to death, destruction, and even genocide. In referring to "destruction sacred and devote," the Father echoes the language of the genocidal slaughters foretold to Moses in the desert, conducted in the land of Canaan by Joshua and his armies, and finished against the Amalekites by Saul and his forces. To be a thing "accursed . . . to the Lord," as Jericho is to Yahweh at Josh. 6:17, is to be to "destruction sacred and devote"; likewise, to be a nation that God promises to "utterly put out the remembrance of" (Exod. 17:14), and to be a people about whom God gives orders to "utterly destroy all that they have; and spare them not, but slay both man and woman, infant and suckling, ox and sheep, camel and ass" (1 Sam. 15:3) is to be to "destruction sacred and devote." The Father is not merely working out a "determinedly non-affective" speech applying a "logical method . . . to a universe of things"[46] here. The Father means business, deadly and destructive business, and his speech is all too full of affect, anger, and genocidal determination to be regarded as having "tonal qualities" that are "merely accidental."[47]

The Son recognizes the mood and import of the Father's speech immediately. Rather than continuing to plead for mercy on behalf of mankind, the Son offers himself as the "rigid satisfaction," volunteering to take the Father's bloodlust upon himself in order to give humanity a second chance *before it has even made its first fatal mistake*.

> Behold mee then, mee for him, life for life
> I offer, on mee let thine anger fall;
> Account mee man; I for his sake will leave
> Thy bosom, and this glory next to thee
> Freely put off, and for him lastly die
> Well pleas'd . . .
>
> (3.236–41)

By offering to die, and to freely put off "glory," the Son has made the leap beyond the concepts and categories of Heaven's monarchical court, and has entered a cognitive and moral realm hitherto unseen in Milton's Heaven: the truly Christian realm in which to be great is to serve others. Service, however, is not here constructed as *fealty*, but as love, interrelation, even interdependence, and as actions that bring the best of oneself and others to the forefront. Though it is the Son who will undergo death, it is through the Father's power that the Son will be raised back to life: "Thou wilt not leave me in the loathsome grave / His prey, nor suffer my unspotted Soul / For ever with corruption there to dwell" (3.247–49). The Son sacrifices himself, not out of fealty to the Father, but out of a complex mixture of love for mankind and love for the Father who made them. The Son's sacrifice, in a sense, forces the best parts of the Father's nature to come to the fore. Adam and Eve have not yet fallen, and already the Father is raging against them the way Yahweh raged against the nascent Israelite nation for whom Moses had to intercede again and again. Hapless humanity cannot—and should not—be held fully responsible for what is about to happen to them; despite the Father's foreknowledge, or the narrator's claim thereof, it is the act of a tyrant to punish subjects for infractions they have not yet committed. In sacrificing himself to save mankind, the Son saves the Father as well, if only just barely, from being what Satan accused him of being—a tyrant who would rather destroy his own creations than see them deviate in the smallest way from "true allegiance, constant Faith or Love" (3.104).

At the same time that he saves or acquits the Father, however, the Son, through his willingness to die, delivers the harshest and most devastating critique of the Father that has yet been made. Satan's complaints about the Father being a tyrant pale in comparison to the Son's implicit accusation that the Father is bloodthirsty. The Father, it seems, absolutely *must* have death. Someone must die. Forgiveness—for infractions not yet committed—is simply out of the question until and unless someone who is now living stops living. The Father has no more dark and wicked moment than this one; he is, like an idol before whom worshippers "burn their sons with fire . . . unto Baal" (Jer. 19:5), a savage god of death and devastation. Satan's malice toward mankind is mild, almost timid, compared to the volcanic quality of the Father's murderous rage. This is what divine evil looks like up close. Far from being a purveyor of strict divine justice, such a god would be, for Milton, "in himself, the cause and author of sin," and those who conceive of such a god are "of all blasphemers the most utterly damned" (*De Doctrina Christiana, CPW* 6:166).

In agreeing to sacrifice himself on behalf of mankind, the Son actually takes a remarkable risk, one that no other resident of Heaven is willing to take: "all the Heav'nly Choir stood mute, / And silence was in Heav'n: on man's behalf / Patron or Intercessor none appear'd, / Much less that durst upon his own head draw / The deadly forfeiture, and ransom set" (3.217–21). The death faced by the Son in this situation is neither a metaphor nor a technical nicety, but a real and present annihilation. When the Son refers to "All that of me can die" (3.246), he doesn't know what part that is, or whether there is any part of him that is exempt from death. Certainly, the remaining angels in Heaven do not care to find out what part of them can die, nor do they seem to differ in any significant way from Belial, who asks, when faced with the prospect of annihilation, "who would lose, / Though full of pain, this intellectual being, / Those thoughts that wander through eternity, / To perish rather, swallow'd up and lost / In the wide womb of uncreated night, / devoid of sense and motion?" (2.145–51). No one is willing to pay the Father's price because no one wishes to "perish" and be "swallow'd up and lost." Even more so, no one wishes to take the risk of trusting the Father to bring him back to life once that life has been rendered forfeit for mankind's sake. Nothing about the Father's previous actions in the war in Heaven, and nothing about the Father's speeches here in Book 3 has created in the "Heav'nly Choir" that kind of trust.

Despite the fact that "while God spake, ambrosial fragrance fill'd / All Heav'n, and in the blessed Spirits elect / Sense of new joy ineffable difuss'd" (3.135–37), the overwhelming sense of relief that the narrator describes as "new joy ineffable"—an all-too-momentary sense of relief based on the hope that the Father is not quite as violent, intractable, and full of rage as he has only recently given every appearance of being—seems to have quite disappeared by the time the Father has gotten around to demanding a death if mankind is not utterly to be destroyed. No one volunteers because no one can *raise himself* from death, and, so it appears, no one trusts the Father enough to do so either. The Son's willingness to die forces the Father's hand: "Thou wilt not leave me in the loathsome grave" (3.247), he says, suggesting that the Father might very well so leave any other volunteer. The Son thus uses his close relationship to the Father, and his dependence on the Father's power, to force the Father to put into action the mercy of which the Father has previously only spoken. It is as if the Son is saying, with all Heaven as his witness, "Father, if it is true that your 'Mercy first and last shall brightest shine' [3.134], then here is the opportunity to put that Mercy to work. I will die for mankind, and you will raise me from death, because once dead, I cannot raise myself." In *De Doctrina Christiana*, Milton stresses the point of the Son's need to rely upon the Father, writing that the Son "felt that not even his divine nature was strong enough for him to endure the pangs of death" (*CPW* 6:270).

Though the Son expresses his willingness to die, Milton refuses to follow the Luthero-Calvinist position on the Father and Son and the necessity of death for satisfaction of justice. Milton simply never writes the Son's sacrifice in either *Paradise Lost* or *Paradise Regained*. In fact, paradise is regained without death, without sacrifice, merely through refusing the temptations of Satan. Calvin, who would have rejected Milton's soteriology as pernicious and heretical nonsense, argued that Christ "purged with his blood those evils which had rendered sinners hateful to God; that by this expiation he made satisfaction and sacrifice duly to God the Father."[48] Calvin goes on to insist that it was not enough for Christ to suffer just any kind of death: "to make satisfaction for our redemption a form of death had to be chosen in which he might free us both by transferring our condemnation to himself and by taking our guilt upon himself."[49] Milton, however, skips over the relationship of death and redemption, having the Son triumph over the accuser (Satan) rather than die before the accuser (the mob before whom Pilate presented Jesus).

Though the Son expresses willingness to die, he does not die. The Son lives, and mankind is redeemed without a drop of blood being spilled.

It is after the Son expresses his willingness to die that the Father seems to wake up from his dreams of death and destruction. Yes, mankind will suffer mortality and death, but the Son's willingness to die, to suffer the "anger" of the Father (3.237), and the "rage" of Death (3.241) will ultimately redeem mankind, and so outdo "Hellish hate" with "Heav'nly love" (3.298). Hate and Love, however, are not so simple an opposition as an unwary reader might first suspect. "Hellish hate" might seem, at first, to be *Satan's* hate, while "Heav'nly love" might seem to be the love of the Son *and* the Father. But Satan is actually relatively peripheral to the drama that has just played out between the Father and the Son in Heaven; furthermore, it is the Father whose "hate" for mankind is so strongly expressed that he simply must have a death in order to appease him: "Die hee or Justice must" (3.210). Because the Father creates Hell,[50] and because the forces of Hell do the Father's bidding,[51] in the final analysis, "Hellish hate" is the *Father's hate.* It is because of the Father's "anger" and the corresponding "rage" of a "Death" that is a servant to the Father's will, that the drama of satisfaction, sacrifice, death, and resurrection must be played out at all. The Father holds it in his power to say *enough*. But despite the fact that he appears to be leaning toward a policy of no-strings-attached mercy in lines 167–202, he abruptly pulls back, and reasserts his anger, his "Justice," and his demand for death. With no other way to save mankind from the Father, and the Father from himself, the Son volunteers to be the victim and object of the Father's ire.

As the Son makes his heroic offer, he returns once more to the language of war, battle, and conquest. In the current context, however, the Son is fighting the common enemy of all, not *Satan*, but *Death*—specifically, Death as it does the bidding of the Father. Despite the fact that Book 2 tells the story of Death being the son of Satan, it is the Father who takes ultimate credit for having "provided Death" (11.61), and Death does the bidding of the Father in the same way that Satan does the bidding of the Father. Each serves so "That with reiterated crimes he might / Heap upon himself damnation" (1.214–15), but each is merely doing the Father's bidding. In fighting against Death, the Son is actually fighting against the Father's own anger. When the Son says that he shall "rise Victorious, and subdue / My vanquisher, spoil'd of his vaunted spoil" (3.250–51), it is ultimately the Father over whom he wins his victory. It is the Father who creates Death, both in Hell—"A Universe of death, which God by curse / Created evil, for evil only good" (1.622–23)—and through Satan's dalliance with Sin as described in Book 2 (746–803). The bizarre portrait painted in this speech by the Son shows him using the Father's power to overcome the effects of the Father's wrath:

> Thou at the sight
> Pleas'd, out of Heaven shall look down and smile,
> While by thee raised I ruin all my Foes,
> Death last, and with his Carcass glut the Grave:
> Then with the multitude of my redeemed
> Shall enter Heav'n long absent, and return,
> Father, to see thy face, wherein no cloud
> Of anger shall remain, but peace assur'd
> And reconcilement; wrath shall be no more.
>
> (3.256–64)

Immediately, the Father seems to soften, as if once he is assured of his price, his anger abates, his rage passes. He gives the Son "all Power" (3.317) at this point, and indicates that once the Son gives up that power, no one will ever need to wield it again: "Then thou thy regal Sceptre shalt lay by, / For regal Sceptre then no more shall need, / God shall be All in All" (3.339–41). Empson took this as the Father's finest moment in the entire poem, a sudden, if belated, realization that his position as "Heav'n's King" was untenable and unsustainable except through military force, and violent application of the "regal Sceptre."

Whether or not the Father is portrayed as realizing the full import of his words, based as they are on Milton's adaptation of 1 Cor. 15:28, Milton himself certainly did. The Son takes the "regal Sceptre" from the Father, but he does not return it to the Father, now or ever. Where Paul is at pains to emphasize that the Son will resubmit himself to the Father, Milton is at pains to elide any such reference to a resubmission to the Father by the Son. A critical turning point has been reached in this relatively early episode of *Paradise Lost*. Mankind is already saved—despite having not yet fallen—and the

Father is no longer he who "Sole reigning holds the Tyranny of Heav'n" (1.124). The Son has done, through reason, patience, long-suffering, and the willingness to suffer death at the Father's own hand, what Satan and all his "puissant legions" (1.632) were unable to do—get the Father to hand over power. What the Son will do with that power is only hinted at in *Paradise Lost*; it remains for *Paradise Regained* to provide the Son a stage from which to redefine power, government, and the proper relation of mankind both to himself and to the divine.

5
"Tempt not the Lord thy God": The End of Kingship and the Awareness of Divine Similitude in *Paradise Regained*

> Yet he who reigns within himself, and rules
> Passions, Desires, and Fears, is more a King;
> Which every wise and virtuous man attains.
> —John Milton, *Paradise Regained*

Milton Eikonoklastes

For the mystics of East and West, from the sages of the Upanishads and Lao Tzu to Meister Eckhart and the Martin Luther who discovered the nature of the divine in a water closet, God is not to be found in the external rites and rituals of any established church, sect, or creed. At best, such rites and rituals serve merely as signposts or guides along the way, pointing to that which cannot be fully expressed or realized in external terms. In this way, the various mysticisms which have appeared across times and cultures (Hindu, Buddhist, Taoist, Gnostic, Kabbalist, Alchemist, and Christian—to name only a few) are all forms of iconoclasm, attempts either to break images of the divine that serve merely to distance worshippers of such images from the divine itself, or to proliferate divine representations to the point that their constructed and metaphorical nature becomes clear. Milton is an iconoclast in both senses. In his poetic work, he is at pains to create, reject, and re-create images of the divine—creating the Father as a military monarch, and the Son as a youthful angelic warrior who matures into a peaceful and private man who shows the way to finding an inward oracle, an inner divinity. Milton does this in order to emphasize that such images are merely images, generated by and for human beings. In the final analysis, God is not to be contained within any single one of these images; rather, God is only to be found by searching within, by heeding the promptings of "the Spirit, which is *internal, and the individual possession of every man*" (*De Doctrina Christiana, CPW* 6:587, emphasis added). Although the infamous English republican, regicide, pamphleteer, and poet does not, after the manner of the Johanine Christ, declare that he and God are one, or, like Theresa of Avila, base a union with divinity on an erotic sense of the divine within, he does, throughout his work, emphasize and prioritize an internal relation to the divine. Beyond images of God, beyond human categories of worship, beyond human ideas of church and state, internal relation to the divine is, for Milton, precisely what the English had not fully developed, despite their controversies about such lesser issues as bishops and presbyters, surplices and stained glass windows.

When Milton suggests, in *Of Education*, that it is possible to "repair the ruins of our first parents" (*CPW* 2:366–67) through a vigorous program of pedagogical self-improvement remarkably like his own, he writes in the language of internal relation to the divine. In so doing, Milton is firmly within a Reformation tradition of imagining salvation as a process of deification, or, less radically, of discovering God within rather than without. Such radical continental Protestants as Caspar Schwenckfeld, the Silesian nobleman, Teutonic knight, and aristocratic evangelist for reform, regarded God within as the true God: "I cannot be one in faith with either the Pope or Luther, because they condemn me and my faith, that is, they hate *my Christ in me*."[1] Schwenckfeld went on to suggest that the purpose of the incarnation was to make it "possible for man to become what God is,"[2] that is, divine. David Joris, a Dutch Protestant of the mid-sixteenth century, argued that the purpose of religion was "to achieve unity with God, a unity which comes only by the inner re-enacting of the incarnation and Passion of Christ."[3] Quintin of Hainaut, a sixteenth century Flemish spiritualist, held that "every Christian becomes, in a pantheistic or mystical sense, a Christ."[4]

English divines in Milton's day made arguments that, though they stop short of asserting that humans will become divine, assert that the divine is to be found by searching within. The Quaker minister Alexander Parker argues that "Christ Jesus is the Truth, and he is the Light, and . . . the Light is within . . . all they who deny to be guided by the light within denies God, Christ, and the Spirit . . . for God is light, Christ is light, and the Spirit is light."[5] The equation is clear: the light is to be discovered within, and God is light, therefore God is to be discovered within. Another famous Quaker, George Fox, writes his 1654 pamphlet "To all that would know the way to the kingdome," as "A Direction to turn your minds within, where the voice of the true God is to be heard, whom you ignorantly worship as afarre off."[6] Fox goes on to maintain that "as the eternal light which Christ has enlightened you withal is loved, minded, and taken heed unto, this earthly part is wrought out."[7] When the earthly part is "wrought out," what is left is the divine light, the inner light provided by God to all those who truly seek. Lydia Fairman specifically identifies the inner light with an inner Christ when she writes of "Christ the light in every one of you."[8]

David Loewenstein has argued that "the early Quakers . . . represented the largest and most dynamic movement of social, political and religious protest"[9] in the mid-seventeenth century, and convincingly demonstrates that *Paradise Regained* and "its striking revision of external forms of politics and kingship; its emphasis on the mighty power of a spiritual kingdom within; and its depiction of Jesus as a pious and inward saint"[10] partakes of many of the same ideas taken up by the Quakers. "The emphasis in early Quaker writings on the interiorization of power and kingship"[11] is one shared by *Paradise Regained*, as "this poem does not simply repudiate worldly kingship; it also makes kingship and power inward . . . redefining them in terms of a spiritual kingdom of the mind."[12] Loewenstein further writes of the "unusual emphasis on interiority in *Paradise Regained* . . . in the manner of religious radicals like the Quakers."[13]

Some such radicals in England went even further than an emphasis on interiority, going so far as to identify themselves with Christ. James Nayler entered Bristol riding upon a donkey as palm branches were strewn before him on the ground. Christopher Hill suggests that in 1656, when he made his Bristol ride, Nayler had "believed it was possible for a man to achieve Christ's perfection and perform

Christ's works."[14] Hill describes the struggles that "all protestant churches" had with the "appeal . . . to the inner voice [conflicting] with the necessity of organization," and suggests that one of the major problems faced by George Fox as he consolidated the Quaker movement in England was that "[t]he absolute individualism of the appeal to Christ within every man had to be curbed."[15] When placed in this larger theological and historical context, Milton's suggestion that true divinity is to be found by listening to an inward oracle (*Paradise Regained* 1.403), by paying attention to the promptings of the inner man (2.477), rather than by seeking for God externally, seems almost tame.

Though hardly as extreme in its presentation as was the 1656 ride of James Nayler,[16] *Paradise Regained* is still quite radical. Milton, by the time he writes *Paradise Regained*, is concerned to point the way to the reality of God behind human images of God, or as Meister Eckhart puts it, "to leave god for God." Christopher Hill describes Milton's "fluid conception of Christ's kingdom" as "a state of mind,"[17] emphasizing the internal nature of Milton's construction of the divine. John Shawcross argues (quoting M. V. Rama Sarma)[18] that *Paradise Regained* depicts "a human's ideal passage through life to salvation: any human being like the Son must first gain 'self-knowledge or awareness of divine similitude.'"[19] I believe that the meaning of the phrase "divine similitude" has far-reaching implications. *Paradise Regained* is ultimately about awareness of divine similitude understood as a connection to the divine, and a participation in the divine.[20] Each man, woman, and child can be divine—in fact, is divine.[21] What prevents us from realizing this divinity is the very human imagination that constructs elaborate church hierarchies designed to separate worshipper and worshipped, that organizes civil society along top-down hierarchical lines, and that imprisons the idea of God within the categories of church and state. To imagine God as a king is to bind the infinite, to circumscribe the eternal, to subject the sacred to the profane. To imagine God at all is to confine the divine within the boundaries of thought. Though Milton spent much of his life and poetic career *creating* such images of God, he does so not in order to confine, but to liberate. The divine is not to be contained in any image, and Milton's poetic characters are merely pointers to the divine. God is not an Unmoved Mover, or an irascibly Yahwistic personality, or a Christ-like figure of meekness and strength. God, as an expression of ultimate value and reality, cannot be identified with any manifestation, confined within any formulation, or restricted to any object, practice, or ritual. In *Paradise Regained*, the Son refuses temptations of food, wealth, kingship, knowledge, and finally a temptation to identify divinity with external displays of power because he realizes that the divine does not reside in these things or in any of the other possible material or abstract temptations Satan might offer. For the Son, as for Milton, true divinity, true God, is only to be found within, through obedience to an inner voice, an inward oracle.[22]

According to Milton, humanity can learn to hear this inner voice. Learning will help restore humanity to "the highest perfection," and set humanity on the road to "regaining to know God aright" (*CPW* 2:367). Knowing God means loving him, imitating him, and finally being like him. Milton goes on to acknowledge, however, that such loving, imitating, and likening cannot be achieved without the aid of what he refers to as "sensible things" (*CPW* 2:368), or the world of everyday forms. It is by "orderly conning over the visible and inferior creature" (*CPW* 2:369) that one can come to "the knowledge of God and things invisible" (*CPW* 2:368–69). It is crucial, however, not to mistake such things visible for anything other than metaphors—God is not an image, nor is God a concept or idea. God is only pointed to by images and ideas. To concretize the metaphor, to mistake the reference for the referent, is to fall into what Milton calls an "ignorantly zealous divinity" (*CPW* 2:375). To discover the divine within, to really and truly be guided by the "Spirit, which is internal, and the individual possession of each man" (*CPW* 6:587), is to have moved beyond the need for divine images—even, and perhaps especially, those contained in scripture.

This is not to say, however, that Milton has no use for divine images—it is merely to argue that Milton grew to regard such images as placeholders, as pedagogical aids, as a kind of Pauline spiritual milk for the immature in reason and faith. When Milton argues in *De Doctrina Christiana* that "God attributes to himself again and again a human shape and form" (*CPW* 6:136), and berates those who would "contradict God" (*CPW* 6:136) on this point, he does so in the context of an acknowledgment of limited human understanding. For Milton, God "transcends everything, including definition" (*CPW* 6:137), and "God is inaudible just as he is invisible" (*CPW* 6:239). So it is not that Milton is arguing that "God, in all his parts and members, is of human form" (*CPW* 6:136), but that "so far as it concerns us to know, he has that form which he attributes to himself in Holy Writ" (*CPW* 6:133). Milton specifically admits that "God is always described or outlined not as he really is but in such a way as will make him conceivable to us" (*CPW* 6:133). Milton's is an argument, not against peering behind the image of God, but against forming anthropomorphic images of the divine that do not already have scriptural warrant as spiritual milk for those who need it. The image of God as a Stuart-era monarch is just such an unwarranted image, one that does not conform to the idea of God "he wishes us to possess" (*CPW* 6:136).

Paradise Lost and *Paradise Regained* can finally be seen as arguments for, and illustrations of, what it means to move beyond the "visible and inferior creature" and reject as inessential such otherwise potentially desirable externals as learning, power, and wealth. In *Paradise Regained*, the Son demonstrates what it is to move beyond images, surfaces, and appearances by refusing to assign ultimate value to things in and of themselves. Learning, for example, though it can serve to bring humanity closer to God, is not the greatest value. Treating learning as the greatest value rather than a lesser value is just like treating an image of God as if it were God. Just as learning—in its proper usage—merely points the way to the divine, so also do divine images merely point toward the divine. Rejecting—or refusing to acknowledge—such distinctions is precisely the move that Satan makes in *Paradise Regained*. Satan's temptations of the Son are all organized around a simple principle: concretize the metaphor, and regard external things that are quite proper as lesser values as if they were the greatest value.[23] In effect, what Satan offers are images, and the Son is Milton's ultimate iconoclast.

As *Paradise Lost* ends, Adam has discovered a "paradise within . . . happier far" (12.587) than the external paradise he has had to leave. Given as clear a signal as this about the relative merits of external and internal locations for paradise, Milton's readers should not be surprised by the vigor of the Son's contempt for Satan's temptations in *Paradise Regained*. What the Son is rejecting is not primarily food or wealth, kingship or knowledge, but the notion that the external, the visible, the tangible is the measure of reality. Just as Adam's "paradise within" is happier than Eden, so the Son's "inner man" is nobler than a King who wears a crown, on earth or in heaven. The Son begins his work in *Paradise Regained* wandering in the desert, away from the world of shows and trappings, "with holiest meditations fed" (2.110). Rejecting externality altogether, the Son "[i]nto himself descended" (2.111). As the Son begins his "great work" (2.112), and his "mission high" (2.114), he seeks divine guidance from the "inward oracle" (1.403), the "spirit of truth" (1.402) that dwells within.

In his discussion of *Paradise Lost*, William Empson questions the notion of hierarchies and external rule in heaven: "Why do angels have to be organized into an elaborate hierarchy at all?"[24] It is precisely such hierarchies that are to be done away with upon the final ascension of the Son to the divine throne. Although in *Paradise Lost* the Father proclaims that all shall bow down to the Son and "Under his great Vice-gerent Reign abide / United as one individual Soul" (5.609–10), in *Paradise Regained*, the Son repeatedly refuses and expresses contempt for the idea of kingship. As early as the age of twelve, the Son felt that his "Spirit aspir'd to victorious deeds" and "heroic acts" to "subdue and quell o'er all the earth / Brute violence and proud Tyrannic pow'r" (1.215–20). He "held it . . . more heavenly," however, even as a child, to "make persuasion do the work of fear" (1.221, 223).

The idea of kingship has been being impressed upon the Son since he was a human child; his mother tells him "Thy Father is th' Eternal King," and further tells him that a "messenger from God" foretold that "Thou shouldst be great and sit on David's throne" (1.238–40). After poring over "(t)he Law and Prophets, searching what was writ" and finding that he was the one "of whom they spake," the Son accepts that he is promised a kingdom, but the question then becomes *what kind of kingdom he is promised.* Is the Son to assume a military throne in heaven? Or is the Son's "kingdom" to be imagined in different terms? The Son's kingdom is, as Donald Swanson and John Mulryan have argued, "a spiritual kingdom that is neither accompanied by eschatological signs nor located in space. . . . The inner or spiritual nature of the kingdom might easily have been inferred from the parable of the seed growing secretly or from Luke 17: 21b: 'for behold, the kingdom of God is within you.'"[25] This is the same argument that is made by such radical reformers as Schwenckfeld, Joris, Quentin of Hainaut, Parker, Fox, and Fairman. The kingdom is to be found within; the kingdom is of the inner man. This inner nature of the Son's kingdom can be seen in his words at the end of Book 2:

> to guide Nations in the way of truth
> By saving Doctrine, and from error lead
> To know, and knowing worship God aright,
> Is yet more Kingly; this attracts the Soul
> Governs the inner man, the nobler part;
> That other o'er the body only reigns,
> And oft by force, which to a generous mind
> So reigning can be no sincere delight.
> Besides, to give a Kingdom hath been thought
> Greater and nobler done, and to lay down
> Far more magnanimous than to assume.
>
> (473–83)

Nations are guided, not by military force or by monarchical authority, but by "saving Doctrine," by the power of the "inward oracle" (1.463) to guide each individual to truth. The end of such guidance is knowing and worshipping God aright, and this appeals primarily to the inner man. Knowing and worshipping God, then, is primarily an affair of the inner man, having little or nothing to do with the shows and trappings of a secular and clerical government that "o'er the body only reigns / And oft by force." For the Son, just as it is far more magnanimous to give a kingdom (to give up a kingdom) rather than to assume one, so it is also "oftest better" (2.486) to relinquish a scepter than to gain one. The Son receives from the Father all of the trappings of regal power, all of the distinctions and prerogatives of absolute rule, *only to lay them down.*

The Son's path in *Paradise Regained* is at once that of an ascetic, an exemplar (in the sense of one who shows the way), and an ordinary man with an extraordinary will to discover the divine will. The Son is emphatically a man[26]—that is the whole point for Milton, who wrote that education could, if pursued with alacrity and seriousness of purpose "repair the ruins of our first parents."[27] If a man can resist the blandishments of Satan, and if a man can regain "lost Paradise" (4.608), then each man can potentially secure his own redemption—once again, Milton confidently strides where all but the "heretical" theologian Pelagius had feared to tread.

Two things must be noted: first, Milton does not write the Son as a savior; the Son does not sacrifice himself on a cross anywhere in *Paradise Regained*. Paradise is regained without the blood the Father had demanded in *Paradise Lost*. Second, nowhere in all of *Paradise Regained* is the Son referred to as Christ. Five times he is referred to as Jesus, an Anglicized transliteration of *Yeshua*, a common name for a first-century Hebrew man, but not once does the word Christ appear anywhere in the poem.[28] By deliberately eliding the title of Christ (a Greek translation of the Hebrew *Mashiach*—or *anointed* [king/priest]), Milton emphasizes the humanity of the Son in a manner that borders on Socinian.[29]

Paradise Regained is a final dismantling of divine kingship and rule. Anti-reign, -glory, and -power, *Paradise Regained* is Milton's ultimate rejection of the image of God as a king. *Paradise Regained* represents a culmination of the hints contained in the enigmatic phrase "God shall be All in All," spoken (in *Paradise Lost*) by the Father to the Son, and the hints by Raphael to Adam and Eve of their eventual "ascension" to the spiritual plane. After the temptations of *Paradise Regained*, authority and separateness are to be no more. Creator and Creation will be one.[30] Milton's ultimate point is that we were once quite close to being as God is; the great task of humanity is to do the hard work necessary to repair the ruins of Adam and Eve and complete the transformation from external to internal, from profane to sacred, from the merely human to the fully divine.

Obedience and Authority:
External and Internal

One of the most important questions for Milton, and one of the most crucial issues in both *Paradise Lost* and *Paradise Regained* is that of obedience. What does it mean to be obedient, and to what or whom is the Son obedient? For Milton, to be obedient, as the Son is obedient, is to listen to the promptings of the "inner man, the nobler part," to follow the guidance of the inner light that is the possession of each Christian on earth.[31] The Son and Satan have remarkably different views on what constitutes obedience; the Son rebukes Satan for claiming that he is obedient to God, as Satan says "what he bids I do" (1.377). The Son's retort reveals the true, internal nature of obedience: "Wilt thou impute to obedience what thy fear / Extorts[?]" (1.422–23). The Son, here as at 1.223 where he expresses his preference to "make persuasion do the work of fear," regards actions taken out of fear as unworthy and hypocritical, equivalent to the actions of Satan who once "fawn'd, and cring'd, and servilely ador'd / Heav'n's awful Monarch" (*Paradise Lost* 4.959–60). True obedience is not rendered out of fear, nor is it rendered by external shows of obsequious behavior; rather, true obedience is an internal orientation, a listening to the promptings of the "spirit of truth" (*Paradise Regained* 1.462) that dwells in "pious hearts, [as] an inward oracle" (1.463). The Son emphasizes this point again when he tells Satan "do as thou find'st / Permission from above; thou canst not more" (1.495–96). *Satan* "canst not more," because Satan confuses obsequiousness with obedience; Satan's entire orientation is external, given to shows of power and submission. Because Satan does not have the "spirit of truth" as "an inward oracle," he is bound to hierarchical authority by his own lack of insight.

In the matter of obedience, and throughout *Paradise Regained*, the Son is not so much a savior as an exemplar—he "saves" by showing the way, by providing a roadmap for mankind to follow.[32] What the Son does, essentially, is to put aside all temporal concerns and imaginative categories—from food and wealth to kingship and knowledge to external displays of divine status—in order to focus on the true, internal nature of the divine.[33] The Son rejects everything that might be considered to make up a more or less normal human life. Satan's temptations begin with the relatively mundane and concrete, and move toward "higher" and more abstract pleasures. The Son rejects these things because they all tend to direct an individual's vision outward—to shows and trappings—and prevent the repair of the "ruins of our first parents" by preventing the necessary awareness of and focus upon the inner light, the inner man, the nobler part that is in some important way the truest connection to God that anyone can have. Directing vision outward is, in fact, the whole point of Belial's suggestion that Satan "Set women in [the Son's] eye" (*Paradise Regained* 2.153), because women can "Draw out with credulous desire" (2.166). Though Satan resists this suggestion as insufficient to try the virtue of the Son, Satan nevertheless shares Belial's insistence on defining everything in external terms—the very shows and trappings that the Son rejects—and he does so in part because he has lost or rejected the inner, nobler part of himself, a loss/rejection dramatized in his soliloquy in Book 4 of *Paradise Lost*. Satan offers, instead of women, "manlier objects" (2.225), objects that have "more show / Of worth, of honour, glory, and popular praise" (2.226–27).

Satan also assumes that the Son is on earth to engage in "High actions" (*Paradise Regained* 2.411) that must be achieved externally: "Great acts require great means of enterprise" (2.412), says Satan as he puzzles over what the Son is to do and how he is to do it. Satan assumes that the Son must be active and achieve external goals. However, the Son has from his childhood on earth been "Private, unactive, calm, contemplative" (2.81), and at the end of *Paradise Regained* the Son returns to "his mother's house private" (4.639). In between, what the Son does is literally *nothing*. He remains passive and resistant in the face of Satan's temptations. At most, what the Son can be seen as *doing* is negating the externals of Satan and descending "[i]nto himself" (2.111) in order to listen to the inward oracle of truth. After the Son refuses food, wealth, power, and even knowledge—all couched, however, in Satan's terms, those of external glory[34]—Satan simply cannot understand what the Son "dost . . . in the world" (4.372).

Satan's definitions—here as so often—are those he has adopted from the Father. The Father, in both *Paradise Lost* and *Paradise Regained*, is a character remarkably free of any hint of interiority. The Father is entirely a what-you-see-is-what-you-get ruler, whose only moments of what might even charitably be described as thought or reflection are delivered as speeches before a dutifully rapt audience. The Father's speeches are performances, studied shows of majesty and power, of external command and demands for elaborate displays of deference and eternally delivered, endlessly repeated thanks. The Father is an object lesson in shows and trappings, a lesson that Satan has learned all too well.

Thus, Satan and the Son regard the temptations in radically different ways. Satan is merely trying to see how high the Son's price is, what choice portion of the shows and trappings of the world will suffice to tempt him to play a role in the grand pageant of pomp and power that—for Satan—is the universe. For the Son, the stakes are much higher than Satan imagines. Not only is he determined to resist Satan's blandishments and refuse to join in the external pageant of earth, but he is trying, above all, to resist the Father's blandishments in order to dismantle the external pageant of heaven, to lay down the regal scepter of a military and monarchical heaven, and finally to redefine heaven and earth in terms of the internal, the private, and the non-hierarchical. It is no accident that the Son returns, not to his Father's house and a heavenly, and therefore public and universal throne, but to "his mother's house private" at the end of *Paradise Regained*. The ending is much like that given to Adam and Eve in *Paradise Lost*—their way is "solitary," and they make their way in the world with Providence as their guide, not gods or angels or kings or magistrates, merely an inner sense of what it means to be related to the divine and to dwell in a paradise within rather than a paradise without.

There is a crucial opposition between disobedience in "the happy garden" (*Paradise Regained* 1.1) and the "firm obedience" (1.4) that "Eden raised in the wild wilderness" (1.7). The suggestion that Eden can be raised in a desert powerfully evokes the idea that it is the internal, not the external, that matters. The settings and circumstances of obedience and disobedience are not the point. In fact, the external paradise of Eden is manifestly inferior to the "paradise within thee, happier far" that Michael tells Adam of in *Paradise Lost* (12.587). With that admonition in mind, it seems that the "wild wilderness" of *Paradise Regained* is actually preferable to the "happy garden" because it provides a setting conducive to a focus on that paradise within.

The focus on the internal, on the development of obedience and Eden as symbols of a "paradise within," is furthered by the insistence in the poem's second stanza that the deeds of the Son are "Above heroic, though in secret done" (*Paradise Regained* 1.15). Defining secret, unrecorded actions as above heroic radically changes the terms of action outlined in *Paradise Lost*. David Loewenstein has made a similar point: "By choosing to dramatize deeds 'Above heroic' done in secret by a deeply introspective Jesus, Milton not only drastically revises the epic heroic ethos: he also signals his poem's relation to radical religious culture in the Interregnum and Restoration."[35] *Paradise Lost* is a symphony of "Sonorous metal blowing martial sounds" (1.540) and actions taken by heavenly and hellish forces are taken with great pomp and public circumstance—including the actions of the Father. *Paradise Regained*, however, begins and ends with an insistence on the "secret" (1.15) and "private" (4.639) nature of the

Son's actions. In highlighting an opposition between public and private, Milton is further amplifying his point about the relative importance of external and internal. Genuine actions and attitudes are those taken without concern for an audience; the Son's actions in *Paradise Regained* are not entirely without an audience—Heaven and Hell watch constantly—but they are not taken with military or monarchical glory in mind. Neither the Father nor Satan ever acts without such a concern for glory, for public approbation, for "glory and benediction" (*Paradise Regained* 3.127). Despite the fact that such glory and "endless gratitude" (*Paradise Lost* 4.52) may be due the Father under the terms of the current system, the insistent focus on externals like hierarchy and the concomitant payer and payee economy of "glory" and "gratitude," is a constant source of conflict in both *Paradise Lost* and *Paradise Regained*. Through the Son, Milton is redefining heroism, paradise, and glory in terms that specifically reject the hierarchical model of the Father's Heaven and the mirror image hierarchy of Satan's Hell.

Similarities between the Father and Satan that were first highlighted in *Paradise Lost* are reemphasized by the respective portrayals of the Father and Satan in *Paradise Regained*.[36] In his first speech, to the "ancient Powers of air and this wide world" (1.44), Satan shows himself to be obsessed with surfaces and appearances, while he misinterprets or misunderstands their import. The "Woman's Seed" (1.64) is "displaying / All virtue" (1.67–68), and "glimpses of his Father's glory shine" (1.93) in this man who must "sudden be opposed" (1.96), before "in the head of nations he appear / Their King, their leader, and supreme on earth" (1.98–99). Satan simply does not know for certain who this man is, and can only imagine the mission of this "Woman's Seed" in terms of the external and hierarchical categories in which he has lived, moved, and had his being, categories which are the Father's creation.

Like his all-too-apish son Satan, the Father also reveals, in his first speech, an obsession with externals, with appearances. The Father's tone is that of a braggart, "Vaunting aloud" much like Satan once did (*Paradise Lost* 1.126), as if to appear in control of a situation that he does not, and cannot control. The Father seems especially concerned that Gabriel and the other angels shall "by proof" (the "ocular proof" demanded by Othello) see that the Father was right all along, that this "Son of God" (*Paradise Regained* 1.136) born of the "virgin pure" (1.134) will "show him worthy of his birth divine / And high prediction" (1.141–42) by being exposed to Satan after the manner of Job. The image raised by the comparison to Job should disturb even readers raised on a pious interpretation of the story and its climactic passage at 42:6: "I have heard of thee by the hearing of the ear: but now mine eye seeth thee. Wherefore I abhor myself, and repent in dust and ashes." Is the Son to be put through the kind of familial, psychological, and physical torture that Job suffered merely so that the Father can prove a point? Yes. In fact, the terms of the Father's speech are shockingly reminiscent of Job.[37] The Father is trying to prove a point to Satan, the angels, and humankind in that order: "He [Satan] now shall know I can produce a man / Of female seed, far abler to resist / All his [Satan's] solicitations" (1.150–52). This is being done so that "all the angels and ethereal powers, / They now, and men hereafter may discern, / From what consummate virtue I have chose / This perfect man" (1.163–66).

The mention of "Salvation for the sons of men" (1.167) is almost an afterthought; what the Father harps upon continually is how he appears in this situation, how angels and men will regard him, how good he will look for having chosen the Son. His speech seems calculated to elicit the approval of his audience, which, in fact, it does: "all Heaven / Admiring stood a space, then into hymns / Burst forth" (1.168–70). One can imagine the self-satisfied smile that plays about the monarch's face while his courtiers engage in yet another of the seemingly endless rounds of flattery, admiration, and hymn-singing to the greatness of their king. Such a speech has nothing in common with "deeds / Above heroic, though in secret done." Such a speech is the equivalent of the trumpet blowing that "hypocrites do in the synagogues and in the streets, that they may have the glory of men" (Matt. 6:2). Just as Satan glories in "monarchal pride / Conscious of highest worth" (*Paradise Lost* 2.428–29), so also does the Father "smiling" (*Paradise Regained* 1.129) deliver a speech designed to highlight his own "monarchal pride." The Father and Satan each "have their reward" (Matt. 6:2), just as do the hypocrites in the synagogues and in the streets.

In stark contrast to the twin kings of pride and glory, the Son's "holy meditations" (1.195) pursue a course that moves steadily away from public glory and thoughts of self-aggrandizement and pride. The Son will blow no trumpets before him in the streets that he may have the glory of men or of angels. The Son's meditation explicitly moves from "public good" (1.204) that might be achieved through "knowledge" (1.213), to public good that might be achieved through "victorious deeds" (1.215) and "heroic acts" (1.216) that would subdue "proud tyrannic power" (1.219), to a rejection of each of these paths. Both knowledge (displayed in public disputations with the "teachers of our Law" [1.212]), and heroic acts (such as rescuing "Israel from the Roman yoke" [1.217]), are paths pursued in search of external reward, to have the glory of men and angels. What the Son is pursuing is more profound than glory, more important than "David's throne" (1.240), and more lasting than a "promised Kingdom" (1.265) or even "Redemption for mankind" (1.266). Mankind is far too limited an object for the Son's efforts; what the Son is trying to redeem is the entirety of a universe gone horribly wrong, a universe in which dominance and submission are the measures of obedience, where knee-crooking, hymn-singing, and "martial sounds" are the daily activities of Heaven and Hell, where kings reign over both Heaven and Earth after the fashion of Nimrod.

What the Son will do, now that he knows the time has come to no more "live obscure, / But openly begin" (1.287–88) depends on the meaning of the following phrase: "as best becomes / The authority which I derived from Heaven" (1.288–89). Conceiving of this authority as somehow military or monarchical is a mistake—the very mistake that Satan makes. For the Son, as for Milton, the authority derived from Heaven is an internal authority, the "double scripture," especially the "internal scripture of the Holy Spirit" that Milton describes in *De Doctrina Christiana* (*CPW* 6:587). He who has "the spirit, who guides truth" (6.583) has the authority derived from Heaven, "the mind of Christ" (6.583), an authority that no "visible church . . . let alone any magistrate, has the right" (6.584) to gainsay or oppose. The Son in *Paradise Regained* is a perfect illustration of what John Shawcross has called "Milton's essential belief," that "[w]orth does not lie in the external, in works for a public arena, in negation and prohibition, nor in a mere following of example, no matter how blest the example might be, if the inner being has not been enlightened."[38]

Divine Similitude

When the Son describes himself as God's "living Oracle" (1.460) sent to teach God's "final will" (1.461), his choice of words reinforces the idea that power is to be exercised one last time, as the Son takes up the regal scepter of divine kingship only to lay it down. The "final will" of God, can of course be taken to mean the primary or even highest will of the divine, but it also means just what it implies at the surface—finality of willing, a kind of last will and testament that represents the last time hierarchical structures will be used to impose the will of a superior (god, king, magistrate) upon inferiors (angels, mankind). Hierarchy has no place in a system in which "an inward oracle" (1.463) is to guide mankind and "dwell / In pious hearts" (1.462–63). When guided by an inward oracle—the "Spirit of Truth" (1.462)—no individual has further need of the kind of top-down hierarchical structures of governance that Milton describes in *Tenure of Kings and Magistrates*. Guided internally, all sentient beings—whether human or ethereal—in Milton's universe would be part of the "All in All" that is God after the Son lays down the regal scepter (*Paradise Lost* 3.339–41). Inward realization of divine similitude—the realization expressed in such disparate traditions as the Chandogya Upanishad's *tat tvam asi* (that thou art), the Muslim martyr Al Hallaj's cry *ana al-Haqq* (I am the Truth), the Christian mystic Meister Eckhart's claim that "there is something in the soul so closely akin to God that it is already one with him and need never be united with him,"[39] and Caspar Schwenckfeld's claim to be guided by "my Christ in me"[40]—this is Milton's great argument and his final recommendation to his "fit audience . . . though few." Stop seeking God in religious institutions and rituals, in forms of government, even in the anthropomorphic terms of Scripture, Milton is saying. Seek God by paying strict attention to the "inward oracle" that guides the "inner man, the nobler part" of each individual who will allow it to do so.

Finding the true God by searching within, and "repairing the ruins of our first parents" in the course of this search is the spiritual imperative behind the Son's rejection of all temptations in *Paradise Regained*. Everything Satan presents, from food and sex, to wealth and power, to knowledge and art is a call to look outward, to focus on forms, rituals, and external appearances. Even though such things as, for example, philosophy and literature are not wrong or sinful in themselves, Satan presents them as if they were in themselves the highest values to which mankind could aspire. In Satan's view, knowledge is for its own sake; philosophy is for its own sake; power is for its own sake. There is, or so Satan suggests, nothing behind or beyond appearances. Satan's temptations are always focused on such appearances, on what must, in the final analysis, be regarded as illusions.[41]

Thus, "awareness of divine similitude" is (or should be) the primary goal of all endeavors. To the extent that food leads an individual's thoughts away from such awareness, food is to be rejected. To the extent that learning—whether of Greek philosophy, literature, art, or even of the debates in the Temple—leads an individual's thoughts away from the awareness of divine similitude, learning is to be rejected. Such rejection, however, is not categorical but conditional.[42] Food, wealth, learning: these things are not evil in and of themselves. There is nothing inherently wrong with Greek drama or a table filled with "dishes piled, and meats of noblest sort" (*Paradise Regained* 2.341), nor is there anything inherently wrong with being found "Among the gravest Rabbis disputant / On points and questions befitting Moses' chair" (*Paradise Regained* 4.218–19). Such things simply are not the greatest value, and have, even for the wise, the dangerous potential to distract the mind away from the awareness of divine similitude. As the Son puts it, "he who receives / Light from above, from the fountain of light, / No other doctrine needs, though granted true" (*Paradise Regained* 4.288–90). Light from above is the awareness of divine similitude, an inner voice that says to anyone who can or will listen, "This is my son—or daughter—in whom I am well pleased." In this sense, everyone who cultivates and maintains the all-important awareness, who receives "Light from above," can say "I and the Father are one." Each human being is connected—though only those who willingly receive the "Light from above" are aware of this connection—to the divine, is part of the divine. Satan's effort, and the sole point of all of his temptations in *Paradise Regained*, is to distract attention away from the awareness of that connection. As John Shawcross has argued, "the Son rejects the necessity of an intervener"⁴³ for all those who receive "Light from above." Such an intervener is yet another Satanic layer of remove from the divine, no better than the kings, bishops, and presbyters who drew attention to themselves and away from God.

Even Satan's temptation of Eve in *Paradise Lost* is designed to draw attention away from an awareness of divine similitude. When Satan tells Eve that she and Adam "shall be as gods" (9.708), his words are at once a denial of divine similitude and an appeal to a narcissistic desire to usurp a divinity that Eve already possesses. Satan's goals—with Adam and Eve in *Paradise Lost*, and with the Son in *Paradise Regained*—are to tempt others into mistaking means for ends, representations for realities, and to encourage a sense of separateness from the divine, the very sense of unbridgeable distance from God that Satan himself feels when he declares "Evil be thou my Good" (*Paradise Lost* 4.110). Adam and Eve learn only too late to recognize and value the "paradise within" (12.587), and it remains for the Son in *Paradise Regained* to lead humanity down the path to divine similitude, a possibility once obliquely hinted at by the archangel Raphael when he promised Adam and Eve that "your bodies may at last turn all to spirit" (*Paradise Lost* 5.497). The Son, however, demonstrates that bodies need not turn into spirit, that *physical* transformation is not at all what is required. What is required is an inward realization that one is *already divine*, and this is precisely what Satan failed to realize—choosing to see divinity in terms of military and monarchical power—and what he tries to prevent others from seeing.

Tempt not the Lord thy God

The arguments over the perplexing end of *Paradise Regained* have tended to cluster around two contrasting positions. One argument suggests the Son is having something of an identity crisis in the poem; he does not know, until the final temptation, who he is, and even after coming to the realization of his identity he is merely declaring his firm faith in God. A contrasting argument suggests the Son is fully aware of who he is, and is openly declaring his divine status.⁴⁴ At the very moment of refusing the final temptation of Satan, the Son utters these enigmatic words: "Also it is written, / Tempt not the Lord thy God" (4.559–60). The crucial question to be asked is what exactly the Son means by this. Are readers to assume that the Son is merely trading biblical quotations with Satan, merely throwing Deut. 6:16 back in the face of Satan's earlier quotation of Psalm 91:11–12? Is the Son declaring his belief in God, or is the Son declaring his divine status, declaring, in effect, that he is God?

If we argue that the Son is actually declaring that he is God, we are left with a number of vexing questions. How might such a declaration be reconciled with Milton's Arianism[45] (a position that holds that the Son is separate from, and inferior to, the Father)? Why must Satan not "Tempt . . . the Lord thy God"? It seems that the Biblical Satan (admittedly a character who is different in many ways from the Miltonic Satan[s] of the epic poems) has engaged in precisely such temptation of God before, aiming his machinations at Yahweh's divine pride-of-ownership during conversations with the deity about Job. Is the injunction quoted by the Son intended to forestall any further such events? Is it because "the Lord thy God" is, in fact, susceptible to temptation that he must not be tempted?

Another issue is the curious fact that the speaker of the injunction against tempting "the Lord thy God" is not referred to as the Son, but as Jesus. This is one of only five times the name Jesus appears in the entire poem, and the only time outside of Book 2, with Andrew's and Simon's concern that "their joy so lately found" (9) had disappeared, and with Satan's temptations of food and wealth, instances that play on the all-too-human and material fears of abandonment, hunger and poverty. Why? Should we place Satan's temptation at the end of Book 4 (the temptation to the Son to prove his status as Son by hurling himself from the top of the temple, thus forcing the issue raised in Psalm 91, with its assurance that angels would prevent the Son from so much as striking his foot against a stone) in the same category of material temptation into which we put the temptations of food and wealth? The answer to this question is intimately related to the question of what, exactly, the Son is doing when he (identified as Jesus) quotes the scriptural injunction not to tempt God.

One line of argument might run this way. Because, in each of the previous occurrences of the name Jesus, the context has been one of markedly material and human fears and temptations—Andrew and Simon's fear of abandonment, of losing their "joy so lately found" (2.9); Satan's temptation of a physically famished Jesus with delectable food and drink; and Satan's temptation of a poor-carpenter's-son Jesus with wealth—this final reference to the Son as Jesus is also in the context of a material and human temptation. Satan believes himself to be testing a man, not a god, and Satan falls from the top of the temple out of sheer amazement to find that this is a truly perfect man, one who cannot, after the manner of Adam, be tempted into a fall. The final temptation, then, is a material and human one, a temptation for a human being to put God to the test, to see, if you will, whether or not God is a man of his word. In falling from the temple, Satan finally recognizes this Jesus, this perfect man, as the Son of God. The poem's narrator encourages this sense of recognition for the reader by describing Satan as he "Who durst so proudly tempt the Son of God" (4.580), directly echoing the description of Satan in *Paradise Lost* as he "Who durst defy the omnipotent to arms" (1.49).

Though this line of argument supports an Arian interpretation of Milton's depiction of the Son, it fails to take into account the order of the temptations with which Satan presents the Son. In following the temptation order of Luke, rather than that of Matthew, Milton has put the temptations in an ascending scale. First, Satan rejects what he considers to be the too grossly obvious temptation proposed by Belial in Book 1, that of women and sex. Satan begins with the concrete temptation of food. What, after all, could possibly be wrong with eating, especially for a man who has been without material sustenance for forty days? From food, a temptation that might be categorized as first-level, Satan moves on to the second-level temptation of wealth. Jesus was born the son of a poor carpenter. How, without wealth, will he ever be able to afford the food and other material items he so evidently lacks? When these temptations fail, Satan moves on to the third-level temptation of earthly kingship. So far the movement in Satan's temptations has been from the more material to the less material.

The temptation of earthly kingship is even less material than is the temptation of wealth. Satan has been moving steadily away from offering material temptations in Milton's presentation. Knowledge, the temptation of classical learning, represents yet another step away from the material temptations with which Satan began. What kind of temptation, then, is Satan's challenge to the Son that he hurl himself "safely if Son of God" from the temple? It is the most abstract, the least "material" temptation of them all—a challenge to the Son to prove his identity through a demonstration of divine power. "Prove who you are; show me that you can command the power of God" is what Satan is saying to the Son at this point. In this sense, it is Satan who is tempting "the Lord thy God." It is the challenge to proof of identity though a display of power that is the temptation, not the testing of God's word concerning the safety of his Son, a testing the Son would set in motion by the act of hurling himself down from the temple. In effect, what Satan is tempting the Son to do is prove that he is, in fact, what Satan has suspected him to be from the beginning of the poem.

Why, then, is Satan "smitten with amazement" (4.562), so smitten that he falls from the temple himself? He is overwhelmed, not simply by having his worst fears confirmed, not simply by having his earlier-expressed suspicions validated, but by the extent to which the answer of the Son goes beyond his worst fears. This is not merely a man (even a perfect man), nor is it merely a Son of God that Satan has been tempting—it is God himself. However, the Son is not God in any Trinitarian sense; rather, he is God (he is divine) in the way that anyone can be, and in fact, already is. What the Son has successfully claimed and defended against the temptations of Satan is the sense of divine similitude that itself constitutes the "fairer Paradise" (4.613) that is superior to the lost paradise of Eden. As he establishes this new, inner Eden, the Son both ascends to the kingly throne of the Father and begins dismantling it. "Tempt not the Lord thy God" is a direct statement from the Son to Satan: *tempt me no further.*

How can such a claim be reconciled to the narrative descriptions of the Son as "True image of the Father" (4.596) and "Son of the most high" (4.653)? This claim is the culmination of the movement from Father to Son that Milton has been writing throughout his two epics. The Son has taken his place, his promised place, in the scheme of dethroning divinity. The Son has become the "True image of the Father" by inhabiting a model of divinity that the Father could, and did, conceive (the future state when God would be "All in All"), but could not himself inhabit. Satan's final temptation is a temptation of the heavenly status quo: identify yourself through, and with, power. It is at the very moment of Jesus' rejection of this temptation that "A fairer Paradise is founded" (4.613) for humankind. The Son's rejection of a display of power is the final nail in

Satan's coffin, and the final dismantling of kingship as a model of divinity.

What Satan is finally forced to realize at the end of Book 4 is what he has resisted seeing until then: the Son's identity and the unimpeachable, untemptable internal mode of the Son's divinity. This is Satan's final, and truest fall, and his ultimate tragedy. Everything he has failed to understand all along is encapsulated for him in the Son's refusal of the final temptation. The Son is what Satan could have been had he only understood that external glory, power, and fame are finally meaningless, and that true freedom, true divinity is found by rejecting them. The hymn of victory at the end of *Paradise Regained* ("A fairer Paradise is founded now . . . ") sums up the issue. The new paradise is fairer than Eden because Eden's paradise was based on *reasonless* obedience to *external* authority, an obedience of fear rather than an obedience of persuasion. At the end of *Paradise Regained*, obedience is *reasoned, internal,* and given to *oneself.* Far from being an example of *license*, this obedience given to oneself is, in fact, the *liberty* of Milton's Sonnet 12. Those who have regained Paradise are so intimately connected to the divine that they are themselves the God to whom obedience is due. The "inner man, the nobler part" of each human being is divine in the same way that the Son's "inner man" is divine. When this divinity is realized and cultivated, no external God or Law is needed. In such a formulation of what it means to be divine, God is taken down from his throne because those who are no longer subjects no longer need a hierarchically imagined divinity.

The full implications of the new-model Divinity outlined at the end of *Paradise Regained* are summed up in the last two lines of the poem. After defeating Satan, rejecting power as a mode of operation and identification, and dismantling the very kingly model upon which both the Father and Satan have built their respective hierarchies and roles, the Son goes home. The home he returns to is not a heavenly throne, but the poor house of his human mother: "he unobserved / Home to his mother's house private returned" (4.638–39). The Son returns not to his father's house, nor to the Father's house, but specifically to his "mother's house private."[46] Private can be read here in two ways. It could refer back to "unobserved," meaning that no one saw, or intruded upon, the Son after his conquest of Satan and his "regaining" of Paradise for humankind. More interestingly, however, "private," read in its sixteenth- and seventeenth-century political sense, implies that the Son, having rejected power and kingship, is returning to a house and a life that has no part in the external government of affairs either earthly or heavenly.[47] This fits quite nicely with the Son's speech on power at the end of Book 2, where he rejects the model of government that "o'er the body only reigns, / And oft by force, which to a generous mind / So reigning can be no sincere delight" (478–80). Instead of this kind of external, and manifestly public reign, the Son prefers the internal, private (in the sense both of individual and non-hierarchical, non-magistratical) government of truth: "to guide nations in the way of truth / By saving doctrine, and from error lead / To know, and, knowing worship God aright, / Is yet more kingly, this attracts the soul, / Governs the inner man, the nobler part" (2.473–77).

In returning to his "mother's house private," the Son closes the door on the model of reign by force, the model of divinity that pictures God as a king and leader of troops, and steps irrevocably through the door that leads to a model of reign as inner accord with truth. In so doing, the Son redefines true government as knowing and worshipping God aright, as an inner government of the inner man, the nobler part, a knowing and worshipping that establishes an inner Paradise, the "fairer Paradise . . . founded now" than that external Paradise of Eden, whose sole test was one of external obedience. Milton, through the Son, has closed the door on kingship, on God imagined as a tyrant, and on the need for hierarchical structures of church and state that serve merely to encourage—after the manner of Satan—a sense of separateness from the divine. Milton's ultimate message to his fit audience is that although they do not currently do so, they can do as the Son does, and be as the Son is—divine beings walking the earth in full accord with each other and the divine source of all being. God is not a king, and worship need not involve pageantry, ceremony, or submissive words and gestures—worship is inner awareness of divine similitude. As William Blake—still one of the finest readers and critics of Milton—expressed the idea, "God becomes as we are, that we may be as he is."

Notes

Chapter 1. Of Miltons and Gods

1. This extreme is not one to which all groups identified as "Gnostic" go, but it is recognizable, for instance, in Marcion. According to Hans Jonas, Marcion's demiurge was primarily conceived in terms of "pettiness" (*The Gnostic Religion*, 2d ed. [Boston: Beacon Press, 1991], 141) and was merely *just* as opposed to *good.* The Valentinian " 'artificer' (demiurge) of the left-hand things" (190) is also recognizable as a devilish kind of anti-God whose main attribute is "ignorance . . . and [the] presumption in which he believes himself to be alone and declares himself to be the unique and highest God" (191).

2. Among those critics who see Milton as favoring heavenly kingship, I will specifically be engaged with three: Joan Bennett, *Reviving Liberty: Radical Humanism in Milton's Great Poems* (Cambridge: Harvard University Press, 1989); Stevie Davies, *Images of Kingship in Paradise Lost: Milton's Politics and Christian Liberty* (Columbia: University of Missouri Press, 1983); and Robert Fallon, *Divided Empire: Milton's Political Imagery* (University Park: Pennsylvania State University Press, 1995).

3. Neither of Milton's great biographers makes much of the phrase "great Taskmaster's eye." William Riley Parker remarks merely that these lines reflect "a humble submission" and that the sonnet as a whole "is one of re-dedication" to "the service of God." See *Milton: A Biography*, 2d ed. (Oxford: Oxford University Press, 1996), 124. David Masson speculates that the sonnet may reflect not only Milton's sense of belatedness in choosing a career, but also a growing diffidence about the prospect of entering the priesthood in the Church of England. See *The Life of John Milton*, vol. 1 (New York: Macmillan, 1946), 325–26.

4. This becomes especially obvious in *Samson Agonistes*. Michael Lieb has called the God of Milton's drama "our living dread." See "'Our Living Dread': The God of Samson Agonistes," *Milton Studies* 33, ed. Albert C. Labriola (Pittsburgh: University of Pittsburgh Press, 1997), 3–25.

5. There are numerous constructions of God in the Hebrew scriptures. The wrathful Yahweh of Exodus 32, for example, is just one construction. The portraits of God in Amos and portions of Isaiah—with the ethical concerns of those books—are radically different from the wrathful deity found elsewhere in scripture.

6. Milton is so often at odds with what might seem on first glance his natural allies that it is difficult to see him uncritically accepting *anything*. John Rumrich's characterization of Milton as a man possessed of a mind "syncretic yet stunningly idiosyncratic"—in *Milton Unbound: Controversy and Reinterpretation* (Cambridge: Cambridge University Press, 1996), 146—seems to me exactly right. Milton didn't much care what other people—especially so-called authorities—thought about anything, unless he could somehow use those thoughts to the advantage of his case. Milton genuflected before no human opinion, and before precious few scriptural opinions. Milton would have hated being an undergraduate in a modern university where what Rumrich calls "the invented Milton" (2) was being taught.

7. Regina Schwartz has made a powerful case for the connection between exclusive personal divinity and nationalism. "[M]onotheism has been caught up with particularism, with that production of collective identity as peoples set apart." See *The Curse of Cain: The Violent Legacy of Monotheism* (Chicago: University of Chicago Press, 1997), 31. This kind of particularism "reduces all other gods to idols," and is "so violent that it reduces all other worshipers to abominations" (33). Schwartz characterizes this tension as a struggle between the One (a construct that suggests both singleness and universality) and the Many; the One in such a struggle is that which truly exists, while the Many are those who are somehow false, whose existence is either an abomination or a lie. Whether the one and the many are gods or humans, the kind of universality contained in exclusive personal monotheism is dangerous; according to Schwartz, "The danger of a universal monotheism is asserting that its truth is the Truth, its system of knowledge *the* System of knowledge, its ethics *the* Ethics" (33).

8. Ibid., 17.

9. Ibid., 54.

10. Michael Lieb's 1981 book, *Poetics of the Holy* (Chapel Hill: University of North Carolina Press, 1981) discusses *Paradise Lost* and its portrait of divinity in terms of an analysis of Milton's concept of holiness.

11. Unless otherwise noted, all quotations of Milton's prose are from *The Complete Prose Works of John Milton*, vol. 8, ed. Don M Wolfe et al. (New Haven: Yale University Press, 1953–1982). Such quotations are cited parenthetically as *CPW*, with volume and page number. All quotations of Milton's poetry are from *John Milton: Complete Poems and Major Prose*, ed. Merritt Hughes (New York: Odyssey, 1957).

12. *Milton and Heresy*, 3.

13. Ibid., 3.

14. John Rumrich, *Milton Unbound: Controversy and Reinterpretation* (Cambridge: Cambridge University Press, 1996), 2.

15. Ibid., 4.

16. John Diekhoff, *Milton's Paradise Lost: A Commentary* (New York: Humanities Press, 1963), 31.

17. Ibid., 10.

18. William Riggs, *The Christian Poet in Paradise Lost* (Berkeley: University of California Press, 1972), 45.

19. William B. Hunter, *Visitation Unimplor'd: Milton and the Authorship of De Doctrina Christiana* (Pittsburgh: Duquesne University Press, 1998), 8.

20. William Empson, *Milton's God* (Norfolk, Conn: Chatto & Windus, 1961), 9.

21. *The Essays of John Dryden*, vol. 2, ed. W. P. Ker (New York: Russell & Russell, 1961), 165.

22. Joseph Addison, *The Spectator*, vol. 3, ed. Donald F. Bond (Oxford: Clarendon Press, 1965), No. 297, 59.

23. Ibid.

24. Ibid., 86.

25. Samuel Johnson, *Samuel Johnson: The Oxford Authors*, ed. Donald Greene (Oxford: Oxford University Press, 1984), 708.

26. Thomas Newton, ed. *Paradise Lost* (Birmingham: Printed by J. Baskerville for J. and R. Tonson, 1759), lxiii.

27. Percy Bysshe Shelley, *Shelley's Poetry and Prose*, ed. Donald H. Reiman and Sharon B Powers (New York: Norton, 1977), 133.

28. *De Doctrina Christiana* is a matter of some recent controversy. Since its "discovery" in 1823 and its first translation into English in 1825, it has long been assumed to be a work by Milton. This position has recently been challenged. William B. Hunter has gone so far as to insist that *De Doctrina Christiana* is not by Milton at all, and even those (still the majority in Milton studies—myself included) who believe this work to be by Milton have recently been forced (by the analyses of Gordon Campbell and others) to acknowledge that it contains numerous and lengthy passages in which the Latin is decidedly un-Miltonic. This project is not the place for presenting arguments that even pose as definitive and/or authoritative on this matter. However, raising questions and casting doubts—even legitimate doubts—is not equivalent to proving a case. I argue that the burden of proof in the matter of the authorial provenance of *De Doctrina Christiana* is on those who would prove that Milton is *not* the author. This case has not, to date, been proven.

29. Henry John Todd, ed. *The Poetical Works of Milton*, (London: Rivingtons, 1852), 193.

30. David Masson, *The Life of John Milton; Narrated in Connexion with the Political, Ecclesiastical, and Literary History of His Time.* (1871; reprint, Gloucester, Mass: Macmillan, 1946), vol. 6, 823.

31. David Masson, ed. *The Poetical Works of John Milton* (London: Macmillan; 1882), 18.

32. Christopher Hill, *The World Turned Upside Down* (New York: Viking Press, 1972), 403.

33. Denis Saurat, *Milton, Man and Thinker* (New York: The Dial Press 1925), 217.

34. Ibid., 219.

35. Christopher Hill, *Milton and the English Revolution* (London: Faber and Faber, 1977), 3.

36. C. S. Lewis, *A Preface to Paradise Lost* (London: Oxford University Press, 1942), 65.

37. Ibid., 69.

38. A. J. A. Waldock, *Paradise Lost and its Critics* (Cambridge: Cambridge University Press, 1947), 18.

39. Ibid., 18–19.

40. Ibid., 19.

41. Empson made no secret of his distaste for the Christian God. "I think the traditional God of Christianity very wicked, and have done since I was in school, where nearly all my little playmates thought the same" (*Milton's God*, 10).

42. Empson's book is in my opinion one of the finest that has ever been written on Milton's epic poem, but curiously, it has been allowed to go out of print, despite the fact that it was published some nineteen years after C. S. Lewis's publication of *A Preface to Paradise Lost*. (Lewis's book, of course, remains in print.) This curious circumstance might be attributed to simple market economics; however, the fact that market economics in this case so neatly coincide with the dominance of the very neo-Christian movement that Empson decried is almost enough to raise suspicions of an interpretive conspiracy. Books that are no longer readily available, whether through commercial or university presses, effectively have been silenced. While it is true, certainly, that many potentially valuable volumes have been allowed, for various reasons, to go out of print (including the Yale Milton Prose volumes), it seems remarkably odd to me that an "orthodox" volume originally published in 1942 remains in print, while a deeply unorthodox volume originally published in 1961 is almost unobtainable outside of a university library.

43. Rumrich's 1996 publication of *Milton Unbound* was an open challenge to the neo-Christian school of late twentieth-century Milton criticism. A champion of reader-response criticism such as Fish is placed in a curious position by the responses of readers who have lived under the kind of despotism that Milton only imagines in his poetry. According to Rumrich, "The Milton to whom the students at Peking University responded was . . . a radical humanist, who not only hated tyranny and superstition but who, unlike more quiescent intellectuals and artists, put himself on the line fighting against them" (xi). I am reminded of the image of the solitary Chinese man who stood in front of a line of Red Army tanks during the Tien An Men uprising; the kind of tyranny that young man died resisting is something that relatively comfortable academic critics in the West will likely never have to encounter except on television.

44. Empson, *Milton's God*, 10. The reactions of non-Christian readers to *Paradise Lost* and its portrait of the Father was of no real concern in the seventeenth, eighteenth, and even nineteenth centuries. Historically informed scholarship that tries to understand the poem and its context together need not be immediately concerned with the place of *Paradise Lost* within a late-twentieth-and early-twenty-first-century context of emerging multiculturalism in literature and education. It seems to me, however, that this is no excuse for ignoring the issue altogether. Demanding that readers take an orthodox Christian position in the interpretation of the poem is a kind of intellectual colonialism.

45. Ibid., 10–11.

46. David Norbrook, *Writing the English Republic: Poetry, Rhetoric and Politics, 1627–1660* (Cambridge: Cambridge University Press, 1999), 445, note 32.

47. Rumrich, *Milton Unbound*, 4.

48. Stanley Fish, *Surprised by Sin: The Reader in Paradise Lost*, 2d ed. (Basingstoke, Hampshire: Macmillan, 1997), 9.

49. Dennis Danielson, *Milton's Good God: A Study in Literary Theodicy* (Cambridge: Cambridge University Press, 1982), ix.

50. Sharon Achinstein, *Milton and the Revolutionary Reader* (Princeton: Princeton University Press, 1994), 68.

51. Alexander Pope, "First Epistle of the Second Book of Horace Imitated," *The Poems of Alexander Pope*, ed. John Butt (New Haven: Yale University Press, 1963).

52. Thomas Newton, *Paradise Lost*, lxiii–lxiv.
53. Fish, *Surprised By Sin*, 4. Fish's contention that the reader is harassed by *Paradise Lost* is anticipated by Samuel Johnson. In his *Prefaces, Biographical and Critical, to the Works of the English Poets*, Johnson describes Milton's epic as "one of those books which the reader admires and lays down, and forgets to take up again" (*Samuel Johnson: The Oxford Authors*, ed. Donald Greene [Oxford and New York: Oxford University Press, 1984], 711). He goes on to say, "We read Milton for instruction, retire harassed and overburdened, and look elsewhere for recreation; we desert our master, and seek for companions" (711).
54. Fish, *Surprised By Sin*, 12.
55. In his 1996 book, *Milton Unbound*, John Peter Rumrich forcefully argues against Fish's model of the effects of *Paradise Lost* on a reader. Fish responded in the preface to the second edition of *Surprised by Sin*, by accusing Rumrich of mistaking the "substantive content" (xv) of his work.
56. Christopher Hill quotes Winstanley as rejecting the Christian God in no uncertain terms: "A traditional Christian who 'thinks God is in the heavens above the skies, and so prays to that God which he imagines to be there and everywhere . . . worships his own imagination, which is the devil.'" *The World Turned Upside Down*, 141.
57. Ibid., 141.
58. In the twentieth century, William Empson has expressed sentiments similar to those of Winstanley: "what Christians are worshipping, with their incessant advertisements for torture, is literally the Devil" (*Milton's God*, 260). Empson went on to lament that he saw "no hope before Christians until they renounce the Devil and all his works; that is, stop worshipping a God who is satisfied by torture, and confess in public that they have done so" (266).
59. Norbrook, *Writing the English Republic*, 477.
60. Bishop Hall described *The Doctrine and Discipline of Divorce* as a "licentious pamphlet" reflecting a "woeful degeneration." *The Works of the Right Reverend Joseph Hall*, ed. Philip Wynter (Oxford: Oxford University Press, 1863), 467. Herbert Palmer vilified Milton as a libertine in a sermon delivered before Parliament in August 1644. Milton received so much criticism, in fact, that in the *Second Defense* he lamented that he had not written the divorce tracts in Latin. Christopher Hill, in *Milton and the English Revolution*, gives an eloquent and concise account of the overwhelmingly negative responses to Milton's divorce tracts.
61. Hill, *Milton and the English Revolution*, 7–8.
62. Norbrook, *Writing the English Republic*, 477.
63. Ibid., 479.
64. "If Milton had allowed himself consciously to accept the view of Winstanley, Erbury and some Ranters, that the God whom most Christians worshipped was a wicked God, his life . . . would have fallen about his head like the temple of the Philistines" (Christopher Hill, *The World Turned Upside Down*, 401). Professor Hill's comment is perceptive, though perhaps not in the manner he intends. I believe Milton and Winstanley are allied on this issue. In differing with Professor Hill over the interpretation of the words "the God whom most Christians worshipped," I contend that for Milton, God was not wicked; however, the *image* of God that most contemporary Christians worshipped—the god of monarchical power—was wicked. Milton not only accepted a view quite similar to that of Winstanley, he made it the central issue of his epic poetry.

65. Norbrook, *Writing the English Republic*, 477.
66. Albert Labriola, " 'All in All' and 'All in One': Obedience and Disobedience in *Paradise Lost*." *All in All: Unity, Diversity, and the Miltonic Perspective*, ed. Charles W. Durham and Kristin A. Pruitt (Selinsgrove, Pa: Susquehanna University Press, 1999), 39.
67. Ibid., 40.
68. Hobbes quotes Psalm 51 to make this point, "against thee I have sinned, 0 Lord"—David's reflection on his arranged murder of Uriah and his resultant marriage to Bathsheba.
69. John Calvin, *Institutes of the Christian Religion*, 2 vols. Trans. Ford Lewis Battles, ed. John T. McNeill (Philadelphia: Westminster Press, 1960), 1511.
70. Milton's definition of a tyrant from *Tenure of Kings and Magistrates* (*CPW* 3:212).
71. Davies, *Images of Kingship in Paradise Lost*, 127.
72. Ibid.,130.
73. Ibid., 130.
74. Ibid., 175.
75. Ibid., 148.
76. Ibid., 148.
77. Ibid., 131.

Chapter 2. "His Tyranny Who Reigns"

1. Empson remarked, in *Milton's God*, that "the intelligence of the Romantic authors has been held in contempt since . . . T. S. Eliot" (13). While this may be an exaggerated claim outside of the realm of Milton studies, I believe it to be a reasonably accurate summation of the neo-Christian reaction to Blake and Shelley and their (in)famous assessments of *Paradise Lost*. Kenneth Gross, in "Satan and the Romantic Satan: a Notebook"—*Re-membering Milton*, ed. Mary Nyquist and Margaret W. Ferguson [New York, London: Methuen 1987], 318–41) argues that modern characterizations of both the Romantic Satan and the Romantics themselves operate as "a slander of the sophisticated work of many nineteenth-century readers" (320). For instance, John Diekhoff refers to Shelley's argument in *A Defence of Poetry* that Milton's Devil being morally superior to Milton's God as "eloquent nonsense"—see *Milton's Paradise Lost* (New York: Humanities Press, 1963), 30. Even the unusually provocative authors Dobranski and Rumrich, in *Milton and Heresy*, a volume deeply Blakean and Shelleyan in its readiness to see heresy in Milton, diffidently declare that they do not "pursue a critical agenda nostalgic for the *excesses* of Romantic readers" (3, emphasis added). For a thorough presentation of the writings of Romantic-era poets and critics on Milton, see Joseph Wittreich's *The Romantics on Milton* (Cleveland: Press of Case Western Reserve University, 1970). Wittreich opposes the dismissal of the Romantics and is much more positive in his evaluations of the Romantics than are the critics mentioned above. For example, Wittreich laments the "assiduous and unrelenting attack on Romantic criticism" (6) of what he refers to as Milton's admirers in the twentieth century. Wittreich goes on to challenge the notions that the Romantics focus narrowly on

Milton's art (leaving his politics and theology out of consideration) and that they are guilty of "magnifying and distorting the character of Milton's Satan" (9). Wittreich contends that Romantic criticism's strength is "its ability to hold Milton—man, thinker, and poet—in balance" (9). Wittreich also upholds the perceptions of those relatively few twentieth-century Milton critics who have not denigrated the Romantics: "The perceptions of Hanford, Empson, and Beer are borne out by the criticism reprinted in this edition; the impressions of their colleagues are corrected by it" (8).

2. Bennett, *Reviving Liberty*, 33.

3. Christopher Hill has complained about what he takes to be a peculiarly American Miltonist groupthink: "There is the immensely productive Milton industry, largely in the United States of America, a great part of whose vast output appears to be concerned less with what Milton wrote . . . than with the views of Professor Blank on the views of Professor Schrank on the view of Professor Rank on what Milton may or may not have written" (*Milton and the English Revolution*, 3). Mary Nyquist and Margaret Ferguson have made a similar complaint, lamenting what they take to be the especially American tendency of writing on Milton to "become so narrowly professionalized that the very weight of its authority tends to crush any efforts not appearing to confirm to its standards. It is often neo-Christian . . . , or at least neo-theological" (*Re-membering Milton*, xv). I find it wonderfully ironic that *any* Milton critic would resort to arguments based on general consensus of critical opinion. Milton's own model was the Berean's insistence on searching the scriptures daily, to prove to *themselves* "whether these things were so" (Acts 17:11). Professors Blank, Schrank, and Rank (as well as Professors Nyquist, Fish, and Ferguson) do immensely valuable work, but that work is not the final word—no one's work is. As is often the case, however, Empson's take is simultaneously provocative and refreshing, as he condemns a mentality that assumes "that a man ought to concur with any herd in which he happens to find himself" (*Milton's God*, 231).

4. Robert Thomas Fallon, *Divided Empire: Milton's Political Imagery* (University Park: Pennsylvania State University Press, 1995), 32.

5. Ibid., 33.

6. Ibid., 32.

7. In evaluating the evidence of Milton's prose, I believe that it is of the utmost importance to keep in mind that Milton is writing *to win*. His prose is a competitive instrument, and as such, it may seem to present inconsistent views of Milton's theological and political attitudes, especially on the matter of kingship. Reuben Sanchez reminds us that Milton's prose involved shifting self-presentational strategies: "Milton's self-presentation varies from prose tract to prose tract because of the type of argument he makes and the type of persona he creates for the better persuasiveness of that argument. The persona and decorum [and, I would add, the emphasis] of a given tract, therefore, are particular aspects of Milton's response to an immediate occasion" ("From Polemic to Prophecy," *Milton Studies* 30, ed. Albert Labriola [Pittsburgh: University of Pittsburgh Press, 1993], 27). Milton's persona, decorum, and rhetorical emphasis are in some sense the equivalent of battle strategies or game plans; individual elements of Milton's overall belief system are subordinated to the goal of *winning* whatever argument he finds himself involved in. Milton's tepid—and somewhat embarrassing—defense

of Jeroboam in *A Defense of the English People* is an excellent example of how Milton, in the pursuit of victory, will make a move that would, in a less immediately agonistic circumstance, be repellent to him. Thus, I think it is problematic at best to focus, as Fallon does, on Milton's flattering of Queen Christina in *A Second Defence*, a strategy Milton pursues in an attempt to both further advertise and consolidate what he considered to be his triumph over Salmasius.

8. Michael Fixler has also argued for a consistency in the purpose of Milton's prose writings, and has noted that inconsistency may appear as a result of Milton's immediate rhetorical situation: "The unity, particularly of the prose, may be obscured by the apparently different objectives he pursued at different times, but in reality these objectives were only so many means to one end." *Milton and the Kingdoms of God* (Evanston, Ill.: Northwestern University Press, 1964), 76.

9. Fallon, *Divided Empire*, 36.

10. Ibid., 31.

11. Robert Thomas Fallon, *Milton in Government* (University Park: Pennsylvania State University Press, 1993), 205.

12. Ibid., 205.

13. Ibid.

14. Empson, *Milton's God*, 111.

15. Fallon, *Divided Empire*, 42.

16. Painting heaven as an impossibly glorious monarchy is the move of a closet (or open) royalist, a move more befitting Filmer and Hobbes than Milton. G. Wilson Knight (though he would have argued that Milton's heaven was a model for human monarchy to imitate, rather than a model intended to shame human monarchy out of existence) constructed much this kind of royalist Milton in the service of arguments designed, in part, as a professorial rallying cry in the British war effort against Hitler. Knight argued that Milton was a defender of constitutional monarchy, claimed that Milton's attitude, even during the Republican years, was "sympathetic to the idea of royalty" (*Chariot of Wrath* [London: Faber and Faber, 1942], 44) and resorted to an argument similar to that of Robert Fallon: Milton said nothing derogatory about numerous monarchs, and had praise for Queen Christina of Sweden (44). Though Milton writes to Christina that he has not "written a word against kings, but only against tyrants" (*CPW* 4:604), it should not be forgotten that Milton is writing here less out of principle than out of polemical purpose—writing both to consolidate and extend the rhetorical victory over Salmasius that Milton feels he has achieved with the earlier *Defence of the People of England*.

17. Bennett, *Reviving Liberty*, 18. This seems ultimately to be a rather small claim. What, after all, are the "essentials" of the world view that Milton ostensibly shares with Hooker? A belief in God? Bennett herself admits that Milton 'did not . . . begin his arguments on the same theoretical footing as did the 'traditionalists' of his own day" (17), traditionalists who would have been closer, in theoretical terms, to Hooker than to Milton.

18. Ibid., 9.

19. Fallon, *Divided Empire*, 33.

20. Bennett, *Reviving Liberty*, 79.

21. Herodotus, *The History of Herodotus*, trans. George Rawlinson (Chicago: Britannica, 1955), 108.

22. Plato, *The Republic*, trans. Benjamin Jowett (Chicago: Britannica, 1955), 419.

23. Thomas Aquinas, *Summa Theologica*, vol. 1, trans. Daniel J. Sullivan (Chicago: Britannica, 1955), 530.

24. Thomas Aquinas, *Summa Theologica*, vol. 2, trans. Daniel J. Sullivan (Chicago: Britannica, 1955), 309.

25. See, for example, Joseph Bentham, *The right of kings by Scripture* . . . (London, 1661); Matthew Griffith, *A sermon preached in the citie of London by a Lover of truth* . . . (London, 1643); G. S., Lover of loyalty. *The Dignity of Kingship Asserted* . . . (London, 1661); John Jones, *Christvs dei, or, A theologicall discourse* . . . (Oxford, 1642); Roger L'Estrange, *No blinde guides* . . . (London, 1660); Richard Mocket, *God and the King:* . . . (London, 1663); Thomas Morton, *The necessity of Christian subjection* . . . (Oxford, 1643); Robert Mossom, *The king on his throne...*(York, 1643); William Prynne, *The title of kings proved to be jure devino* . . . (London, 1660); R. H. (Richard Hooke), *The royal guard, or, The King's salvation* . . . (London, 1662); James Ussher, *The power communicated by God to the prince, and the obedience required of the subject* . . . (London, 1661).

26. Christopher Kendrick has argued that Milton was a proto-nationalist: "His whole epic vocation was intertwined with what we might call a form of proto-nationalism. . . . Milton's . . . is a religiously coded patriotism for which the ideal English church . . . is simply one with the nation, and for which the nation represents only a peculiarly chosen member of the collective saintly body." *Milton: A Study in Ideology and Form* (New York: Methuen, 1986), 84.

27. Achinstein, *Milton and the Revolutionary Reader*, 17.

28. Barbara Lewalski, *Protestant Poetics and the Seventeenth-Century Religious Lyric* (Princeton: Princeton University Press, 1979), 131.

29. The Jubilee year, which came every fifty years, provided relief to families that had fallen into poverty, as well as serving as a reminder that all land really belonged, not to the Israelites themselves, but to Yahweh. The Jubilee Law, outlined in Leviticus 25, prevented land from being sold in perpetuity; the law provided that if a man sold any hereditary land, the sale price was to be calculated according to the number of years left until the next Jubilee year. Thus, sale of land was rather more like *leasing* land and its produce. The relation between the Jubilee law and the bitter fight against enclosure of lands in England becomes especially clear when considering the *exceptions* to the Israelite law: land and houses in walled cities were not included in those properties returned at Jubilee. (The only exception to this exception was houses and lands originally belonging to members of the Levite priest class.)

30. Gleaning, outlined at Lev. 19:9–10 and Deut. 24:19–21, was the process of gathering whatever portion of a crop had been either intentionally or unintentionally left behind. Like the provision of return of lands during the Jubilee years, it has its roots in the recognition that the land and its produce belong to Yahweh and are distributed by Yahweh as provisions for his people. The land and its wealth were not the exclusive possessions of the wealthy and powerful, but shared possessions given to all the people as a gift from their God.

31. Fallon, *Divided Empire*, 36.

32. Christopher Hill has argued that the popular myth of the Norman Yoke posited an originally democratic and non-monarchical constitution as the native

English model of society and government. Monarchy was an imposition of the invading Normans of 1066, and thus monarchy is a *foreign* institution, and the rejection of the Stuart monarchy is rejection of a foreign tyranny. See "The Norman Yoke," in *Puritanism and Revolution* (London: Secker & Warburg, 1969), 50–122. I do not believe that Milton would reject such a notion—especially since it appears in his antimonarchical tracts and his *History of Britain*—nor do I believe that Milton could have failed to see the analogy between the myth of the Norman Yoke, with its narrative of kingship as a foreign innovation and imposition, and the Biblical narratives of the eventual fall of the Israelites from a commonwealth into kingship "in the manner of all the nations."

33. Regina Schwartz, "Citation, Authority, and *De Doctrina Christiana*," in *Politics, Poetics, and Hermeneutics in Milton's Prose*, ed. David Loewenstein and James Grantham Turner (Cambridge: Cambridge University Press, 1990), 233.

34. Ibid., 230.

35. Fallon, *Divided Empire*, 42.

36. Nimrod is also, for Milton, "the first that hunted after Faction" (*Eikonoklastes, CPW* 3.466), and faction is an indispensable ingredient in Milton's recipe for tyranny.

37. Baruch Halpern, *The Constitution of the Monarchy in Israel* (Chico, Calif.: Scholars Press, 1981), 71. Other works useful for an understanding of the development of the idea of Yahweh as a king include: Zafrira Ben-Barak, *The Manner of the King and The Manner of the Kingdom: Basic Factors in the Establishment of the Israelite Monarchy in the Light of Canaanite Kingship.* (Jerusalem: Hebrew University, 1972); Marc Zvi Brettler, *God is King: Understanding an Israelite Metaphor* (Sheffield: JSOT Press, 1989); and Audrey K. Gordon, *Religious Dimensions of Kingship in Canaan and Israel.* M.S. (History and Literature of Religions), (Evanston, Ill.: Northwestern University), 1967 (Diss 378 NU 1967).

38. Halpern, *The Constitution of the Monarchy in Israel*, 71.

39. Ibid., 73.

40. For a discussion of the *Enuma Elish*, Genesis, and Milton, see Regina Schwartz, *Remembering and Repeating: On Milton's Theology and Poetics* (Chicago: University of Chicago Press, 1993). Also see J. Martin Evans, *Paradise Lost and the Genesis Tradition* (New York: Oxford University Press, 1968).

41. Judges describes a period in Israelite "history" (perhaps "prehistory" would be a more accurate term) in which Israel might be more accurately described as the *nations* of Israel rather than as the *nation* of Israel. This loose confederation of related tribes had no centralized system of government, being governed instead by a series of local chieftains, or "judges" (Othoniel, Ehud, Deborah, Barak, Samson, etc.) who are portrayed in the narrative as having a tendency to arise when needed and then ride off into the sunset, fade away into obscurity, or die gloriously when their useful time is over.

42. Israel and the surrounding nations would not be identified as "oriental" by modern readers with a reasonably fine-tuned geographical sense. However, Milton is using a definition of the term that originally focused on a particular site's location in relation to Rome. The Roman empire, both in its classical and its "Holy" incarnations, was often thought of as split into "Occidental" (west of Rome) and "Oriental" (east of Rome) territories. The *Oxford English Dictionary* cites numerous examples of this usage during and before Milton's time. Milton considered the

near–middle eastern milieu in which Israel existed to be "oriental" in precisely this sense, as is made clear in *Tenure of Kings and Magistrates*: "the people of Asia, and with them the Jews also, especially since the time they chose a King against the advice and counsel of God, are noted by wise Authors much inclinable to slavery" (*CPW* 3:202–3).

43. Christopher Hill, *The English Bible and the Seventeenth-Century Revolution* (New York: Penguin, 1993), 223.

44. Ibid., 208.

45. Ibid., 209.

46. Ibid.

47. G. W. Knight, *Chariot of Wrath*, 27.

48. J. H. Hanford, *A Milton Handbook*, 4th edition (New York: Appleton-Century-Crofts, 1954), 79.

49. Hill, *Milton and the English Revolution*, 91.

50. Regina Schwartz has written that "Milton was preoccupied with origins" (*Remembering and Repeating*, 1). Milton "wrote of the origin of the cosmos, the birth of his god, the birth of the first man and the first woman, the first utterance, the first interpretation, the first temptation, the first rebellion, the first home, and the first exile. And he did so by returning to the work he regarded as the first of texts, the Bible, and, even then, to its beginning, Genesis" (1).

51. Empson, *Milton's God*, 103.

52. On the nature of the Son's rule, Michael Fixler has argued for a four-fold definition of "Christ's Kingdom" in Milton's time: 1) "spiritual and inward, experienced by each Christian within himself as the justification through faith in Christ"; 2) "The Church, or the community of the faithful bound in fellowship"; 3) "a society transformed in its institutions and spirit by piety, righteousness, virtue and charity"; and 4) "the eschatological one, or the kingdom of Glory" (*Milton and the Kingdoms of God*, 77–78). I contend that by the end of his life Milton had lost patience with #2, held out little hope for #3, and waited for #4 while otherwise focusing exclusively on #1.

53. Newton, *Paradise Lost*, lxiii.

54. Bennett, *Reviving Liberty*, 9.

55. Aristotle, *Politics*, trans. Benjamin Jowett (Chicago: Britannica, 1955), 495.

56. Empson, *Milton's God*, 74.

57. The way in which this critical commonplace is passed on to students is particularly revealing, I think. *The Norton Anthology* (Major Authors 6th ed. M. H. Abrams, General Editor [New York: W. W. Norton & Co., 1996]) provides the following footnote to Satan's description of the "tyranny of Heaven" (*Paradise Lost* 1.124): "The accusation is bold, but one of the aims of the poem is to show that Satan is a tyrant and God is not" (668, note 9). In his *Riverside Milton* (Boston: Houghton Mifflin, 1998), Roy Flannagan is concerned enough to provide a footnote to this same line that offers "a corrective to everything Satan says here" (358, note 48). In contrast to the requirements of ordinary scholarship, in these pedagogical situations, no effort whatsoever is made to acknowledge the long tradition of opposing viewpoints on the matter of the tyrants and the tyrannies represented in *Paradise Lost*.

58. Norbrook, *Writing the English Republic*, 480.

59. Ibid.

60. Ibid.

61. For other descriptions of the Father–Son dialogue in Book 3 of *Paradise Lost* as containing a challenge by the Son, see Michael Lieb's "Reading God: Milton and the Anthropopathetic Tradition," *Milton Studies* 25, ed. James D. Simmonds (Pittsburgh: University of Pittsburgh Press, 1989), 213–43, and "Milton's 'Dramatick Constitution': The Celestial Dialogue in *Paradise Lost*, Book III," *Milton Studies* 23, ed. James D. Simmonds (Pittsburgh: University of Pittsburgh Press, 1987), 215–40.

62. Labriola, "'All in All' and 'All in One,'" 39.

63. Gordon Campbell has pointed out this parallel previously. See "Popular Traditions of God in the Renaissance," *Reconsidering the Renaissance: Papers from the Twenty-First Annual Conference*, ed. Mario A DiCesare (Binghamton, N.Y.: Medieval and Renaissance Texts and Studies, 1992), 501–20.

64. Michael Lieb, "Milton and the Anthropopathetic Tradition," 225.

65. Ibid., 229.

66. Empson, *Milton's God*, 120.

67. Davies, *Images of Kingship in Paradise Lost*, 175.

68. Fish, *Surprised By Sin*, 62.

69. Davies, *Images of Kingship in Paradise Lost*, 30–31.

70. Ibid.

71. Fallon, *Divided Empire*, 42.

72. The argument that Milton became increasingly disappointed with, and even enraged against the English people who failed to live up to his expectations of them, is made in (among many places) Don M. Wolfe, *Milton in the Puritan Revolution* (New York: Humanities Press, 1963), 240–46; Joan Bennett, *Reviving Liberty* (Cambridge: Harvard University Press, 210 n. 49); James Turner, "The Politics of Engagement," *Politics, Poetics, and Hermeneutics in Milton's Prose*, ed. David Loewenstein and James Turner (Cambridge: Cambridge University Press, 1990), 257–75; Hugh Trevor-Roper, "Milton in Politics," *Catholics, Anglicans and Puritans: Seventeenth-Century Essays* (Chicago: University of Chicago Press, 1988), 231–82; and Christopher Hill, *Milton and the English Revolution* (London: Faber and Faber, 1977), 182–221.

73. Stella Revard, *The War in Heaven: Paradise Lost and the Tradition of Satan's Rebellion* (Ithaca: Cornell University Press, 1980), 218.

74. Empson, *Milton's God*, 24

75. Lieb, "Milton's 'Dramatick Constitution': The Celestial Dialogue in Paradise Lost, Book III," 229.

76. Augustine, *On Christian Doctrine*, trans. J. F. Shaw (Chicago: Britannica, 1955), 626.

Chapter 3. "Who durst defy th' Omnipotent to Arms"

1. Revard argues cogently that Milton's Satan shares many of the traits of the Satans or Lucifers common in Renaissance literature. There is much of Vondel's Lucifer in Milton's Satan, but the relations grow strained when Milton's character is compared to the Satans of DuBartas or Tasso, for example. DuBartas's Satan is a mean and petty figure, and Tasso's Satan is a carnival grotesque. Milton's Satan,

until the temporary transformation into a serpent in book 10, retains grandeur of form and purpose that even defeat in Heaven and the fall into Hell does not entirely remove from him. In this way, Milton's Satan has more in common with Iago, Edgar, Macbeth, and even Hamlet, than he does with the devils of DuBartas and Tasso.

2. Harold Bloom, *The Western Canon* (New York: Harcourt Brace, 1994), 180.

3. John Carey, "Milton's Satan," in *The Cambridge Companion to Milton*, ed. Dennis Danielson (Cambridge: Cambridge University Press, 1989), 132.

4. Ibid., 131.

5. S. Musgrove, "Is the Devil an Ass?" *Review of English Studies* 21 (London, 1945), 302–15. The propagandistic Satan-as-Axis-Powers-General tone of this article is certainly understandable, given the World War II context in which it was written, but Empson's critique (*Milton's God*, 30–33) of Musgrove's argument remains telling nevertheless.

6. A more immediate example from Hollywood might be to watch *Star Wars* only after a good morning's hatred of Darth Vader. Imagine, if you will, recommending such a thing to a college student today.

7. The argument that *Paradise Lost* is, in fact, a religious text is frequently made. Samuel Johnson argued that the poem's "every line breathes sanctity of thought and purity of manners" and both readers of the poem and characters in the poem "are compelled to acknowledge their subjection to God in such a manner as excites reverence and confirms piety" (708). Such modern critics as Danielson argue that Milton's purpose was to present a "Good God" fit for the reverence and worship of the fit though few who might understand his message.

8. Jeffrey Burton Russell, *The Devil: Perceptions of Evil from Antiquity to Primitive Christianity* (Ithaca: Cornell University Press, 1977), 198.

9. Revard, *The War in Heaven*, 198.

10. Ibid., 220.

11. Again, I refer the reader to Empson's account of Japanese and Chinese students and their reactions to *Paradise Lost*. Empson writes that "those of my students who became interested in *Paradise Lost*, though too polite to express their opinion to me quite directly, thought 'well, if they worshipped such a monstrously wicked God as all that, no wonder that they themselves are so monstrously wicked as we have traditionally found them' " (10). Later, Empson describes the reaction of a Chinese university audience in the late 1930s to Satan's first great speech in *Paradise Lost* (1.85–124): "It was received with fierce enthusiasm. . . . The audience, you understand, really did mean to resist to the end however powerless, exactly like Satan and with the same pride in it; also, not being Christian, they would not require a separate theological argument before they could sympathize with him" (45).

12. Empson, *Milton's God*, 76.

13. Revard, *The War in Heaven*, 210–11.

14. Joost van den Vondel, *Lucifer*, trans. Leonard Charles Van Noppen (New York and London: Continental Publishing Co., 1898) 2.143–46.

15. Maurice Kelley argues for the view that "begot" is a figurative expression that simply means an exalting or raising in rank. The Father did not literally create the Son that day, in Kelley's view, but is instead "creating a new thing—a king" when he proclaims the Son ruler over the angels. See *This Great Argument: A Study*

of Milton's *"De Doctrina Christiana"* as a Gloss upon *"Paradise Lost"* (Princeton: Princeton University Press, 1941), 105.

16. Empson, *Milton's God*, 82–83.

17. Regina Schwartz, among others, has also made the link between Hamlet and Milton's Satan: "Like Hamlet, Satan could be bounded in a nutshell and count himself the king of infinite space—'the mind is its own place, and in itself / can make a Heav'n of hell' (I.254–55)—were it not that he has bad dreams—'which way I fly is Hell, myself am Hell' (IV.75)" (*Remembering and Repeating*, 96).

18. In *Milton's Epic Characters* (Chapel Hill: University of North Carolina Press, 1968), John Steadman clearly establishes a difference between "likeness" and "equality." Basing the distinction on Milton's *Art of Logic*, Steadman writes that the two categories represent "two distinct types of comparison" (160). "Likeness" implies a similar nature or kind of being, while "equality" implies true parity or even sameness of nature and being. Steadman argues that Satan's arguments pose as calls for likeness (angels are "like" God, and therefore equally free because of that likeness) when they are actually calls for equality (angels are just the same as God and therefore equally free because God is not inherently superior).

19. Fish, *Surprised by Sin*, x.

20. Shelley, *Shelley's Poetry and Prose*, 133.

21. Ibid., 133.

22. Ibid.

23. Kenneth Gross, "Satan and the Romantic Satan: a Notebook," *Re-membering Milton*, ed. Mary Nyquist and Margaret Ferguson (New York: Methuen, 1988), 324.

24. Ibid., 324. For Gross, Lewis's "loving attention to the details of Satan's self-degradation and absurdity," is evidence of a willful critical blindness that renders Lewis unable to see "the unconscious and less impersonal disgust which his arguments can release—as when he speaks (authoritatively) of Satan's systematic degradation from heroic rebel, to party politician, to intruding thief, to toad-like seducer-spy, and finally to nothing more than 'a thing that peers in at bedroom or bathroom windows.' It is Lewis' eye, and not Satan's, which has here converted the sacred Bower of Adam and Eve into a bourgeois bedroom or bathroom" (324).

25. Arnold Williams, "The Motivation of Satan's Rebellion in *Paradise Lost*," *Milton: Modern Judgments*, ed. Alan Rudrum (Nashville, Tenn.: Aurora Publishers, 1970), 136–50.

26. Ibid., 140.

27. Schwartz, *The Curse of Cain*, 54.

28. Empson, *Milton's God*, 103.

29. Though "his former name / Is heard no more in Heav'n," Satan's former name is heard three times in *Paradise Lost*, at 5.760, 7.131, and 10.425.

30. Empson, *Milton's God*, 103.

31. Steadman argues that "although Satan's argument *seems* reasonable, its conclusion is patently false, for it contradicts the Biblical conception of the angelic nature and office. As Milton points out in the *Christian Doctrine*, angels are 'ministering spirits' (Heb. 1:14) and . . . are 'ordain'd...to serve,' and in denying this fact Satan is contradicting the traditional Christian view of their true function" (*Milton's Epic Characters*, 264). Steadman's argument, thorough and precise though it is, conflates the Bible with *Paradise Lost*. Milton's Satan, not being a Christian, can hardly be expected to uphold the "traditional Christian view" of

anything. Additionally, within the timeframe of the poem itself, the Bible has not yet been written, therefore there is, as yet, no "Biblical conception of the angelic nature and office" for Satan to consult. It is less than fair to expect a literary character to have the same cultural and historical facts at his fingertips that readers of that character may have. Criticizing Milton's Satan for not taking Biblical conceptions and Christian views into account reduces the critic to undignified gloating over possessing knowledge that is deliberately withheld from a fictional character.

32. John Calvin, *Institutes of the Christian Religion*, trans. Lord Lewis Battles, ed. by John T. McNeill, vol. 2 (Philadelphia: Westminster Press, 1960), 1489.

33. Magistrates do not simply get a free ride from Calvin. There are requirements they must live up to in order to fulfill their sacred responsibilities. They should "remember that they are vicars of God, [and] they should watch with all care, earnestness, and diligence, to represent in themselves to men some image of divine providence, protection, goodness, benevolence, and justice" (1491). In other words, kings and magistrates are under obligation to stand in, in a way, for God, represent God to the people.

34. Thomas Müntzer, "Sermon Before the Princes," *Spiritual and Anabaptist Writers: Documents Illustrative of the Radical Reformation*, ed. George Huntston William, *The Library of Christian Classics*; v. 25 (Philadelphia: Westminster Press, 1957), 69. In Müntzer's formulation, the power of rulers, both superior and inferior, is the power to "wipe out the godless" through the "power of God" (68). The princes, the civil magistrates, rather than those whom Müntzer sneeringly refers to as "false clerics" (65), and "learned divines" (67), are to eliminate "the wicked who hinder the gospel" (65). If they do not do so, "the sword will be taken from them," as "the godless have no right to live except as the elect wish to grant it to them" (68, 69). Though Müntzer outlines the possibility of rebellion against a prince who fails in his duty, those empowered to overthrow such a ruler are not "private persons," but the "elect," specifically, and only, those who qualify as "true friends of God" (69). Who are the "true friends of God"? For Müntzer, they are the very princes who take seriously their duty to God's church, as opposed to those "godless rulers who should *be killed*, especially the priests and monks who revile the gospel as heresy for us and wish to be considered at the same time as the best Christians" (69 emphasis added). Those empowered to rebel, those empowered to overthrow and even kill a "godless ruler" are *other rulers*, not the people themselves.

35. Stephen Marshall, "A Letter Written by Mr. Stephen Marshall . . . of the Parliament's taking up Defensive Arms," (London, 1643), 3.

36. Ibid., 6.

37. Ibid., 17.

38. Ibid., 14. Marshall goes on to define this power as, in England, the King and Parliament together. Thus, the taking up of defensive arms by Parliament against Charles I is not an example of the kind of rebellion of private persons against a legal monarch to which Calvin is so adamantly opposed, but an example of one part of the "higher power" trying to subdue another part of that same power to its proper role and function.

39. Steadman provides an alternative explanation for Satan's use of titles as a persuasive tool: "In appealing to title and birthright as arguments for rebellion, Satan is abusing a familiar *topos* of Renaissance rhetoric . . . a favorite theme of the

humanists was nobility, and as its chief cause they would favour merit more often than birth" (*Milton's Epic Characters*, 266).

40. Calvin, *Institutes of the Christian Religion*, vol. 2, 1519. Calvin insists that absolute obedience is due not only to the benevolent ruler, but also to the tyrant. A wicked ruler can, in fact, be the judgment of God:

> We are not only subject to the authority of princes who perform their office toward us uprightly and faithfully as they ought, but also to the authority of all who, by whatever means, have got control of their affairs . . . whoever they may be, they have their authority solely from him." (1512)

Calvin does appear to open a loophole, however. Sometimes God "raises up open avengers from among his servants, and arms them with his command to punish the wicked from miserable calamity" (1517). This appears to open the door to a possibility of justified overthrow of a wicked ruler. This kind of "avenger" is "armed from heaven" and subdues "the lesser power [the unjust ruler] with the greater [the power and justice of God], just as it is lawful for kings to punish their subordinates" (1517).

41. Empson, *Milton's God*, 60.

42. Marshall, "A Letter Written by Mr. Stephen Marshall," 3.

43. Calvin tries to stuff the genie back in by saying that "unbridled despotism is the Lord's to avenge" and that we "private individuals" should not "at once think that it is entrusted to us, to whom no command has been given except to obey and suffer" (1518). Only "magistrates of the people, appointed to restrain the willfulness of kings" (1519), such as the ephors of Sparta, the tribunes of Rome, and the demarchs of Athens, are to take up this call from God to subdue the lesser power with the greater. Calvin is less successful, however, than is Satan at holding back the forces he has helped unleash. The notion of resistance by divine mandate, once loosed upon the world, gains tremendous currency in the later sixteenth and throughout the seventeenth and eighteenth centuries. Many claim, as did the Puritan preachers and pamphleteers of the mid-seventeenth century in England (among them one John Milton, whose *Tenure of Kings and Magistrates* takes Calvin's argument and runs with it to justify the deposition and execution of tyrants), that they have (or that they represent a group that has) just such a mandate from God.

44. Calvin, *Institutes of the Christian Religion*, vol. 2, 1489.

Chapter 4. "That far be from thee"

1. Gary D. Hamilton, who grounds Milton's portrayal of God in the Arminian–Calvinist controversies of the seventeenth century, argues that "Milton reflects in God's defense of himself [in Book 3 of *Paradise Lost*] the restlessness of an age that had come to have doubts about the goodness of its Calvinist God. In Book III God is defending himself against Calvinism . . . " See "Milton's Defensive God: A Reappraisal," *Studies in Philology* 69, no. 1 (1972), 89.

2. Alexander Pope, "First Epistle of the Second Book of Horace," Poems, ed. John Everett Butt (New Haven: Yale University Press, 1963), 850, line 102.

3. William Blake, *The Complete Poetry and Prose of William Blake*, ed. David V. Erdman (Garden City, N.Y.: Anchor Books, 1988), 96.

4. "Defence of Poetry," *Shelley's Poetry and Prose*, 498.

5. G. K. Knight, *Chariot of Wrath*, 44.

6. Hill, *Milton and the English Revolution*, 364.

7. Ibid.

8. Ibid.

9. Draco's seventh-century B.C.E. law code was an attempt at a transition from a kind of "frontier" justice in which Athenian families settled accounts by violence against those with whom they were at odds. To enforce his laws, and to gain acceptance for them as surer remedies than were already provided under the existing ad hoc system, Draco instituted severe punishments, usually death, for even the most minor infractions.

10. *Meister Eckhart: A Modern Translation*, trans. Raymond B. Blakney (New York and London: Harper & Brothers, 1941), 204.

11. Danielson, *Milton's Good God*, ix.

12. Regina Schwartz has argued in *The Curse of Cain* that characterizations in biblical narratives are not synonymous with the divine. Schwartz critiques those who serve political agendas by willfully confusing the divine with representations (see especially the introduction on this point). This distinction is made with added force in her "Questioning Narratives of God: The Immeasurable in Measures," in *Questioning God*, ed. John Caputo, Mark Dooley, and Michael Scanlon (Bloomington: Indiana University Press, 2001).

13. Danielson, *Milton's Good God*, ix.

14. Regina Schwartz has previously discussed the relationship between evil and creation in Genesis and *Paradise Lost* in the first chapter of her work *Remembering and Repeating: On Milton's Theology and Poetics*.

15. Lieb, "Milton and the Anthropathetic Tradition," 225.

16. Ibid., 229.

17. Christopher Ricks, ed. *Paradise Lost and Paradise Regained*. (New York: New American Library, 1989), 47.

18. Richard Baxter, "Aphorismes of Justification: with their explication annexed: wherein also is opened the nature of the covenants, satisfaction, righteousnesse, faith, works, &c." (London, 1649), 135.

19. Ibid.

20. In *The Alternative Trinity: Gnostic Heresy in Marlowe, Milton, and Blake* (Oxford and New York: Clarendon Press; Oxford: Oxford University Press, 1998), A. D. Nuttall writes at some length about Milton's theodicy in *Paradise Lost*. He refers to the "turning inside-out of 'justify' " (90) in Milton's great epic, and also argues that the justifying of God in the poem is Milton's attempt to defend God against a Calvinist notion of predestination that cast God in the position of the author of evil. Nuttall's analysis supports my own to the extent that our arguments share a concern with Milton's attempt to defend God; however, I would like to take my argument a bit further, insisting that the implication of "justifying" God is a two-edged sword: as justification is at once an accusation and an acquittal, so Milton's justifying of God is an accusation of wickedness and a poetic acquittal from the same. This standing in judgment of God is the real "audacity of Milton justifying God" (105).

21. Milton, in his invocation to Book 1 of *Paradise Lost*, reinterprets the fundamental tenet of the Reformers' doctrines of justification and grace. Calvin vehemently disallows the possibility that there could be any such thing as an "upright heart and pure" (*Paradise Lost* 1.18), arguing that fallen man is incapable of possessing an upright or pure heart: "In order that we may rightly examine ourselves, our consciences must necessarily be called before God's judgment seat. For there is need to strip entirely bare in its light the secret places of our depravity, which otherwise are too deeply hidden" (*Institutes of the Christian Religion* 1:759). Rather than bringing before God a pure and upright heart, Calvin insists that fallen man brings before God the "secret places of [his] depravity." Milton suggests that an "upright heart and pure" is a real possibility; such a heart can legitimately be the Spirit's "Temple," and the possessor of such a "Temple" can legitimately attempt to "justify the ways of God to men."

22. Alister E. McGrath, *Iustitia Dei: A History of the Christian Doctrine of Justification* (Cambridge: Cambridge University Press, 1986), vol. 1, 6.

23. Ibid., vol.1, 12.

24. Ibid., vol. 1, 13.

25. Ibid., vol. 1, 15.

26. Ibid., vol. 2, 13.

27. In *Love Known: Theology and Experience in George Herbert's Poetry* (Chicago: University of Chicago Press, 1983), Richard Strier argues that the "'aim and mark of the whole discourse'" of Herbert's "Sepulchre" is "the contrast between God's treatment of man and man's treatment of God" (17). Here, Strier has neatly expressed a dynamic that the theologically and biblically informed poetry of Herbert and Milton share. However, Strier has also deftly delineated a crucial difference between the two poets, a difference that illustrates just how radical is Milton's appropriation of the justification doctrine. Strier argues that an examination of "Sion" allows us to "distinguish Herbert's from Milton's sense of what it means for God to choose the heart as His special dwelling, for in Herbert we shall see that God does not choose the heart 'before all Temples' because it is 'upright' or 'pure'" (179).

28. Justification was one of the raging theological issues in England before, during, and after the time Milton was composing *Paradise Lost*. Richard Baxter's 1649 publication of *Aphorismes of Justification* set off a firestorm among English Protestant divines that would continue until 1658, only to be revived again in the early 1670s. Baxter's opinion that justification resulted from the faith of the individual Christian was in direct opposition to the opinions of John Owen, John Eedes, William Eyre, and John Crandon, all of whom argued that the faith of the individual Christian was a *result*, not a *cause* of the imputation of righteousness involved in justification. Though Baxter did receive some support from such writers as John Goodwin and George Walker, he was largely alone in defending the idea that faith was instrumental (an instrument or cause) in the justification of believers.

Milton's own opinions on this issue are closer to Baxter's than they are to the majority of English protestant divines. See John Crandon, *Mr. Baxters Aphorisms Exorized and Anthorixed* (London, 1654); John Eedes, *The Orthodox Doctrine concerning Justification* (London, 1642); William Eyre, *Vindiciae Iustificationis Gratuitae* (London, 1654); John Owen, *Of the Death of Christ* (London, 1650). In *De Doctrina Chris-*

tiana, Milton outlines a threefold process of the reconciliation of mankind to God. The first step is regeneration: "the old man is destroyed and . . . the inner man is regenerated by God through the word and the spirit so that his whole mind is restored to the image of God, as if he were a new creature" (*CPW* 6:461). Following regeneration is ingrafting in Christ—"the process by which God the Father plants believers in Christ by God the Father. That is to say, he makes them sharers in Christ, and renders them fit to join, eventually, in one body with Christ" (*CPW* 6:477). Finally, after regeneration and ingrafting comes justification—a "relative or external" measure that follows the "absolute or internal" effects of regeneration and ingrafting; in justification, "we receive [Christ's] righteousness, imputed to us, as a gift" (*CPW* 6:486).

It is when Milton comes to the issue of the role of faith in justification that his proximity to Baxter becomes clear. After following his usual method of copious citation and quotation of relevant scriptures, Milton writes "In all these passages the Bible tells us that we are justified by faith and through faith and of faith. But whether we are justified through faith as an instrument, which is the orthodox view, or in some other way, the Bible does not specify" (*CPW* 6:489). What Milton cites as "the orthodox view"—faith as a cause or an instrument of justification—is not the common doctrine at all; rather, it is closer to the position defended by Baxter against by far the majority of English protestant divines in the 1650s. Milton further argues that "[if] faith is an action, or rather a habit acquired by frequent actions, not merely infused [then it] is by that we are justified." However, if "faith were not acquired but infused, we should be less reluctant to admit that it is *the cause of justification*" (*CPW* 6:489, emphasis added).

29. Fish, *Surprised By Sin*, lxxi.

30. Hamilton argues that the Son's speech "should not be labeled 'suasive, as if he has to work on God to prevent him from changing his mind and delivering a sterner sentence," and further contends, "The Father's future course of action has already been firmly declared, and the Son now seeks to spell out the significance of this declaration in the context of other less praiseworthy alternatives." See "Milton's Defensive God: A Reappraisal," *Studies in Philology* 69, no. 1 (1972), 95–96.

31. Irene Samuel has forcefully contended that the Son is arguing with the Father in this scene: "the Son *argues* . . . In Milton's Heaven the independent being speaks his own mind, not what he thinks another would like to hear." See "The Dialogue in Heaven: A Reconsideration of Paradise Lost, III.1–417, "*Publications of the Modern Language Association of America* 72, no. 4, part 1 (September 1957), 604.

32. While stopping short of arguing for a lying Father, Irene Samuel does argue that the Father changes his point of view after the Son's speech: "he immediately sanctions and adopts the view presented by the Son, incorporating it into his new statement and modifying the first" ("The Dialogue in Heaven," 606).

33. Russell, *The Devil*, 198.

34. Empson, *Milton's God*, 74.

35. Irene Samuel refers to the Father as "the monarch Satan thought to emulate" ("The Dialogue in Heaven," 606). The issue facing the Son (and the rest of Heaven and Earth) in this scene is to what extent (if any) Satan's emulation is in error.

36. Lieb, "Milton's 'Dramatick Constitution,'" 229.

37. Ibid.

38. Empson, *Milton's God*, 130.
39. Norbrook, *Writing the English Republic*, 475.
40. Danielson, *Milton's God*, 144.
41. Revard, *The War in Heaven*, 218.
42. "On the New Forcers of Conscience under the Long Parliament," line 6.
43. Ibid., line 20.
44. Fish makes much of this passage in *Surprised by Sin*, arguing that in it "Milton emphasizes the 'selfness' of Satan's concern" (339). I agree; however, the Father's speech in 3.167–73 reveals at least as much (if not more) "selfness" of concern.
45. Empson, *Milton's God*, 208.
46. Fish, *Surprised By Sin*, 62.
47. Ibid., 62.
48. Calvin, *Institutes of the Christian Religion*, vol. 1, 505.
49. Ibid., vol. 1, 509.
50. Hell is described as "A Universe of death, which God by curse / Created evil, for evil only good" (*Paradise Lost* 2.622–23).
51. At 10.629–31, the Father refers to Sin and Death as "My Hell-hounds," and states that he "call'd and drew them thither / . . . to lick up the draft and filth / Which man's polluting Sin with taint hath shed." Satan's attempts at revenge are allowed so that his efforts "shall redound / Upon his own rebellious head" (3.85–86). Even the narrator gets in on this act, claiming that Satan was only able to raise himself from of the burning floor of Hell "by the sufferance of supernal Power" (1.241).

Chapter 5. "Tempt not the Lord thy God"

1. George Huntston Williams, *The Radical Reformation* (Philadelphia: Westminster Press, 1962), 258.
2. Ibid., 335.
3. Ibid., 483.
4. Ibid., 599.
5. Alexander Parker, "A testimony of the Light within. . . ." (London: Printed for Giles Calvert at the Black spread-Eagle at the west end of Pauls, 1657).
6. George Fox, "To all that would know the way to the kingdome," (London: Printed for Robert Wilson, 1654), title page.
7. Ibid., 2.
8. Lydia Fairman, "A few lines given forth and a true testimony of the way which is Christ . . . " (London: Printed for Thomas Simmons, 1659).
9. David Loewenstein, "The Kingdom Within: Radical Religious Culture and the Politics of Paradise Regained," *Literature and History* 3:2 (Autumn 1994): 64.
10. Ibid., 63.
11. Ibid., 64.
12. Ibid., 74.
13. Ibid., 72.
14. Hill, *The World Turned Upside Down*, 251.
15. Ibid., 252.

16. Nayler recanted his radical identification of himself with Christ after "M.P.s spent six weeks denouncing Nayler with hysterical frenzy; many demanded sentence of death and Nayler was ultimately flogged and branded with a brutality from which he never recovered" (Hill, *The World Turned Upside Down*, 249).

17. Hill, *Milton and the English Revolution*, 416.

18. Rama Sarma's book is entitled *The Heroic Argument: A Study of Milton's Heroic Poetry* (Madras: Macmillan, 1971).

19. John Shawcross, *Paradise Regain'd: Worthy T'Have Not Remain'd So Long Unsung*. (Pittsburgh: Duquesne Univesity Press, 1988), 1.

20. John Rumrich observes that "Milton's cosmos begins with 'one first matter all' and ends when 'God shall be All in All' . . . The Son's material being may originally be more refined and exalted than that of other creatures, but eventually parakeets and pachyderms would also qualify as participants in the Godhead." "Milton's Arianism: Why it Matters," *Milton and Heresy*, eds. Stephen B. Dobranski and John P. Rumrich (Cambridge: Cambridge University Press, 1998), 83.

21. The notion of an essential unity between humanity and divinity, between worshipper and worshipped, is comparatively rare in the Christian tradition, but it is well-represented in Western philosophy. Epictetus, the so-called "slave philosopher," represents this unitary view particularly eloquently:

> "You are a superior thing; you are a portion separated from the deity; you have in yourself a certain portion of him. Why then are you ignorant of your own noble descent? Why do you not know whence you came? Will you not remember when you are eating, who you are who eat and whom you feed? When you are in conjunction with a woman, will you not remember who you are who do this thing? When you are in social intercourse, when you are exercising yourself, when you are engaged in discussion, know you not that you are nourishing a god, that you are exercising a god? (*Discourses*, trans. George Long [Chicago: Britannica, 1955], 146).

22. I agree with David Loewenstein that this emphasis on an inward oracle, or an inner light, brings Milton very near to the early Quaker tradition. In this tradition, as Christopher Hill puts it, "Christ within every man" (*The World Turned Upside Down*, 252) was the driving force in the lives of believers, and religious hierarchies of the kind that George Fox eventually imposed were considered "an infringement upon individual liberty that . . . denied the continuing presence of Christ within *all* believers" (255).

23. Stanley Fish has argued that Satan promotes a false hierarchy of values throughout *Paradise Regained*: "In each of the plots that Satan constructs, one or more of these things has been put forward as the highest possible value; and therefore to resist the appeal to act in its name is to resist the temptation to substitute that value for the value of obedience to God." See "Things and Actions Indifferent: The Temptation of Plot in *Paradise Regained*," in *Milton Studies* XVII, ed. Richard S. Ide and Joseph Wittreich (Pittsburgh: University of Pittsburgh Press, 1983), 167.

24. Empson, *Milton's God*, 103.

25. Donald Swanson and John Mulryan, "The Son's Presumed Contempt for Learning in *Paradise Regained*: A Biblical and Patristic Resolution," in *Milton Studies* XXVII, ed. James D. Simmonds (Pittsburgh: University of Pittsburgh Press, 1991), 250.

26. As Barbara Lewalski has pointed out in *Milton's Brief Epic: The Genre, Meaning, and Art of Paradise Regained* (Providence: Brown University Press, 1966), 135–38, there has long been controversy over the nature—human or divine—of the Son in *Paradise Regained*. Among those who argue that the Son is divine, Allan Gilbert, in his 1916 article "The Temptation in *Paradise Regained*" (JEGP, XV, 606), maintains that the Son was taught directly by God, and therefore had no need for ordinary human education. Douglas Bush refers to the Son as a "sinless divine protagonist" (*English Literature in the Earlier Seventeenth Century, 1600–1660* [Oxford: Clarendon Press, 1962], 412). Elizabeth Pope, in *Paradise Regained: The Tradition and the Poem* (Baltimore: Johns Hopkins University Press, 1947), argues that Milton himself viewed the Son as not a man but a divine being: "Milton was working under the influence of the tradition that Christ deliberately withheld from Satan all evidence of his own identity" (39). On the side of those who see the Son as human are such scholars as M. M. Mahood, who describes the Son as a "perfect man, as yet scarcely aware of His divine progeniture" (Lewalski 137), Northrop Frye, who argues that the Son "withstands the temptations as a human being until the tower temptation, at which time the omnipotent divine power 'takes over' the human will" (Lewalski 137), and A. S. P. Wodehouse, who maintains that the Son "actually progresses from human beginnings to a full realization of his divinity in the tower scene" (Lewalski 137).

27. Speculation about whether Milton believed in the divinity of Christ is not necessarily fully relevant to a consideration of the "divinity" of the Son in *Paradise Regained*. Critics seems to conflate the two figures, often referring to the Son as Christ, when he is nowhere referred to as such in Milton's poem. Elizabeth Pope, for example worries over the fact that Milton's "preoccupation with the lower aspect of Christ's dual nature may well raise the question of whether, by the time Milton wrote *Paradise Regained*, Milton still believed in the Lord's divinity at all" (*Paradise Regained: The Tradition and the Poem*, 22).

28. To continually refer to the Son as Christ is to run the risk of emphasizing personal religious faith at the expense of what Milton wrote. One notable example of this trend is Barbara Lewalski, who refers to the Son of *Paradise Regained* as Christ throughout her book *Milton's Brief Epic*. In a discussion of the introduction to *Paradise Regained*, Lewalski writes of "Christ's action of overcoming the satanic temptations in the wilderness," and suggests that "Christ comes to understand himself," and that the "temptation process itself serves as a stimulus to Christ's growth toward complete understanding" (133).

29. Socinians were a sixteenth- and seventeenth-century group who believed that Jesus was divine only in his office or his function, but not in his nature. For the Socinians, Jesus was a man, no more, and no less, and the fact of his humanity made Jesus' mission and accomplishments all the more efficacious as a divinely inspired example for humankind.

30. Stanley Fish has written that "the impulse behind Milton's art [is] to lose the self in a union with God." See "Inaction and Silence," in *Calm of Mind: Tercentenary Essays on Paradise Lost and Samson Agonistes*, ed. Joseph Anthony Wittreich (Cleveland: Press of Case Western Reserve University, 1971), 27. Though Fish has in mind something rather more traditional—a giving over of a separate self to God—I think his formulation is apt. To lose the self in a union with God is, for Milton, to lose the Satanic sense of separation from God and to realize that one is always already part of the divine.

31. This is what Milton refers to as "the Spirit, which is internal, and the individual possession of each man" (*De Doctrina Christiana, CPW* 6:587).

32. John Shawcross disagrees with the idea that the Son is an exemplar: "The Son in *Paradise Regain'd* has, it seems, always been viewed as an exemplar, whom Milton is urging his faithful, God-loving reader to emulate. I think that is wrong" (*Paradise Regain'd: Worthy t'have Not Remain'd so Long Unsung*, 82). Shawcross goes on to suggest that the Son is "never offered as an example," and that the "Son is not example: he is above example" (82). In using the word exemplar, I mean to suggest not so much someone who is to be *imitated* as someone who is quite literally to be *followed*. The Son points the way to salvation by following the way. It is up to each man and woman to follow the same path the Son took. As Shawcross puts it, "humankind must internalize the heroism of the Son" (8), and follow on its own the path the Son took. In this sense, humankind must not *imitate* the Son, but *become* the Son.

33. Peggy Samuels has argued that "Milton's Son of God seems to be constructing a space of 'radical interiority' within which he cultivates a private relationship with God." See "Labor in the Chambers: *Paradise Regained* and the Discourse of Quiet," in *Milton Studies* XXXVI, ed. Albert C. Labriola (Pittsburgh: University of Pittsburgh Press, 1998), 154.

34. "Be famous then / By wisdom" (4.221–22) is what Satan, exasperated, is finally reduced to appealing.

35. Loewenstein, "The Kingdom Within," 73.

36. Jeffrey B. Morris describes the shift from Satan to the Father in *Paradise Regained* as "subtle and abrupt," and as part of a narrative technique that leaves readers with a "sensation . . . of disruption." See "Disorientation and Disruption in *Paradise Regained*," in *Milton Studies* XXVI, ed. James D. Simmonds (Pittsburgh: University of Pittsburgh Press, 1990), 219, 222. I agree that the shift is subtle, but I argue that it is intended to highlight similarities between Satan and the Father.

37. David Loewenstein has argued for a connection between the Jesus of *Paradise Regained* and Job, referring to Job as a model whom "Milton's Jesus surpasses" ("The Kingdom Within," 65).

38. Shawcross, *Paradise Regain'd*, 76.

39. Eckhart, *Meister Eckhart: A Modern Translation*, 205.

40. Williams, *The Radical Reformation*, 258.

41. All of Satan's blandishments are, as Stanley Fish has observed, "allied in their inferiority to an inner word and an inward kingdom" ("Inaction and Silence," 41).

42. This argument has been made many times before. For example, Douglas Bush has written that "It is only in comparison with the divine light of humble Christian faith and virtue that Greek philosophy . . . appears as the product and instrument of arrogant human pride . . . [The Son's] condemnation is relative rather than absolute." *English Literature in the Earlier Seventeenth Century 1600–1660*, 398. In an interesting twist on the issue of the Son's seeming contempt for classical learning, Donald Swanson and John Mulryan argue that the Son's "rejection" of learning is a sham designed to deceive Satan, writing of "Jesus' deliberate distortion of his (and hence Milton's) perspective on Greco-Roman thought" ("The Son's Presumed Contempt for Learning," 248).

43. Shawcross, *Paradise Regain'd*, 113.

44. John Shawcross, for example, believes that the Son "knows he is the Son of God, despite the unintelligible readings of some critics who have tried to hinge the poem on that question" (*Paradise Regain'd*, 39). Christopher Hill, on the other hand, takes the view that it is not until "the miracle of the pinnacle [that] Jesus arrives at full understanding of his own nature" (*Milton and the English Revolution*, 422).

45. The question of Milton's "Arianism" has been taken up recently by John P. Rumrich in *Milton and Heresy*. Rumrich refutes the arguments of Patrides and Hunter (from the volume *Bright Essence*) and concludes that "Early readers recognized Arianism in *Paradise Lost* and, once *de doctrina Christiana* was discovered and published, various Milton scholars, Maurice Kelley most notably, recognized the consistency of its heretical theology with Milton's poetic fiction" (89). Rumrich asks a cogent question: "Is Milton scholarship so committed to the orthodoxy of *Paradise Lost* that it will continue in its refusal to acknowledge Milton's Arianism, even if it means denying the evident provenance of his theology?" (89).

To call Milton an "Arian" is not to imply, however, that Milton lines up with the fourth-century presbyter on every theological point. Milton, in fact, differs from Arius over several important points. Arius, for example, insists that the Son (as well as the rest of creation) was formed ex nihilo (out of nothing), while Milton, in *De Doctrina Christiana*, asserts that the Son was formed ex Deo (out of the divine nature). This difference alone, though it might seem minor at first glance, is already a serious compromising of Arius' absolutely uncompromising monotheism.

46. Lowenstein characterizes this move as "among the more provocative sociopolitical aspects of Milton's Puritan epic" ("The Kingdom Within," 70).

47. Changing the terms of true government from external to internal makes for a radical challenge to Calvin's notion that private citizens were to have no voice in governmental affairs: "private citizens . . . may not deliberately intrude in public affairs . . . or undertake anything at all politically. If anything in a public ordinance requires amendment . . . let them commit the matter to the judgment of the magistrate, whose hand alone here is free" (*Institutes*, vol. 2, 1511).

Works Cited

Achinstein, Sharon. *Milton and the Revolutionary Reader, Literature in History.* Princeton: Princeton University Press, 1994.
Addison, Joseph, and Richard Steele. *The Spectator.* Edited by Donald Frederic Bond. 5 vols. Oxford: Clarendon Press, 1965.
Aquinas, Thomas. *Summa Theologica.* Translated by Daniel J. Sullivan. Edited by Robert Maynard Hutchins. 2 vols. Vol. 19–20, *Great Books of the Western World.* Chicago: Britannica, 1955.
Aristotle. *Politics.* Translated by Benjamin Jowett. Edited by Robert Maynard Hutchins. 2 vols. Vol. 8–9, *Great Books of the Western World.* Chicago: Britannica, 1955.
Augustine. *On Christian Doctrine.* Translated by J. F. Shaw. Edited by Robert Maynard Hutchins. Vol. 18, *Great Books of the Western World.* Chicago: Britannica, 1955.
Baxter, Richard. *Aphorisms of Justification, with Their Explication Annexed . . .* London: Printed for Francis Tyton, 1649.
Bennett, Joan S. *Reviving Liberty: Radical Christian Humanism in Milton's Great Poems.* Cambridge: Harvard University Press, 1989.
Blake, William, David V. Erdman, and Harold Bloom. *The Complete Poetry and Prose of William Blake.* Garden City, N.Y.: Anchor Books, 1982.
Bloom, Harold. *The Western Canon: The Books and School of the Ages.* New York: Harcourt Brace, 1994.
Bush, Douglas. *English Literature in the Earlier Seventeenth Century, 1600–1660.* 2d, revised ed., *Oxford History of English Literature,* 5. Oxford: Clarendon Press, 1962.
Calvin, John. *Institutes of the Christian Religion.* Translated by Ford Lewis Battles. Edited by John T. McNeill. 2 vols. Philadelphia: Westminster Press, 1960.
Campbell, Gordon. "Popular Traditions of God in the Renaissance." In *Reconsidering the Renaissance: Papers from the Twenty-First Annual Conference,* edited by Mario A. DiCesare. Binghamton, N.Y.: Medieval and Renaissance Texts and Studies, 1992, 501–20.
Danielson, Dennis Richard. *Milton's Good God: A Study in Literary Theodicy.* Cambridge and New York: Cambridge University Press, 1982.
Davies, Stevie. *Images of Kingship in Paradise Lost: Milton's Politics and Christian Liberty.* Columbia: University of Missouri Press, 1983.

Diekhoff, John Siemon. *Milton's Paradise Lost: A Commentary*. New York: Humanities Press, 1946. Reprint, 1963.

Dobranski, Stephen B., and John Peter Rumrich. *Milton and Heresy*. Cambridge and New York: Cambridge University Press, 1998.

Dryden, John. *Essays*. Edited by W. P. Ker. New York: Russell & Russell, 1961.

Du Bartas, Guillaume de Salluste. *Du Bartas: His Devine Weekes and Works, 1605*. Translated by Josuah Sylvester. Edited by Francis C. Haber. Gainesville, Fla.: Scholars' Facsimiles & Reprints, 1965.

Eckhart, Meister. *Meister Eckhart: A Modern Translation*. Edited by Raymond Bernard Blakney. New York and London: Harper & Brothers, 1941.

Empson, William. *Milton's God*. London: Chatto & Windus, 1961.

Epictetus. *Discourses*. Translated by George Long. Edited by Robert Maynard Hutchins. Vol. 12, *Great Books of the Western World*. Chicago: Britannica, 1955.

Fairman, Lydia. *A Few Lines Given Forth and a True Testimony of the Way Which Is Christ . . .* London: Printed for Thomas Simmons, 1659.

Fallon, Robert Thomas. *Milton in Government*. University Park, PA: Pennsylvania State University Press, 1993.

———. *Divided Empire: Milton's Political Imagery*. University Park: Pennsylvania State University Press, 1995.

Fish, Stanley. "Inaction and Silence." In *Calm of Mind: Tercentenary Essays on Paradise Regained and Samson Agonistes in Honor of John S. Diekhoff*, edited by Joseph Anthony Wittreich. Cleveland, OH: Press of Case Western Reserve University, 1971, 25–47.

———. "Things and Actions Indifferent: The Temptation of Plot in *Paradise Regained*." In *Milton Studies*, edited by Richard S. Ide and Joseph Wittreich. Pittsburgh: University of Pittsburgh Press, 1983, 17:163–85.

———. *Surprised by Sin: The Reader in Paradise Lost*. 2d ed. Basingstoke, Hampshire: Macmillan, 1997.

Fox, George. *To All That Would Know the Way to the Kingdome . . .* The fourth edition corrected and amended. London: Printed for Robert Wilson, 1660.

Gross, Kenneth. "Satan and the Romantic Satan: A Notebook." In *Re-Membering Milton: Essays on the Texts and Traditions*, edited by Mary Nyquist and Margaret W. Ferguson. New York, London: Methuen, 1987, 318–41.

Hall, Joseph, and Philip Wynter. *The Works of the Right Reverend Joseph Hall*. Oxford: Oxford University Press, 1863.

Halpern, Baruch. *The Constitution of the Monarchy in Israel*. Chico, CA: Scholars Press, 1981.

Hamilton, Gary. "Milton's Defensive God: A Reappraisal." *Studies in Philology* 69, no. 1 (1972): 87–100.

Hanford, James Holly. *A Milton Handbook*. 4th ed. New York: Appleton-Century-Crofts, 1954.

Herodotus. *The History of Herodotus*. Translated by George Rawlinson. Edited by Robert Maynard Hutchins. Vol. 6, *Great Books of the Western World*. Chicago: Britannica, 1955.

Hill, Christopher. *Puritanism and Revolution*. London: Secker & Warburg, 1969.

———. *The World Turned Upside Down: Radical Ideas During the English Revolution*. New York: Viking Press, 1972.

———. *Milton and the English Revolution*. London: Faber and Faber, 1977.

———. *The English Bible and the Seventeenth-Century Revolution*. New York: Penguin, 1993.

Hunter, William B. *Visitation Unimplor'd: Milton and the Authorship of De Doctrina Christiana*. Pittsburgh, PA: Duquesne University Press, 1998.

Johnson, Samuel. *Samuel Johnson*. Edited by Donald Johnson Greene. *The Oxford Authors*. Oxford and New York: Oxford University Press, 1984.

Jonas, Hans. *The Gnostic Religion: The Message of the Alien God and the Beginnings of Christianity*. 2d, revised ed. Boston: Beacon Press, 1963. Reprint, 1991.

Kelley, Maurice. *This Great Argument: A Study of Milton's De Doctrina Christiana as a Gloss Upon Paradise Lost*. Princeton: Princeton University Press, 1941.

Kendrick, Christopher. *Milton: A Study in Ideology and Form*. New York: Methuen, 1986.

Knight, George Wilson. *Chariot of Wrath: The Message of John Milton to Democracy at War*. London: Faber and Faber, 1942.

Labriola, Albert C. "'All in All' and 'All in One': Obedience and Disobedience in *Paradise Lost*." In *All in All: Unity, Diversity, and the Miltonic Perspective*, edited by Charles W. Durham and Kristin A. Pruitt. Selinsgrove [Pa.] and London: Susquehanna University Press, 1999, 39–47.

Lewalski, Barbara Kiefer. *Milton's Brief Epic: The Genre, Meaning, and Art of Paradise Regained*. Providence: Brown University Press, 1966.

Lewis, C. S. *A Preface to Paradise Lost*. London, New York: Oxford University Press, 1942.

Lieb, Michael. "Milton's 'Dramatick Constitution': The Celestial Dialogue in *Paradise Lost*, Book Iii." In *Milton Studies*, edited by Albert C. Labriola. Pittsburgh: University of Pittsburgh Press, 1987, 23:215–40.

———. "Reading God: Milton and the Anthropopathetic Tradition." In *Milton Studies*, edited by Albert C. Labriola. Pittsburgh: University of Pittsburgh Press, 1989, 25:213–43.

Loewenstein, David. "The Kingdom Within: Radical Religious Culture and the Politics of *Paradise Regained*." *Literature & History* (Autumn 1994): 63–89.

Marshall, Stephen. *A Copy of a Letter Written by Mr. Stephen Marshall . . . In Which . . . The Lawfulnesse of the Parliaments Taking up Defensive Arms Is Briefly and Learnedly Asserted and Demonstrated . . .* London: Printed for John Rothwell, 1643.

Masson, David. *The Life of John Milton*. 7 vols. London: Macmillan and Co., 1871.

———. *The Poetical Works of John Milton*. 3 vols. London: Macmillan, 1882.

McGrath, Alister E. *Iustitia Dei: A History of the Christian Doctrine of Justification*. 2 vols. Cambridge and New York: Cambridge University Press, 1986.

Milton, John. "The Reason of Church Government." In *Complete Prose Works of John Milton*, edited by Don M. Wolfe. 10 vols. New Haven: Yale University Press, 1953, 1:745–861.

———. *Paradise Lost*. Edited by Merritt Yerkes Hughes, *Complete Poems and Major Prose*. New York: Odyssey Press, 1957.

———. *Paradise Regained*. Edited by Merritt Yerkes Hughes, *Complete Poems and Major Prose*. New York: Odyssey Press, 1957.

———. "Areopagitica." In *Complete Prose Works of John Milton*, edited by Ernest Sirluck. 10 vols. New Haven: Yale University Press, 1959, 2:485–570.

———. "Of Education." In *Complete Prose Works of John Milton*, edited by Ernest Sirluck. 10 vols. New Haven: Yale University Press, 1959, 2:361–415.

———. "Eikonoklastes." In *Complete Prose Works of John Milton*, edited by Merritt Y. Hughes. 10 vols. New Haven: Yale University Press, 1962, 3:337–601.

———. "Tenure of Kings and Magistrates." In *Complete Prose Works of John Milton*, edited by Ernest Sirluck. 10 vols. New Haven: Yale University Press, 1962, 3:189–258.

———. "A Defence of the People of England." In *Complete Prose Works of John Milton*, edited by Don M. Wolfe. 10 vols. New Haven: Yale University Press, 1966, 4:298–537.

———. "Christian Doctrine." In *Complete Prose Works of John Milton*, edited by Maurice Kelley. 10 vols. New Haven: Yale University Press, 1973, 6.

———. "The Ready and Easy Way to Establish a Free Commonwealth." In *Complete Prose Works of John Milton*, edited by Robert W. Ayers. 10 vols. New Haven: Yale University Press, 1980, 7:396–463.

———. "Treatise of Civil Power." In *Complete Prose Works of John Milton*, edited by Robert W. Ayers. 10 vols. New Haven: Yale University Press, 1980, 7:238–72.

———. "A Defence of the People of England." In *John Milton: Political Writings*, edited by Martin Dzelzainis. Cambridge: Cambridge University Press, 1980.

———. "Of True Religion." In *Complete Prose Works of John Milton*, edited by Maurice Kelley. 10 vols. New Haven: Yale University Press, 1982, 8:416–40.

Morris, Jeffrey B. "Disorientation and Disruption in Paradise Regained." In *Milton Studies*, edited by James D. Simmonds. Pittsburgh: University of Pittsburgh Press, 1991, 26:219–38.

Müntzer, Thomas. "Sermon before the Princes." In *Spiritual and Anabaptist Writers: Documents Illustrative of the Radical Reformation*, edited by George Huntston Williams. Philadelphia: Westminster Press, 1957, 25.

Musgrove, S. "Is the Devil an Ass?" In *The Review of English Studies*. London: Clarendon Press, 1945, 21:302–15.

Newton, Thomas, ed. *Paradise Lost*. (Birmingham: Printed by J. Baskerville for J. and R. Tonson in London, 1759).

Norbrook, David. *Writing the English Republic: Poetry, Rhetoric, and Politics, 1627–1660*. Cambridge and New York: Cambridge University Press, 1999.

Nuttall, A. D. *The Alternative Trinity: Gnostic Heresy in Marlowe, Milton, and Blake*. Oxford, New York: Clarendon Press; Oxford University Press, 1998.

Nyquist, Mary and Margaret Ferguson, eds. *Re-Membering Milton: Essays on the Texts and Traditions*. New York, London: Methuen, 1987.

Parker, Alexander. *A Testimony of the Light Within . . .* London: Printed for Giles Calvert at the Black spread-Eagle at the west end of Pauls, 1657.

Parker, William Riley, and Gordon Campbell. *Milton: A Biography*. 2nd ed. 2 vols. Oxford and New York: Clarendon Press; Oxford University Press, 1996.

Plato. *The Republic*. Translated by Benjamin Jowett. Edited by Robert Maynard Hutchins. Vol. 7, *Great Books of the Western World*. Chicago: Britannica, 1955.

Pope, Alexander. "First Epistle of the Second Book of Horace Imitated." In *Poems*, edited by John Everett Butt. New Haven: Yale University Press, 1963, xxix, 850.

Pope, Elizabeth Marie. *Paradise Regained: The Tradition and the Poem*. Baltimore: Johns Hopkins University Press, 1947.

Revard, Stella Purce. *The War in Heaven: Paradise Lost and the Tradition of Satan's Rebellion*. Ithaca: Cornell University Press, 1980.

Ricks, Christopher B. *Paradise Lost and Paradise Regained*. New York: New American Library, 1989.

Riggs, William. *The Christian Poet in Paradise Lost*. Berkeley: University of California Press, 1972.

Rumrich, John Peter. *Milton Unbound: Controversy and Reinterpretation*. Cambridge and New York: Cambridge University Press, 1996.

Russell, Jeffrey Burton. *The Devil: Perceptions of Evil from Antiquity to Primitive Christianity*. Ithaca: Cornell University Press, 1977.

Samuel, Irene. "The Dialogue in Heaven: A Reconsideration of Paradise Lost, III.1–417." *Publications of the Modern Language Association of America* 72, no. 4, part 1 (1957): 601–11.

Samuels, Peggy. "Labor in the Chambers: Paradise Regained and the Discourse of Quiet." In *Milton Studies*, edited by Albert C. Labriola. Pittsburgh, PA: University of Pittsburgh Press, 1998, 36:153–76.

Saurat, Denis. *Milton, Man and Thinker*. New York: L. Macveagh The Dial Press, 1925.

Schwartz, Regina M. *Remembering and Repeating: Biblical Creation in Paradise Lost*. Cambridge [UK], New York: Cambridge University Press, 1988.

———. "Citation, Authority, and De Doctrina." In *Politics, Poetics, and Hermeneutics in Milton's Prose*, edited by David Loewenstein and James Turner. Cambridge and New York: Cambridge University Press, 1990, xiv, 282.

———. *The Curse of Cain: The Violent Legacy of Monotheism*. Chicago: University of Chicago Press, 1997.

Shawcross, John T. *Paradise Regain'd: Worthy T'have Not Remain'd So Long Unsung*. 1st ed. Pittsburgh, PA: Duquesne University Press, 1988.

Shelley, Percy Bysshe. *Shelley's Poetry and Prose*. Edited by Donald H. Reiman and Sharon B. Powers. New York: Norton, 1977.

Steadman, John M. *Milton's Epic Characters: Image and Idol*. Chapel Hill: University of North Carolina Press, 1968.

Strier, Richard. *Love Known: Theology and Experience in George Herbert's Poetry*. Chicago: University of Chicago Press, 1983.

———. "Milton's Fetters, or, Why Eden Is Better Than Heaven." In *Milton Studies*, edited by Albert C. Labriola and Michael Lieb. Pittsburgh: University of Pittsburgh Press, 2000, 38:169–97.

Swanson, Donald, and John Mulryan. "The Son's Presumed Contempt for Learning in Paradise Regained: A Biblical and Patristic Resolution." In *Milton Studies*, edited by Albert C. Labriola. Pittsburgh: University of Pittsburgh Press, 1991, 27:243–62.

Todd, Henry John, ed. *The Poetical Works of John Milton*. 5th ed. (London: Rivingtons, 1852).

Vondel, Joost van den. *Lucifer*. Translated by Leonard Charles Van Noppen. Edited by Leonard Charles Van Noppen. New York, London: Continental Publishing Co., 1898.

Waldock, Arthur John Alfred. *Paradise Lost and Its Critics*. Cambridge [UK]: Cambridge University Press, 1947.

Williams, Arnold. "The Motivation of Satan's Rebellion in Paradise Lost." In *Milton: Modern Judgments*, edited by Alan Rudrum. Nashville, TN: Aurora Publishers, 1970, 136–50.

Williams, George Huntston. *The Radical Reformation*. Philadelphia: Westminster Press, 1962.

Wittreich, Joseph Anthony. *The Romantics on Milton*. Cleveland, OH: Press of Case Western Reserve University, 1970.

Index

Abdiel, 29; argument with Satan, 74–75, 82, 85–86, 88, 96, 98–99, 134; as "private person," 37; and relation of strength and liberty, 137–38
Abimelech, 54
Abraham, 10, 52–53; as model for the Son, 67, 70, 117, 126
Achilles, 33, 80, 83, 135
Achinstein, Sharon, 23, 48
Adam, 19; anxiety over God's goodness, 113, 125; conversing with Raphael, 59–60, 96, 124; creation related to angelic rebellion, 106–7; divine similitude and Satan's temptation, 165, 167; fall of, 58, 61, 92, 100, 142; God not referred to as King by, 52; Medieval Latin treatments of, 90; and "Paradise within," 153, 159; and possible ascension, 76, 156, 165; and "solitary way" (model for the Son), 159; threatened with destruction, 124–26, 142; in Vondel, 85
Addison, Joseph, 19
Aeschylus, 80
Agamemnon, 80
Ahriman, 79
Al Hallaj, 163
All in All, 34, 66; as awareness of divine similitude, 35, 163, 168; contested interpretation of, 35; and Milton's alteration of 1 Corinthians, 131–32, 135; and relinquishing of monarchical power, 146, 156
Andreini, Giambattista, 79

Andrewes, Lancelot, 61–62
Angra Mainyu, 79
Annunaki, the, 9
Aquinas, Thomas: on kingship, 46–47
Arianism, 20, 31, 166, 191 n. 20, 194 n. 45
Aristotle: definition of tyranny, 64–65
Atrahasis, 9
Augustine, 10, 21; and the nature of God, 76; and justification, 121–22; and Satan, 91
authority, 27, 34; and the Ante-Nicene Fathers, 47; and the Bible, 47, 50–51, 60; external, 34, 57–59, 87, 103, 110, 135; internal, 162; Milton's attitudes toward, 30, 34–38, 60; and obedience, 155–57, 162, 169; Protestant theories of, 103–5, 107, 109–10, 135. *See also* government; inner man; obedience; rule

Baxter, Richard: justification, 120, 188–89 n. 28
Beelzebub, 70, 79
Belial, 79, 143, 157, 167
Bennett, Joan, 43, 45–46, 49, 178 n. 17
Beowulf, 82
Bereans: as Milton's preferred model of Christian belief, 30–31, 59
Bible, 13–14, 16, 79–80, 95; books of, Acts, 59; —, 1 Corinthians, 34, 131, 135, 146; —, Deuteronomy, 14, 53–54, 166, 179 n. 30; —, Exodus, 14–15, 52–53, 67, 79, 103, 117–18,

121, 124, 141, 171 n. 5; —, Ezekiel, 126; —, Genesis, 52, 67, 117, 124; —, Isaiah, 80, 119, 121, 127; —, Jeremiah, 143; —, Job, 79–80, 118–19, 127, 161; —, John 13, 15; —, 1 John, 13; —, Joshua, 141; —, Judges, 14, 53–54, 180 n. 41; —, 1 Kings, 79, 126–27; —, Lamentations, 119, 127; —, Leviticus, 179 nn. 29, 30; —, Matthew, 55, 161; —, Numbers, 126; —, Psalms, 53, 55, 93–95, 103, 166; —, Revelation, 14–15; —, Romans, 104; —, 1 Samuel, 54, 56, 141; —, 2 Samuel, 79, 126; —, 1 Timothy, 55; —, 2 Thessolonians, 127; and divine evil, 117–19; and divine kingship, 49–51, 54–56; Milton's attitude toward, 47, 50, 56; and models for civil government, 60, 63

Blake, William: critical reactions to, 176 n. 1; and divine evil, 10; and *Milton*, 113; and *Paradise Lost*, 20, 80; and divine similitude, 170

Bloom, Harold, 77

Bolingbroke, Henry, 95

Bush, Douglas, 192 n. 26, 193 n. 42

Calvin, John, 36–37, 185 nn. 33 and 38, 194 n. 47; and justification, 120, 188 n. 21; and the sacrifice of Christ, 144; and secular power, 101–10, 186 nn. 40 and 43, 194 n. 47

Campbell, Gordon, 173 n. 28, 182 n. 63

Canaan, 15, 52–53, 141

Carey, John, 77–78

Chaos (anarch), 72

Charles I, King of England, 31–33, 185 n. 38; and God in *Paradise Lost*, 42–45, 99–100; and Milton's attitudes toward kingship, 39, 57, 62, 71; and Satan's rebellion in *Paradise Lost*, 102, 110–11

Charles II, King of England, 32–33, 44, 80, 111

Charles X, King of Sweden, 43

Chemosh, 14

Christ: forbidding of kingship, 11, 72; and freedom of conscience, 139, 162; Milton's Arian view of, 20, 166–67, 194 n. 45; and Milton's use of the justification doctrine, 120; and Milton's view of Kingship, 61–64; and radical Protestantism, 149–51, 163; sacrifice of (Calvin's view), 144; title never applied to the Son, 156

Christina, Queen of Sweden, 178 nn. 7 and 16

Cromwell, Oliver, 28, 43, 130

custom: Milton's arguments against, 60, 76; and monarchy, 50–52, 63–64; and the rule of the Father in *Paradise Lost*, 84, 97; and tyranny, 60, 136

Danielson, Dennis, 23–24, 116, 183 n. 7

Dante, 79

David, King of Israel, 72

Davies, Stevie, 23; Milton's argument with Salmasius, 71; on Milton's attitudes toward kingship, 38–41, 43, 46, 49–50, 114

Diekhoff, John, 18, 176 n. 1

divine similitude. *See* similitude, divine

Dobranski, Stephen, 18, 176 n. 1

Draco, 115, 187 n. 9

Dryden, John, 19–20, 89

Du Bartas, Guillaume de Salluste, 79, 182–83 n. 1

Duryodhana, 82

Eckhart, Meister, 115, 148, 151, 163

Empson, William, 13; and Asian readers of *Paradise Lost*, 183 n. 11; dislike of the Christian God, 173 n. 41, 175 n. 58; the herd mentality of critics, 177 n. 3; publication status of *Milton's God*, 174 n. 42; on *Paradise Lost*, 21–22, 30, 39, 45, 61, 65, 68, 74, 84–85, 100, 102, 106, 111–12, 128, 130, 141, 146, 154; recent criticisms of, 18–19, 114; on the Romantics, 176 n. 1

England: as new Israel, 47–49

Enuma Elish, 9, 53, 55

Epictetus, 191 n. 21

Euthyphro, 65

Eve: creation related to angelic rebellion, 106–7; divine similitude and Satan's temptation; 165, 167; dream given her by Satan, 113; Medieval Latin treatments of, 90; and "Paradise within," 153, 159; and possible ascension; 76, 156, 165; and the promise to be like God, 76; and "solitary way" (model for the Son), 159; threatened with destruction, 124–26, 142

evil: as destruction and violence, 59, 67, 74; the Father as the source of, 78–79, 86, 113, 118–19, 124–27, 129–30, 143, 146; the Gnostic view of the demiurge, 10–11, Milton's view of the god imagined by his contemporaries, 11–12; necessary for knowledge, 16–17, 45; Satan's motivation for, 91; as separation from God, 165; Yahweh as source of, 118–19, 130

Fairman, Lydia, 150, 154
Fallon, Robert, 43–46, 49, 114, 178
Father, the: combination of good and evil, 17–18; critiques by Waldock and Empson, 20–21; demands death, 141–44; disturbing to readers, 11–12, 24; and hate, 145; and ire, 128; obsessed with self and appearances, 140, 160–61; portrayal of kingship in *Paradise Lost*, 64–70; 73–78, 81–85, 88–90, 92–103; similarity to Satan. 160–61; and the tradition of personal deity, 15; Yahweh as model, 112–20, 123–30, 149. *See also* God
Ferguson, Margaret, 177 n. 3
Filmer, Robert, 36, 178 n. 16
Fish, Stanley: on Milton's art, 192 n. 30; on *Paradise Lost*, 22–25, 28, 69–70, 89, 123, 175 n. 53, on *Paradise Regained*, 191 n. 23, 193 n. 41
Fixler, Michael, 178 n. 8, 181 n. 52
Flannagan, Roy, 119, 181 n. 57
footnotes, *Norton Anthology* and *Riverside Milton*, 181 n. 57
Fowler, Alastair, 22, 119
Fox, George, 150–51, 154, 191 n. 22
Frederick III, King of Denmark, 43
Frye, Northrop, 192 n. 26

Gideon, 54

Gilbert, Allan, 192 n. 26
gleaning, 49, 179 n. 30
Gnostics: views of God, 10–11
God: changing images of, 9–10, 14–18, 148–53, 171 n. 5; found within, 163–65, 178; Gnostic views, 10–11; imagined as a King, 37–59, 61–76, 103; as lying spirit, 79, 125–28; as personal and exclusive, 13–15; providing motivation for rebellion, 92–100; relation to human authority, 102–11; as tyrant, 81, 83–85, 181 n. 57. *See also* Father, the
government: external, 44, 58, 136, 170; internal, 35, 89, 136. *See also* authority; inner man; obedience; rule
Gross, Kenneth, 90, 184 n. 24
Guevara, Che, 82

Haggar, Henry, 28
Hall, Joseph, 175 n. 60
Halpern, Baruch, 52–53
Hamilton, Gary D., 186 n. 1, 189 n. 30
Hamlet, 26; as model for Satan, 77–78, 87, 94, 184 n. 17
Hamlet, 87
Hanford, James Holly, 57
heaven: absence of "private persons" from, 107; fomenting of rebellion in, 92–95; as oppressive regime, 44–45; problem of kingship in, 25, 32–76, 97–100; relation of Milton's portrayal to Protestant theories of political power, 37, 101–11; similarity to Hell, 81–82, 160, 162
hell: created evil by the Father, 96; monarchy in, 25, 72; relation of Milton's portrayal to Protestant theories of political power, 37, 101–11; reflections on the Father's monarchy in, 65, 72; Satan's leadership in, 85–86, 106, 108; similarity to Heaven, 81–82, 160, 162
henotheism, 14–15
Henry IV, Part 1, 136
Herbert, George, 188 n. 27
Herodotus, 46
heterodoxy, 20
Hilkiah, 14–15

Hill, Christopher: groupthink among critics, 177 n. 3; Milton's early opposition to monarchy, 57; Milton of the devil's party, 20; Milton portrayed as an authoritarian by C. S. Lewis, 21; Milton and twentieth-century neo-Christians, 31; the Norman Yoke and monarchy, 179–80 n. 32; Protestant radicalism in England 150–51; Quaker tradition and "Christ within every man," 191 n. 22; radicalism of the Son, 115; Winstanley and the Bible, 56; Winstanley and the Christian God, 175 n. 56, 175 n. 64
Hobbes, Thomas, 37, 176 n. 68
Homer, 79–80, 133
Hooke, Richard, 28
Hooker, Richard, 46, 178 n. 17
Hughes, Merritt, 119
Hunter, William, 18, 51–52, 173 n. 28
Hyppolytus, 10

Iago: as model for Satan, 77–78, 91
Iblis, 79
Iliad, the, 9, 19, 83
inner man: as the basis of true government, 58, 68, 72, 87, 100, 155, 170; defined as the "nobler part" in *Paradise Regained*, 36, 41, 62, 73, 82, 87, 98, 155, 169–70; as inward oracle, 163; listening to the promptings of, 155–56; no role in the monarchies of heaven and hell, 82; redeemable by education, 58; rejects unquestioning obedience, 59; Satan's failure to understand importance of, 87, 98; and the Son, 68, 72–73, 153, 170; as the true connection to God, 103, 151, 155, 169–70. *See also* authority; government; obedience; similitude, divine
Israel: defined as "oriental" by Milton, 56–57, 180–81n. 42; development of the idea of Yahweh as king, 52–55; England as recapitulation of, 48–49; given a king as punishment, 57, 64, 79; relation to Yahweh, 14–15, 79, 120–21, 126

Jeroboam, 71, 177–78 n. 7
Jesus: as an image of God, 12–13, imagined as king, 28; as "Light within," 150; name applied to the Son in *Paradise Regained*, 156, 166–68; relation to exclusive conception of deity, 15; sacrifice of, 144
Job (biblical character): as accuser of God, 11; on God as source of good and evil, 118; and temptation, 161, 166
John IV, King of Portugal, 43
Johnson, Samuel, 19, 175 n. 53
Jonas, Hans, 171n. 1
Joris, David, 149, 154
Josiah, 14, 32, 54
jubilee year, 49, 179 n. 29
justification doctrine: history of, 119–22; Milton's use of, 122–23, 132, 187 n. 20, 188 nn. 21 and 27, 188–89 n. 28

Kelley, Maurice, 183–84 n. 15, 194 n. 45
Kendrick, Christopher, 179 n. 26
kingly: definition of, 73–76
kingship: as a consequence of the Fall, 56–64; on earth, 27, 29, 32, 34, 38–39, 42–43, 56, 64, 70, 72, 167; in heaven, 25, 27, 29, 32–76, 97–100, 115, 178 n. 16; in hell, 25, 65, 72, 85–86, 101–11; Milton's argument against identifying Christ with, 61–63; the Son's attitude towards, 32, 41, 135–36, 154–55
Knight, G. Wilson, 178 n. 16
Koran, the, 79

Labriola, Albert, 35, 66
Lao Tzu, 148
Lenin, V. I., 82
Lewalski, Barbara, 48, 192 nn. 26 and 28
Lewis, C. S.: and the Father, 112; and *Paradise Lost*, 21–24; publication status of *A Preface to Paradise Lost*, 174 n. 42; on Satan, 69, 78, 81, 90, 184 n. 24
Lieb, Michael, 171 n. 4; on the passibility of the Father in *Paradise Lost*, 67–68, 119; the Son's challenge to the Father, 75, 129

Loewenstein, David, 150, 159, 191 n. 22, 194 n. 46
Louis XIV, King of France, 43
Lucifer: in Isaiah, 80; in Milton, 84, 95–97; in Vondel, 85–86, 91, 95
Luther, Martin, 36, 120, 122, 148–49

Macbeth, 77, 78
magistrates: Calvin's view of, 103–4, 185 n. 33; chosen as the deputies of the people, 36–37; lower in authority than the spirit, 162; Satan as, 100–111; soon to be abolished, 163
Mahabharata, the, 82
Mahood, M. M., 192 n. 26
Marduk, 9, 52–53, 55
Marshall, Stephen: on kings and magistrates, 101–5, 107–8, 110, 185 n. 38
Masson, David, 20, 171 n. 3
McGrath, Alister, 120–21
Milton, John, 9, 172 n. 6, and Arianism, 20, 31, 166–67, 194 n. 45; attitudes toward kingship, 34–50, 56–76, 178 n. 16, 179–80 n. 32; the competitive nature of his prose, 177–78 n. 7; controversy with Salmasius as background for the Father in *Paradise Lost*, 99–100; critical history, 18–25; definition of his "fit audience," 30–33; definitions of obedience and authority, 156–62; disappointment with the English people, 182 n. 72; divine similitude, 170; forcing of conscience, 139; good and evil as images of the divine, 15–18, 115; as iconoclast and radical, 148–53; as nationalist, 179 n. 26; Poetry, *Paradise Lost*, 11–13, 15, 17–28, 30–35, 37, 40, 42, 44–47, 49–51, 59–61, 63–65, 67–73, 76–81, 83, 96, 99, 100, 102–3, 107–20, 124–25, 128, 130–33, 135, 137–39, 141, 144, 146–47, 153–54, 156–61, 163, 165, 167, 178; *Paradise Regained*, 11, 13, 18, 23, 25–28, 30, 32–34, 36, 38, 40–41, 58, 62, 68–69, 72–73, 82, 86–87, 115, 132, 139, 144, 147–48, 150–65, 169; —, Psalm 2, 93–95; —, Sonnet 7, 12–13; —, Sonnet 19, 73–74; Prose, *Areopagitica*, 16, 28, 35–36, 48, 59–60; —, *De Doctrina Christiana*, 9, 20, 28, 31, 38, 47, 56, 67, 112, 127, 143–44, 149, 152, 162, 173 n. 28; —, *Defence of the People of England*, 38, 48, 63, 71, 99, 102, 178 n. 16; —, *Doctrine and Discipline of Divorce*, 175 n. 60; —, *Of Education*, 35, 58, 73, 75, 149; —, *Eikonoklastes*, 18, 32, 41–42, 48, 51, 57, 62–63, 132, 148; —, *Letter to a Friend*, 66; —, *The Ready and Easy Way*, 28, 30, 36, 41, 45, 48, 57, 62, 64, 72, 110, 132, 137, 138; —, *The Reason of Church Government*, 57, 60–61, 63, 69, 139; —, *A Second Defense of the English People*, 177–78 n.7; —, *The Tenure of Kings And Magistrates*, 32, 35, 37–38, 41–43, 48, 55–56, 58, 60, 63, 65, 71, 81–82, 99–102, 107–11, 136, 163; —, *A Treatise of Civil Power*, 139; —, *Of True Religion*, 36; rejection of god imagined as a king 11–12, 175 n. 64; and the sacrifice of the Son, 144; theodicy, 28–30 (*see also* justification); theory of political power, 107–11; treatment of the Father and Son as literary characters, 26, 115–16; treatment of kingship in poetry and prose works, 56–76; use of Psalm 2 to establish motivation for Satan's rebellion, 91–95; use of Yahweh as model for the Father, 126–30
Molech, 52, 55
monarchy: classical and scholastic defenses of, 46–47; critical portrayals of Milton as approving of, 39, 43–46, 50, 63, 114, 178 n. 16; and the Father, 99; in heaven, 44; in hell, 50, 72; in Israel, 52, 54, 58, 73; Milton's fight against, 11, 29, 32, 42, 44, 47, 49, 51, 63–64, 74, 80; and Milton's use of 1 Corinthians, 34, 131; and Nimrod, 51; and the Norman Yoke, 179–80n. 32; and Satan, 109, 111; Satan's and the Father's compared, 25, 39, 66; and Satan's objections to the raising of the Son, 84, 87–88; the Son's re-

nouncing of, 41, 67–68, 73. *See also* kingship
monotheism, 14–15
Morris, Jeffrey B., 193 n. 36
Moses, 60, 141, 164; and the image of Yahweh as a king, 52–53, 56; as model for the Son, 67, 117–18, 125–26, 142
Mulryan, John, 154, 193 n. 42
Müntzer, Thomas: on kings and magistrates, 101–4, 107–8, 110, 185 n. 34
Musgrove, S., 78, 81, 183 n. 5

Nayler, James, 150–51, 191 n. 16
Newton, Thomas, 19–20, 24, 63
Nimrod: founder of monarchy, 32, 42, 51–53, 55, 162; founder of tyranny, 180 n. 36
Nisroch, 105, 138
Norbrook, David: "All in All" as the Son's resubmission to the Father, 34; comparisons between heavenly and earthly kingship in Milton's work, 29, 33; critical reaction to Empson, 22; divine abdication in *Paradise Lost*, 130; participation in the heavenly regime of *Paradise Lost*, 65
Nuttall, A. D., 187 n. 20
Nyquist, Mary, 176 n. 3

obedience: Calvin's attitude toward, 186 n. 40; external, 157, 162, 169, 170; The Father's pleasure in, 97, 123; in heaven, 44, 59, 70, 162; in hell, 162; internal, 152, 156–57, 159, 169; as negative for Milton, 59; and persuasion, 58–59, 69, 139, 157, 169; and possible ascension to heaven, 76; and Satan, 111, 156–57; and Satan's temptation of the Son, 191 n. 23; and the Son, 111, 115, 152, 156. *See also* authority; government; inner man; rule
Odyssey, the, 9, 17
Othello: as model for Satan, 77; as model for the Father, 78, 160
Othello, 78, 91

Palestinians, 95

Parker, Alexander, 150, 154
Parker, William Riley, 171 n. 3
Paul, 38, 59; God as "All in All," 35, 146; the lies of God, 127
Pelagius, 58, 155
Philip IV, King of Spain, 43
Philistines, 94–95
Plato, 46–47, 139
Pope, Alexander, 24, 113
Pope, Elizabeth, 192 nn. 26 and 27
private persons: Calvin's opposition to the political involvement of, 37, 185 n. 38; definition of, 36; in Milton's portrayal of divinity, 26; in Milton's theory of political power, 36–37, 102, 107; in Satan's rhetoric; 109; in Thomas Müntzer's theory of rebellion against tyranny, 103, 185 n. 34
Prometheus (of Aeschylus): as model for Satan, 80, 82, 90
Prometheus Unbound, 20

Quintin of Hainaut, 149

Rama Sarma, M. V., 151, 191 n. 18
Raphael, 59–60, 76, 84, 96, 113, 124–26, 128, 156, 165
rebellion: against Charles I, 31; origins of kingship in, 51; Satan and, 69, 78, 80, 82, 90–93, 95–98, 114; Satan and Protestant theories of, 37, 100–111
regicide, 24, 31, 46, 77, 149
Republic, the, 16, 46
Revard, Stella: on Abdiel's argument with Satan, 74, 138; Milton's Satan compared to Vondel's Lucifer, 84–85, 138, 182 n. 1; Satan as classical hero, 80
Richard II, 95
Ricks, Christopher, 119
Riggs, William, 18
rule: external, 34–38, 41, 68, 131, 154; internal, 25, 34–35, 38. *See also* authority; government; obedience
Rumrich, John, 18, 176 n. 1; and Asian readers of *Paradise Lost*, 22, 174 n. 43; on Milton's Arianism, 194 n. 45; on Milton's cosmos, 191n. 20; and Stan-

ley Fish's reading of *Paradise Lost*, 22, 175 n. 55; on syncretism of Milton's mind, 172 n. 6
Russell, Jeffrey Burton, 126

Salmasius, 46, 71, 177–78 n. 7, 178 n. 16; polemical statement as background for the Father in *Paradise Lost*, 99–100
Samuel, Irene, 189 nn. 31, 32, and 35
Samuels, Peggy, 193 n. 33
Sanchez, Reuben, 177–78 n. 7
Satan: and external temptations, 152–53, 155–58; failure of his temptations, 165–69; and freedom, 87; as hero, 19–20, 77, 79–90, 112; and hierarchy, 88; as magistrate, 37, 100–111; and monarchy, 25, 39, 66, 109, 111; and power, 87–88; as rebel, 69, 78, 80, 82, 90–98, 114; as tyrant, 106–11, 133, 181 n. 57
Saurat, Denis, 20–21
Schwartz, Regina: distinction between biblical narratives and the divine, 187 n. 12; Milton and origins, 181 n. 50; Milton's relation to Biblical authority, 50; monotheism in the Bible, 187 n. 14; relation between evil and creation, 187 n. 14; relation between Hamlet and Satan, 184 n. 17; relation of monotheism to nationalism, 172 n. 7; on Yahweh, 14, 94
Schwenckfeld, Caspar, 149, 154, 163
Shakespeare, William, 77–78, 91
Shawcross, John, 119; on divine similitude, 151, 164–65, Milton and internal worth, 162, the Son not an exemplar, 193 n. 32; the Son's self-knowledge, 194 n. 44
Shelley, Percy: on the Father, 112–13; recent critical reactions to, 176 n. 1; on Satan, 20, 89–90, 92
similitude, divine (*see also* inner man): as meaning of "All in All," 35, 66; in *Paradise Regained*, 148, 151; and the Son, 163–65, 168; as the true meaning of worship, 170
Socinian, 156; Socinians, 192 n. 29

Socrates, 16
Son, the: challenge to the Father, 64–70; dialog with the Father in Book 3, 67–68, 70, 116–17; and divine similitude, 163–65; as hero, 115, 132–47; and kingship, 32, 41, 135–36, 154–55; as Miltonic radical, 114–15; as "private person," 169–70; renouncing of monarchy, 41, 67–68, 73; "Tempt not the Lord thy God," the meaning of, 165–69
Steadman, John, 184 n. 18, 184–85 n. 31, 185 n. 39
Strier, Richard, 188 n. 27
Swanson, Donald, 154, 193 n. 42

Tasso, Torquato, 79, 133, 182–83 n. 1
Tertullian, 10
theodicy, 28, 39
Theresa of Avila, 149
Tiamat, 9
Todd, Henry John, 20
tyrant: Aristotle's definition of, 64–65; Milton's definition of, 65
tyranny: of custom and blind affections, 60, 136; definition of, 58, 68; development of, 60–64; foreign invention linked to kingship, 52; Milton's theory of resistance to, 36–38; Protestant theories of resistance to, 100–111; Satan's failed struggle against, 81–83; as self-perpetuating, 90; the Son's elimination of, 131, 146–47, 170

Upanishads, the, 148; Chandogya Upanishad, 163
Uriel, 128

Vader, Darth, 183 n. 6
Virgil, 80, 133
Vondel, Joost van den, 79, 84–86, 91, 95, 182 n. 1

Waldock, A. J. A., 21–22
Williams, Arnold, 90–91, 184, 190
Winstanley, Gerrard: on the origin of kingship, 56; on the text of the

Bible, 56; view of the Christian God, 27, 33, 175 n. 64
Wittreich, Joseph, 176–77 n. 1
Wodehouse, A. S. P., 192 n. 26

Yahweh: imagined as a King, 37–59, 61–76, 103; as lying spirit, 79, 125–28; as model for the Father in *Paradise Lost*, 112–20, 123–30, 149; as personal and exclusive, 13–15; as source of good and evil, 118–19, 130. *See also* evil; Father, the; God
Yudhisthira, 82

Zend Avesta, the, 79
Zeus, 9, 17, 80, 82